Dalit Capital

This is a perceptive and important work that is a must read for anyone interested in the prospects of Dalit capitalism. This book details the discrimination and unfavourable treatment that Dalit entrepreneurs encounter in the functioning of markets in modern India. In so doing, it refutes the optimistic notion that the process of modernization and capitalist development in India will automatically undermine the significance of social identities and their role in the economic sphere.

Kevin Brown
Richard S. Melvin Professor,
Indiana University Maurer School of Law

Although the main thesis of the book is established in relation to Dalit entrepreneurship, analysing how castes operate at the intersection of state, market and civil society, it is equally valuable in understanding the entire gamut of contemporary castes.

Anand Teltumbde
Writer and civil rights activist

This account of 'unfavourable inclusion' marks a new frontier of scholarship on Dalit entrepreneurship. Prakash's study of the business histories of 90 Dalit entrepreneurs in six states provides a fine-grained narrative of how social discrimination is reproduced in the state and market.

Niraja Gopal Jayal
Jawaharlal Nehru University

Dalit Capital

*State, Markets and
Civil Society in Urban India*

Aseem Prakash

Routledge
Taylor & Francis Group
LONDON AND NEW YORK

First published 2015
by Routledge

2 Park Square, Milton Park, Abingdon, Oxfordshire OX14 4RN
711 Third Avenue, New York, NY 10017

Routledge is an imprint of the Taylor & Francis Group, an informa business

First issued in paperback 2017

Typeset by
Glyph Graphics Private Limited
23 Khosla Complex
Vasundhara Enclave
Delhi 110 096

British Library Cataloguing-in-Publication Data
A catalogue record of this book is available from the British Library

ISBN 978-1-138-82253-5 (hbk)
ISBN 978-0-8153-7310-0 (pbk)

To

Mummy
For her immense love and care

Bhaia
Who guided me through most things in life

Guddu Da
Who made my shift from Lucknow to Delhi possible

Padma, Ramila and Jodhka Sir
For their affection and faith in me

Shilpa
For being with me always

&

For all the self-respecting Dalit entrepreneurs who are
fighting it out in the markets for an equal opportunity

Contents

List of Tables and Figures   ix

Foreword by Barbara Harriss-White   xi

Acknowledgements   xxxi

1. Introduction   1

2. Dalits, Theories of Caste and Transformative
   Recognition and Redistribution   22

3. Dalit Entrepreneurs in Urban Markets
   of Middle India   55

4. Dalit Entrepreneurs and the Role of the
   State in the Markets   118

5. Market-based Profit Accumulation and Civil Society   167

6. Intersectionality, Discrimination and
   Unfavourable Inclusion   196

7. Conclusion: Caste and Markets   228

Bibliography   236

About the Author   254

Index   255

List of Tables and Figures

Tables

3.1   Location and Number of Dalit
      Businesspersons Interviewed   67
3.2   Type and Size of Economic Ventures   68
3.3   Market Impediments Created by Former Employers   92
3.4   Factors Facilitating Access to Initial Capital   104

6.1   Dominant Theories of State, Markets and Civil Society   211

Figures

5.1   Dalit Entrepreneurs in Market Networks   172
5.2   Social Networks, Resources and Market Outcomes   175

Foreword

It is an honour to be asked to write a Foreword to this important study of *Dalit Capital: State, Markets and Civil Society in Urban India* which seeks to set it in the context of other field-based research on the persistent and remarkable social regulation of India's economy.

Most of India's economy is non-corporate, non-metropolitan and as fugitive from the statistical record as it is from tax compliance. It is the India of the 80 per cent of the population that lives in small towns and villages — 'Bharat', 'Middle', 'Moffusil' India, whose towns are 'subaltern'. Its selectively unregistered economy has long been referred to as 'informal', and more recently as 'non capitalist', the 'needs economy', the 'reserve army', *'jugaad'*, the domain of 'time pass' and of the beneficiaries of state resource transfers.[1] Yet analysts of the agrarian question in India find that the agricultural economy has long been penetrated and indeed dominated by capitalist production relations,[2] making it difficult to maintain that capitalism has failed to penetrate and dominate the non-agricultural informal economy as well. Then the fundamental question is how order is maintained in this large part of the capitalist economy that lies outside the direct regulative control of the state — or to put it more plainly still — how order is maintained in most of India.

This is the question that this book seeks to answer. In what follows I try to respond to the author's request to locate it in a historical, social and political-economic context.

In my book *India Working* (2003) I explored the roles of class and the economic reworking of non-class institutions of identity by piecing together hundreds of micro-level field studies. I took each of the institutions that were most prominent in the literature in isolation, with a view to capturing the essence of relations of authority, and then looked at them in relation to class; at which point the expressions and practices of authority that were not based on class revealed nuanced complexity, both inside and outside the economy. Unequal *gender* relations were one kind of pervasive regulator, preventing all but a few women from managing the disproportionately little property they own. Informal family business and business families were and are sustained as much through the oppressive control of female workers in both productive and reproductive work as through the exercise of hierarchical authority relations between men (patriarchy in its oldest sense). *Religions* — and India has a plurality of them — also give rise to collective identities that provide institutional bases for both the regulation of capital accumulation and the collective redistribution of resources. India's particular form of secularism actually ensures that religions play a role in the economy that ranges from co-existence through competition to violent confrontation. And the role of *caste* as a regulator differs according to the social status of occupations and their labour forces. It ranges from an expression of caste difference, more or less mapped into occupations and statuses in the economy, to oppressive relations of control, severely constraining economic opportunity and choice on caste lines, for example caste is still used to decide who gets access to work in labour gangs as well as entry to particular occupational sectors — as we shall see in this book.

Competition in markets is impossible without collective action to set the parameters of competition. If the state does not supply these preconditions, then society must; and the distribution of castes (especially business castes), combined with the local structure of property ownership form the basis of corporatist ideologies that characterise the *trade or business associations/modern guilds* that are central to the regulation of informal commercial life. Caste relations then may serve to define proper contracts, settle disputes, organise collective insurance, mobilise representation to the state, create rents and share them with state officials, control labour, and influence price-formation. All these forms of regulation also have *a spatial dimension*, which is closely related to India's distinctive spatio-sectoral 'clustering'. Clusters vary in character according to the local structure of land and property ownership, the distribution of (business) castes, and state regulative competence and capacity. These forms of regulation keep the social structure of the informal economy localised and 'embedded' in civil society, even in the era of globalisation.

In India, the dominant *class* institutions onto which caste, religion and gender are mapped are not confined to capital and labour. The polar classes of capital and labour are forming at a pace slow enough to allow a number of controversial 'awkward classes'[3] to form too.[4]

For example, 95 per cent of Indian firms employ fewer than five workers. Intermediate classes, in which capital and family labour are combined in small businesses and exist in contradiction to both corporate capital and wage labour,[5] account for a numerically large share of India's capital. They drive the Gross Domestic Product (GDP) growth and livelihood creation[6] and have survived the arrival of liberalisation, which was expected to crush them.[7] The reason for their survival is political. Intermediate classes defend non-competition with the help of the identity-based social networks through which market exchange is organised; they defend their economic interests with the help of their social contacts in the state; they manipulate local party politics (tending to fund all political parties, rather than being identified with any one); they enforce market contracts through the authority relations we have summarised earlier rather than through state sanctions; and they engage in small acts of philanthropy or the provision of services to people in need of them — in parallel to the transfers of the State.

A second example of an 'awkward class' is the way the peasantry has been transformed into a class of petty commodity producers and traders through their incorporation into generalised commodity economy. Constituting as they do the single largest category of livelihoods (some 65 per cent), petty commodity producers on and off the land are able to operate with a range of different economic logics; even though they are prevented from accumulating capital by unequal relations of exchange, by incoherent state interventions and by contradictory political mobilisations, they are able to expand through sheer multiplication.[8] The continuum of the self-employed stretches from autonomous petty commodity producers to an unknown but sizable force of disguised wage workers, dependent on brokers or merchants for their raw materials and access to markets for their products, and indebted to them and not free to sell their labour power.

A third awkward class is the labour force of casual workers who are really subsumed under capital but who do not form a recognisable, let alone politically organized, proletariat: there is no consensus on whether seasonally indebted/'neo-bonded' (migrant) wage workers are de-proletarianised or members of a 'precariat'.[9] And fourth, with wholesale and retail trade the most numerous kind of business-cum-employment category it is not clear whether merchant's capital is a precursor to industrial capital, confined to the earliest phase of capitalist development, or is a fully modern and durable form of capital, necessary but unproductive. And when it is discovered that this merchant's capital does not exist in a pure form but is almost always suffused with productive activity — transport, processing, even storage[10] — it seems that in India actually existing commercial capital is able to play a role in class formation. Indeed its local dominance is likely to be a major cause of the persistence of petty production.[11] Basile[12] has gone further, finding in the societal corporatist form of market regulation that is so characteristic of India's commercial capital a hegemonic political control over petty production and trade and over the wage labour force that she argues is reminiscent of fascist Italy.

India's neo-liberal states have been described as de-regulated and competitive — with SEZs rationalising *de jure* the regime of informal concessions that had flourished *de facto*. In the informal economy *de jure* compliance with formal law and regulation has long co-existed with *de facto* defiance. A firm may be registered but it typically flouts the labour and environmental laws and pays tax with great reluctance, delays and under-estimation. *The local state is thus often starved of resources.*[13] Yet state-supplied infrastructure is a vital support to the socially regulated economy, as is the skeletal social safety net helping targeted portions of the workforce to survive. But in doing this it becomes commodified by illegal rental markets (serving private interests) and is suffused with relations of private status. The parallel shadow state governing the informal economic order could not exist without the formal state and vice versa. The hybrid result drives the economy but undermines the legitimacy of the public sphere.

Taken as a whole, the state, the shadow state, the awkward classes, the institutions of social identity and local business organisations together form a structure which not only brings order but also stabilises capital accumulation: a *social structure of accumulation*.[14]

But all such structures change and develop over time, and in the case of the informal economy it has long been conventional wisdom that liberalisation would dissolve inherited informal structures of this kind. Yet in practice, while liberalisation does create new institutions (NGO-SHG credit hybrids) and destroy old ones (collective management of common property such as water bodies), it also reworks those that are in harmony with capitalist accumulation (caste and religion) and barely touches others (e.g. gendered property relations). In the informal economy, liberalisation does not map onto the kink-point of 1991 but instead shows much regulative continuity. The 'animal spirits' of liberated markets and the retreat of the state have not accelerated the destruction of old forms. Rather, liberalisation may be better understood as increasing the tension between forces dissolving social forms of regulation and forces that seek to reinforce them. This is what makes the Indian economy 'Indian'.

Yet even a decade ago, when *India Working* appeared, this account of the actually existing structure of accumulation of India's informal economy — extremely condensed here — was far from complete. So to put Aseem Prakash's book in its context also requires summarising how some of the missing elements have subsequently been explored — and what has been revealed.

First, consider *language*. For John Searle, the philosopher of mind, there is no more fundamental social institution than language.[15] But the languages of economic exchange have not yet been explored and urgently need mapping. Local transactions deploy local languages — there are 1,635 mother-tongues in total, 122 spoken by more than 10,000 and 29 by more than a million. Many tribal languages still lack official state recognition, and the lack of recognition affects education, and poor education affects capacity to negotiate the economy. Without a national language, India's official languages are Hindi and English. Non-English speakers face barriers in the southern Dravidian belt, just as non-Hindi speakers do in the north. Throughout India low-caste, labouring families go into debt to invest in private English education without which neither national markets nor local state services can be accessed. How far this is a good investment is something that needs to be researched. The starter hypothesis is that citizens with a language capability that is confined to the local are excluded from the national market and are subordinated to brokers when attempting to escape the local (unregistered) economy.

Second, *ethnicity*. The role of ethnicity in the structure of accumulation reflects forms of authority different from those of caste[16] or religion. Most people think of ethnicity as something characterising certain geographical regions and their local economies. Adivasis for instance are seen as occupying 'remote' sites and regions, their material culture and their kinship patterns and religion differentiating them from the Hindu social order — tribal groups whose agriculture is hardly touched by capital.[17] In the border state of Arunachal, however, ethnicity takes both territorial and networked forms. It structures a distinctive kind of capitalist accumulation regulated by a highly politicised and rich diversity of institutions. Within the state, but outside their tribal territory, local tribal people face discrimination in customary practices of exchange: Indian outsiders, who cannot enter freely, even more so. Due to the diversity of forms of authority inside a given tribal territory — and there are over a hundred in Arunachal — the elements of capitalism develop in idiosyncratic combinations: private property (occupancy and inheritance) without markets; markets without private property(e.g. forest products), rental markets without sale and purchase (e.g. land). Markets in one production factor exist without others (e.g. private ownership of cattle while grazing/forest is either privately or collectively owned; land/forest sales prevented by headmen). A (neo-bonded) wage labour force and share-tenantry has been imported ready-made (from Assam, Nepal and Bangladesh) rather than pre-dating or emerging from local differentiation. Petty commodity production and trade has emerged without primitive accumulation and co-exists with land seizure and grand-scale tribal accumulation (by contractor-politicians). Property rights and practices of market and non-market exchange are increasingly male-gendered. Non-land property of all kinds is the base for competitive rentier accumulation by different ethnic groups. It is differentiation in the non-agrarian economy that drives agrarian differentiation, not the other way round.'Institutional adaptation, continuity and hybridity are as integral to the emergence of the market economy as are processes creating new institutions and destroying others'[18] (Mishra 2014). The state is essential to this, lubricating the economy through the multiplier effect of the military budget and through financial transfers, aid and loans. Unlike other tribal regions of India: '(c)apital did not enter Arunachal Pradesh in search of raw materials, labour or markets; it entered this border State to strengthen state power'.[19] Through a high level of reservations, ethnicised contracts and business licences, the Arunachali state legitimates and protects all this local institutional diversity, and entry to the state's territory is strictly regulated.[20] Even so, the state is unable to prevent outsiders from investing in the management of much of the non-farm economy. For Dalit and Tibetan migrants, Biharis and traders from West Bengal and Assam, once they have been admitted it is a zone of short term profit for rapid repatriation. Ethnic Marwaris, whose forebears ventured eastwards in the 18th and 19th centuries from Rajasthan to places where there were no business castes, and who are exclusively networked through their trade and migration bases, and their banking and information systems, dominate the non-farm economy and also remit their profits elsewhere.[21] The ethnicised state has thus created space for a structure of accumulation deeply marked by institutional diversity which is not a transitional form but a deep structure of North-East border capitalism.

Third, the role of the *middle class* in the accumulation process. Defined in terms of assets and income, numbering anywhere from 50–200 million and growing rapidly, the middle classes are an element in the structure of accumulation driving it through consumption — what Weber termed 'styles of life'. The middle classes are mostly urban, 'ideological' groups, expressing governing ideas but occupying intermediate, contradictory class locations. On the one hand they overlap with the bourgeoisie (business families, informal capitalist firms owning and/or managing financial, manufacturing, service and commercial property); on the other hand they align with labour (the salariat accounts for a quarter of all employment, and the self-employed over half). They also include the ancillary classes that are necessary to the reproduction of society but are not materially productive: the bureaucracy (in slow decline in the 21st century) and the 'capability-rich' professions (law, medicine, education).[22] Yet India's middle classes have strengthened many features of its pre-liberalisation economy. Till recently supporting, and supported by state capitalism, the middle classes have generated domestic incentives for the expansion of a kind of capitalism that is biased towards the provision of services that are in turn polarised between capital and labour intensiveness. While capital continues to benefit from state subsidies — prime among which is tax evasion — labour-intensive activity is left to fend for itself in the informal economy. Not socially exclusive, but internally differentiated, and 'straddling the contradiction between the economics of markets and the politics of democracy',[23] the middle classes express contradictory political demands. While the upper-caste middle class is retreating into private 'gated communities', commercial and leisure spaces in the cities,[24] the lower-caste middle class in cities and small towns aspires to wrench state patronage away from upper-caste control and so, even in a neoliberal era, they continue to call for an economically interventionist state.

Fourth, there is the *actually existing state,* the object of these demands. Whereas the informal economy beyond the reach of the state is socially regulated and politically governed by a shadow or parallel state, the formal or official state is penetrated by private interests and forms a nexus with local capital that protects and profits from the selective and partial implementation of regulative interventions. The liberalising impact of the neo-liberal state is no different in this respect. It doesn't deregulate so much as 're-regulate', and to the extent that it 'retreats' it increases space for informal regulation. It does so not just informally but also formally and explicitly.[25]

This is where Aseem Prakash is making another important contribution.[26] While Akhil Gupta has characterised these relations as forming a 'blurred boundary' and stressed their porosity,[27] Prakash has identified the frontier where economic laws that should regulate an entire territory and/or society fizzle out, and other non-state regulative practices take their place, as a distinctive *political space*. His field material will lead to higher order theories about the intentions and regulative capacities of the state-in-society. In the North Indian rural economy he has studied, irrespective of land laws, tenancy is still regulated through caste relations. Agricultural wages are held below the legal minimum. Migrants and low-caste workers face more severe wage discrimination than local labour and their rights to organise are savagely repressed. Here, no attempt is made to enforce the laws regulating production. So they are ignored. Where agricultural land meets the expanding city, the master-plans through which land-use is regulated are besieged by insider lobbying at every stage. Exceptions are conceded before the plan is even conceptualised, not to mention during successive rounds of modification, and so become normalised. Here the state is at the mercy of conflicts within the capitalist class. And at the first off-farm transaction which determines returns to production, sellers of the marketed surplus face the collusion of commission agents and the use of producers' indebtedness to flout the law specifying contracts and price formation. The Regulated Markets Act is implemented but it may be evaded without sanction. Socially regulated exchange then displaces the legal regime. In agro-processing, 'extra-service fees' (bribes) are exacted by regulators for granting multiple licences, flouting pollution controls and chicanery on quality standards. A fraudulently non-compliant economy is assisted by the creation of illegal private markets and livelihoods inside the state. In transport, this consists of an illegal economy of brokerage. On one side, liaison agents create a 'single window' for bribes; on the other, a system of prepaid cards has been developed by means of which these bribes are paid and accounted for. Returns from illegal overloading are shared between owners, booking agents, commission agents, informal bankers, officials, politicians and local caste leaders in a nexus of economic, political and cultural power. Once more, interests in the state create illegal markets and benefit privately from them. Payment for rent and bribes can also shift from cash to goods, such as luxury cars and real estate. The narrative of rents and extortion is very well known, even to the office peons. Open gloating is done with sure impunity.[28]

More work like this is needed to check whether it is very different in other sectors and regions because the question how general such politics are is one that policy-makers should care about. Meanwhile it seems that the politics of regulation uses rent in a process of double capture — regulatory independence is captured by the state and the state is captured by local capital. In the process, informal institutions such as the credit card revolve around the formal institutions such as the weigh bridge or check-post. Informal relations evolve into institutions that are now deeply rooted. The actually existing state cannot be reformed without destroying these institutions, economic flows and livelihoods. In policy for urban and regional planning, faced with severe distortions of both intent and practice, two responses have been developed: on the one hand 'flexible' regulation, on the otherever more detailed specification. But both approaches to the informal economy fail to impose an alternative order on the regulative frontier. The process of enforcement is captured by local capital.[29]

It is against the background of these developments that, last but not least, the social structure of accumulation has been re-examined as a *structure of discrimination*, in particular against Muslims, Adivasis and Dalits, in which even citizens with comparable endowments obtain different outcomes.[30] This structure of discrimination operates in three main domains: markets, political institutions and practices of capillary social power.

First, discrimination persists as an organising principle of markets. Instead of being a social expression of mere difference, low caste is still a matter of social and economic hierarchy, lack of choice, and contempt. Credit flows neither fairly nor adequately to Dalits and Adivasis;[31] in the marketplace, entry and site are scrupulously policed against them. Second, a set of political institutions and practices impose discrimination in spite of laws and political movements and demands to the contrary.[32] Although positive discrimination in education and state employment allows for the economic and political participation of Dalits, Adivasis and Muslims, their under-representation anywhere but at the foot of the status/skill ladder ensures 'that emerging voices do not translate into successful and effective social and economic engagement; and that striving for representation does not transform itself into practical control over productive socio-political and economic resources'. Earmarked but underfunded schemes face a structure of indifference and evasion; the preconditions of effectiveness are missing or sabotaged.[33] Third, a truly vast diversity of capillary powers, institutions and practices, ranging from endogamy to patronage, from land and forest alienation to eviction, and from discriminatory terms of exchange to atroci-ties, are deployed in order to ensure that the removal of low esteem remains a battle to be won.[34] In what Satish Saberwal has called its 'micro-cellular' organisation,[35] civil society has strengthened rather than dissolved the distinctions of religion and caste — or it has both dissolved and strengthened them simultaneously. Dominant castes/religious groups are growing increasingly intolerant of assertion from lower caste groups. And Dalit assertiveness and activism in particular is seen as deviance and punished.

Dalits comprise a quarter of India's population. The word 'dalit' means 'oppressed'. It is the modern — some say 'western' — political label for groups of people who have suffered centuries of contemp-tuous treatment as 'untouchables' or 'outcasts'. Gandhi had named them *harijans* (children of God) — though that label is now widely regarded as patronising. In the eye of the state they are subdivided into 'scheduled castes' (SCs, 16 per cent of the population) and 'scheduled tribes' (STs, 8 per cent of the population). Both the groups are conventionally lumped together and also called 'backward' or 'depressed'. Scheduled tribes now occupy forest and mountain ter-ritory (under which there may be rich mineral deposits, their rights to which are protected by law but are being eroded). By contrast, the work that Dalits have historically done is needed all over India: sanitary work, labouring in agriculture, down mines and in quar-ries, on construction sites, around brick kilns and under lorries, in butchery, meat, carcass and leather work, and in other low-skilled and often physically dangerous and dirty occupations — most of them carried out under the beating sun.[36]

Modern India has been built on their backs.

As we noted earlier, after Independence, development was widely expected to dissolve archaic forms of social organization — either through the rationalities of planning or the requirements of markets for competence rather than crony-ism. In both the state and market, contract was expected to replace custom, acquired characteristics to replace ascribed ones: 'The private sector . . . rewards merit and performance' — and by implication, rewards these at the expense of 'traditional' values and ascribed characteristics.[37] As India's incorporation into the global capitalist system accelerated in the 1990s, much of the social–economic theorising of the last 150 years (that of Marx, Weber, Veblen, Schumpeter, Myrdal, Akerlof and North), together with the observations made by the founding fathers of modern Indian sociology (Madan and Srinivas) and the work of anthropologists such as Parry, Searle-Chatterjee and Sharma, suggested that capitalist modernity — market and state — would destroy inherited forms of exchange and economic regulation.

Yet despite India's system of public education, and legal provisions to protect and compensate for centuries of contemptuous treatment, despite positive discrimination ('reservations') in higher education and the public sector, and despite the fact that some Dalits have reached the highest positions in the state, despite the emergence of exceptional Dalit billionaires and an Dalit Indian Chamber of Commerce and Industry (DICCI), neither the state nor the market economy has treated Dalits well. At the start of the 21st century, SCs and STs were roughly twice as likely to be poor, unemployed and illiterate as non-SCs and non-STs; 88 per cent of all Dalits are in the four most intense poverty groups — compared with only 55 per cent of non-Dalits and non-Adivasis,[38] — and this holds irrespective of the political regimes or the levels of economic development of the region/state they are in.[39] As progressively fewer Indians languish under the poverty line, more of those that remain poor are Dalits and Adivasis, often forced to migrate long distances for menial and punishing work, gutter wages and debt-bondage.[40] They face systematically more oppressive and disadvantaged terms and conditions in their transactions about land, labour, capital, credit, inputs, products, and services than the upper-castes. Unable to satisfy banks' demands for collateral, and facing outright discrimination by bank managers, they are rarely given loans for land and so they toil disproportionately as tenants and labourers. Dalit women and men are on the frontline of the battle against Other Backward Castes and Most Backward

Castes for day-to-day control over agricultural production. And Dalit men are on the frontline of the conflict against upper caste men for control over the work and sexuality of Dalit women. As Ambedkar wrote: the 'caste system is not merely a division of labour. It is also a division of labourers'.[41]

But not all Dalits or Adivasis remain manual workers. A small but significant number now own and manage firms in India's business economy. This book is about their experience while clawing their way out of poverty and oppression and their role in the social structure of accumulation.

Aseem Prakash has already contributed extensively in previous publications to our understanding of both India's middle classes[42] and its labouring classes[43] — especially the latter's poor progress in human development,[44] their attempts to claim their rights and their difficult, contested movement towards political, social and economic citizenship.[45] In this study he examines the achievements of Dalits as *owners of enterprises and as entrepreneurs*,[46] documenting through dedicated and taxing fieldwork conducted in 2006–07 the business histories of over 90 Dalit entrepreneurs in six states and 13 districts of north and central India, businesses which had been identified by fellow Dalits to be conspicuously successful. At the outset, I think the project was expected to be a 'feel-good' project, showcasing Dalit entrepreneurship, teaching readers about the resourceful ways Dalit businessmen have triumphed over the problems they have faced, and perhaps even inspiring educated young Dalits to follow the trails they have blazed. But as the fieldwork unfolded it became evident that the story is not that simple, and is not that story. It became impossible to interpret their narratives other than as showing how markets, state and civil society combine to disadvantage even these exceptional people.

There is no doubting that globalisation, liberalisation and 'free markets' have opened up opportunities for Dalits. Yet the Dalit capital researched here is confined to relatively small firms[47] and dominated by occupations linked to caste. One in 10 firms have broken into a formerly closed activity; another 10 per cent deal in new goods, and just 5 per cent are in lines needing high formal skills, such as firms related to medicine. Dalit entry happens through savings from labour, or as a junior working partner (where an upper caste partner is useful for bank credit), rather than from mercantile accumulation or agricultural profits. Access to prime sites and tenancies is often reported to have been blocked. Obstacles are strewn in the way of purchase of supplies and sales of products. Formal credit, irrespective of collateral, is often blocked and requires political brokerage, bribery and rent payments to make it flow. Financial obstruction can pitch entrepreneurs into informal loans at high interest which reduce their rates of return relative to their upper caste competitors. As Karl Polanyi observed, the state is the ultimate planner of markets. In 2002, the Dalit political movement insisted in the 'Bhopal Declaration' that the Indian state must support with credit and infrastructure the development of a Dalit bourgeoisie so that it may seize the opportunities of liberalisation. But the Indian state itself reflects and reproduces the existing social order and Dalits are disproportionately cooped up in public health departments and in sanitary work. For Dalit businesses, apart from state banks, the most relevant parts of the state are the police, the commercial taxes department, electricity boards, and the municipal government. These govern licences, sites and the infrastructure without which Dalit businesses cannot operate. Dalit businesses experience them as a set of departments governed through upper caste patronage — a private status and private interest state. This fortress is approached by Dalits through costly relations of multiple clientage. By contrast for upper castes, political access is networked across departments. Outside the scattering of very recently-formed Dalit chambers of commerce, Dalit organisations are not funded well enough to organise effectively. Politics is seen by Dalits, accurately enough, as lubricated by upper caste black money. In turn (local) politicians enable their upper caste backers to flout municipal laws, jump queues, obstruct Dalits, and protect the perpetrators of violence. Dalits watch mobility and business success being brokered through caste networks, through networks formed through religious/regional identities and family or clan contacts and marriage alliances, all of which cement political access to the state — and exclude them.

So for Dalits, kinship and the family — which the anthropologist Andre Betille has argued replaces caste in the reproduction of inequality — are experienced as mutually reinforcing caste inequalities. Caste endogamy — which proves to be perfectly compatible with capitalism — blocks the transfer of property and resources amassed by Upper Castes to Dalits — and Dalits too are forced into caste endogamy which constricts their economic roles to ones they experience as servile to Upper Castes. Social capital involves kin and caste relations; cultural capital involves street wisdom, tacit knowledge and specific skills. Both forms of capital are reinforced by wealth and very difficult to access if you lack it.

In deconstructing the practices of market, state and civil society that oppress Dalit business, Dr Prakash also examines the dual politics of what he terms the intersectionality of the three overarching institutions of regulation — state, market and civil society — together with the intersectionality of caste, gender, religion, and place through which India's informal economy is construed.

This book is original and path-breaking — in its methodological approach as well as in its substance. Dr Prakash reveals an exceptional capacity to grasp field realities and to situate them in the wider theoretical literature, while at the same time constantly striving to take a back seat, privileging the accounts of Dalit entrepreneurs themselves. And while his approach is that of a critical scholar, he gives Dalit businesses their voices in a double way — first in their narratives of their business histories, and second in the explanations they give for their experiences. But he builds on this base to make higher-order statements about institutions and their politics. Above all, his book reveals how institutional change is not, despite millions of words and speeches to the contrary, not a matter of relative prices or exogenous technology, but of political struggle and resistance.

Especially for Dalits, but also for all citizens, India's liberalised economy is far from depoliticised, and anything but socially disembedded. Reservations and inclusive development have been tried, to minimal effect. What else is to be done? Dr Prakash deals with normative questions of policy as a critical realist. He sees the need to graduate from political to economic citizenship as a process of assertion of needs and rights, and of making formal and substantive claims involving the state, since markets on their own cannot establish guarantees of economic citizenship. He would start, for example, by ensuring that earmarked credit is distributed by development banks to Dalits, Adivasis and Muslims in ratios proportional to their population shares. The experiment in Madhya Pradesh of distributing assured business from the state government in proportion to the Dalit and Adivasi populations[48] should not be confined to manufacturers, but should include distributors — and should be replicated in all states.

For this, for sure: educate, agitate, organise! But education itself needs a curriculum based on the kind of understanding that is yielded by trail-blazing research such as this and — it is to be hoped — the further research that it will stimulate.

Barbara Harriss-White
4 June 2014 Emeritus Professor and Senior Research Fellow, Area Studies, Founder-Director, Contemporary South Asian Studies Programme, University of Oxford

—

Notes

1. See E. Altvater, *The Future of the Market: An Essay on the Regulation of Money and Nature after the Collapse of 'Actually Existing Socialism'*, London: Verso, 1993; P. Chatterjee, Democracy and Economic Transformation, *Economic and Political Weekly*, 2008, XLIII (16): 19–25; Barbara Harriss-White, *India Working: Essays on Economy and Society*, Cambridge: Cambridge University Press, 2003; M.A. January, 'Ideal-types' and the diversity of capital: A review of Sanyal', Work in Progress Paper no. 12, 2012, http://www.southasia.ox.ac.uk/sites/sias/files/documents/ali%20jan%20sanyal-review-final.pdf (accessed on 7 June 2014); C. Jeffrey, *Timepass: Youth, Class and the Politics of Waiting*, Stanford, CA: Stanford University Press, 2010; N. Radjou, J. Prabhu and S. Ahuja, *Jugaad Innovation: A Frugal and Flexible Approach to Innovation for the 21st Century*, Noida: Random House India, 2012.
2. See A. Shah, J. Lerche and Barbara Harriss-White (eds), 2013, *Agrarian Questions and Left Politics in India Journal of Agrarian Change*, Special Issue, 13 (3).
3. The phrase is Teodor Shanin's *The Awkward Class-Political Sociology of Peasantry in a Developing Society: Russia 1910–1925*, London: Oxford University Press, 1972.
4. Space prevents us from discussing the role of primitive accumulation in class formation in contemporary capitalism but, for this, see S. Adnan, 'Land Grabs and Primitive Accumulation in Deltaic Bangladesh: Interactions between Neoliberal Globalization, State Interventions, Power Relations and Peasant Resistance', *Journal of Peasant Studies*, 2013, 40 (1): 87–128.
5. 'Wage workers have a vital interest in keeping the price of wage goods low against their wages, while the intermediate classes have an interest in keeping such goods scarce, their prices high relative to wages; and in

profiting from that scarcity . . . ICs seek rent while the big bourgeoisie seeks profit. Under conditions of "shortage", the ICs can engage in mark-up pricing of their products. Small-scale business and traders can avoid central price controls by engaging in parallel trade and speculation and by siphoning resources into the black economy. The small entrepreneur can gain directly from such activity, unlike the shareholder — or the manager — of a professionally managed company' (Harriss-White, 2003, Ch 3).

6. A. Sinha, K. A. Siddiqui and P. Munjal, in B. Harriss-White and A. Sinha (eds), *Trade Liberalisation and India's Informal Economy*, New Delhi: Oxford University Press, 2007.

7. M. McCartney, 'The "Intermediate Regime" and "Intermediate Classes" Revisited: A Critical Political Economy of Indian Economic Development from 1980 to Hindutva', Working Paper 34, Queen Elizabeth House, Oxford, 2000, http://www3.qeh.ox.ac.uk/pdf/qehwp/qehwps34.pdf (accessed on 7 June 2014).

8. Barbara Harriss-White, 'Capitalism and the Common Man', *Agrarian South: Journal of Political Economy*, 2012, 1 (2): 109–60.

9. T. Brass,'Class Struggle and the Deproletarianisation of Agricultural Labour in Haryana (India)', *Journal of Peasant Studies*, 1990, 18 (1): 36–67; G. Standing, *The Precariat: The New Dangerous Class*, London: Bloomsbury, 2011.

10. Storage isn't simply a mode of speculation. Insofar as it prevents deterioration in the way Marx allowed for the repair of factory machinery, it is productive.

11. Harriss-White, 2012, n. 8.

12. E. Basile, *Capitalist Development in India's Informal Economy*, London: Routledge, 2013.

13. R. de Bercegol, *L'émergence des municipalités. Analyse de la réorganisation des pouvoirsissus de la décentralisationsur la gouvernance de petites villesd' Uttar Pradesh*, Doctoral Thesis, Paris-Est University, 2012.

14. T. McDonough, M. Reich and D. Kotz,*Contemporary Capitalism and its Crises: Social Structure of Accumulation Theory for the 21st Century*, New York: Cambridge University Press, 2010.

15. Discussed in G. Hodgson, 'What are Institutions?' *Journal of Economic Issues*, 2006, XL (1): 1–25.

16. On the difference, see I. N. Gang, K. Sen and M-S Yun, 'Poverty in Rural India: Caste and Tribe', *Review of Income and Wealth*, 2008, 54 (1): 50–70.

17. V. Kumar, 'Defining the Dalits', New Delhi: Centre for the Study of Social Systems, Jawaharlal Nehru University, 2008; A. Shah, 'The Agrarian Question in a Maoist Guerrilla Zone: Land, Labour and

Capital in the Forests and Hills of Jharkhand, India', *Journal of Agrarian Change*, 2013, 13 (3): 424–50.

18. D. Mishra, 'Agrarian Relations and Institutional Diversity in Arunachal Pradesh', in B. Harriss-White and J. Heyer (eds), *Indian Capitalism in Development*, London: Routledge, 2014.

19. Ibid.

20. B. Harriss-White, D. Mishra and V. Upadhyay, 'Institutional Diversity and Capitalist Transformation: The Political Economy of Agrarian Change in Arunachal Pradesh', *Journal of Agrarian Change*, 2009, 9 (4): 512–47; Mishra, 'Agrarian Relations and Institutional Diversity'.

21. The state was unable to prevent/capture and connive with/the environmentally destructive timber trade until the Supreme Court banned it (Mishra 2014). For the role of Marwari networks see B. Harriss-White, *Rural Commercial Capital: Agricultural Markets in West Bengal*, Chs 2 and 3, New Delhi: Oxford University Press, 2008.

22. For a full discussion see S. Jodhka and A. Prakash (eds), *The Middle India: The Politics and Economics of Middle Class in India*, Short Introduction Series, Delhi: Oxford University Press, forthcoming.

23. Jodhka and Prakash, *The Middle India*.

24. Of course, the state led the way: many early 'gated communities' were residential colonies for state employees.

25. See the analysis in Harriss-White, *Rural Commercial Capital*. A new study of the politics of planning in Bangalore sees the dualism between formality and informality as misconceived: 'private and public interest networks [produce] private and public interest outcomes' such that *plan violations* and *planning for violations* support each other and form an integrated system' . . . public interest policy and private interest plans are continuously negotiated (pp. 297, 303 in J. Sundaresan, *Urban Planning in Vernacular Governance*, PhD Thesis, London School of Economics, 2014). Nonetheless the recognition of informal practice draws attention to limits of the role played by formal laws.

26. A. Prakash, 'The Regulation of Markets and the Interface between Formality and Informality',Working Paper 14, forthcoming, http://www.southasia.ox.ac.uk/working-papers-resources-greenhouse-gases-technology-and-jobs-indias-informal-economy-case-rice (accessed on 7 June 2014).

27. A. Gupta, 'Blurred Boundaries: The Discourse of Corruption, the Culture of Politics and the Imagined State', in A. Sharma and A. Gupta (eds), *The Anthropology of the State: A Reader*, United Kingdom: Wiley-Blackwell, 2006.

28. Prakash, 'The Regulation of Markets'.

29. Champaka Rajagopal, personal communication, 2013.

30. S. Thorat, and P. Attewell, 'The Legacy of Social Exclusion: A Correspondence Study of Job Discrimination in India', *Economic and Political Weekly*, 13 October 2007a 13, XLII (41):4141–45; S. Thorat, and K. Newman,'Caste and Economic Discrimination: Causes, Consequences and Remedies', *Economic and Political Weekly*, 13 October 2007b, XLII (41): 4121–24; B. Harriss-White and A. Prakash, 'Social Discrimination and Economic Citizenship', in S. Janakarajan, R. Maria Saleth and L. Venkatachalam (eds), *Indian Economy in Transition: Emerging Issues and Challenges-Essays in Honour of C.T. Kurien*, New Delhi: Sage, 2014.

31. Surjit Singh, 'Financial Exclusion and the Underprivileged in India', in Aseem Prakash (ed.), *Towards Dignity: Access, Aspiration and Assertion of Dalits in India*, forthcoming.

32. B. Harriss-White and Aseem Prakash,'Social Discrimination and Economic Citizenship', Oxfam India Working Paper 8; O Khalidi Khalidi for Muslims, 2010.

33. B. Fernandez, *Transformative Policy for Poor Women: A New Feminist Framework*, Farnham: Ashgate, 2012.

34. B. Harriss-White, K. Vidyarthee, and A. Dixit, 'Regions of Dalit and Adivasi Discrimination in India's Business Economy', in B. Harriss-White, E. Basile, A. Dixit, P. Joddar, A. Prakash, and K. Vidyarthee, *Dalits and Adivasis in India's Business Economy: Three Essays and an Atlas*, New Delhi: Three Essays Press, p. 49, 2014.

35. S. Saberwal, *Roots of Crisis: Interpreting Contemporary Indian Society*, New Delhi: Sage, 1996.

36. In the business economy, India has a series of distinctive regions of relative advantage and disadvantage for SCs and for STs, un-related to the regions where relatively 'pro poor' policies are in force. There are inverse — though different and specific — spatial relationships between the relative density of Dalits and Adivasis in the population and their relative participation in the non-farm economy as owners of firms (Harriss-White et al., 2014).

37. P. Chatterjee, 'Against Corruption = Against Politics', 2011, http://kafila.org/2011/08/28/against-corruption-against-politics-partha-chatterjee/ (accessed on 30 August 2011).

38. Deaton and Dreze: cited in A. Sen, 'Agriculture, Employment and Poverty: Recent Trends in Rural India', in V. K. Ramachandran and M. Swaminathan (eds), *Agrarian Studies: Essays in Agrarian Relations in Less Developed Countries*, New Delhi: Tulika, 2002.

39. K. P. Kannan, 'Dualism, Informality and Social Inequality: An Informal Economy Perspective of the Challenge of Inclusive Development in India', *Indian Journal of Labour Economics*, 2009, 52 (1).

40. J. Bremen, I. Guerin and A. Prakash (eds), *India's Unfree Workforce: Of Bondage Old and New*, New Delhi, Oxford University Press, 2009.
41. http://ccnmtl.columbia.edu/projects/mmt/ambedkar/web/section_4.html (accessed on 7 June 2014).
42. A. Prakash, 'Understanding the Nature of Indian State and the Role of Indian Middle Class', in Surinder Jodhka and Surjit Singh (eds), *Culture and Economic Transformation: Perspectives from India and China*, New Delhi: Rawat Publication, 2013; also see Jodhka and Prakash, *The Middle India*.
43. A. Prakash, 'Workers and Right to Strike', *Economic and Political Weekly*, 25 September 2004, XXXIX (39): 4317–20; A. Prakash, 'How (Un)free are the Workers in the Labour Market? A Case Study of Brick Kilns', in Jan Breman, Isabelle Guerien, Aseem Prakash (eds), *India's Unfree Workforce: Of Bondage Old and New*, New Delhi: Oxford University Press, 2009, pp. 198–232.
44. B. Harriss-White and A. Prakash, 'Social Discrimination in India: A Case for Economic Citizenship', in S. Janakarajan, S. L. Venkatachalam, and R. Maria Saleth (eds), *Indian Economy in Transition: Emerging Issues and Challenges-Essays in Honor of C.T. Kurien*, New Delhi: Sage, 2014.
45. A. Prakash with Barbara Harriss-White and Deepak Mishra, 'Globalisation, Economic Citizenship and India's Inclusive Development', in Jakub Zajączkowski, Jivanta Schöttli and Manish Thapa (eds), *India in the Contemporary World*, New Delhi: Routledge, pp. 127–59, 2013.
46. In the rice mundi of Vellore in Tamil Nadu, in 1973, I came across a Dalit rice retailer. Though retailing rice is as old as time, as he told his business history I was left in no doubt of his entrepreneurship. First in his caste, first in the region, he had had to brave hostility, take risks and be resourceful. I learned not just how innovation is embedded in social institutions but also that entrepreneurship is a socially relative phenomenon.
47. The finding about relative smallness is reinforced by S. S. Jodhka, 'Dalits in Business: Self-employed Scheduled Castes in North West India', *Indian Institute of Dalit Studies Working Paper*, 2010, IV (2). Examining towns in Uttar Pradesh and Haryana in 2010, he interviewed 118 Dalit businessmen and records a huge new wave of entry during the last 10–15 years — overwhelmingly male. But firms start small and remain relatively small, 80 per cent having labour forces of under four employees. They are focussed on petty shop-keeping, workshops, contracting — and for the most part unregistered.
48. See also S. Pai, *Developmental State and the Dalit Question in Madhya Pradesh: Congress Response*, New Delhi: Routledge, 2010.

Acknowledgements

This book is an outcome of what was initially a research project motivated by the writings and intellectual thoughts of Professor Barbara Harriss-White. Later it was pursued as a doctoral thesis at the Centre for Political Studies (CPS), Jawaharlal Nehru University (JNU), New Delhi. Barbara's idea was simple yet intellectually powerful. Drawn from her decades of research on India in general and markets in particular, she has consistently argued that markets in India have not replaced 'customs' with 'contract'. Economic exchanges in the markets are invariably embedded in social relationships. More often than not these social relationships acquire their roots and sustain themselves in ascriptive identities. Although, dominant economic theories and modernist sociological discourses expected social identity to gradually wane, this hope has not really materialised. Barbara's book *India Working* (2003) showed that India's market society is regulated through social structures of accumulation based on identity which are being reworked so as to regulate modern capitalism. This book builds on this idea and is concerned with understanding what happens when a historically marginalised and socially ostracised community, namely Dalits, enter the markets as owners of capital. Do markets discriminate against them on traditional sociological grounds or accept them as individuals on their own merit and efficiency?

In this endeavour, I travelled the length and breadth of the country, meeting and interacting with fascinating entrepreneurs, committed social activists, caste leaders, local small time mafias, scheming local political leaders, 'technically efficient' bankers, lethargic government officials, university professors, research activists, journalists etc. I met more than 100 Dalit entrepreneurs in 13 districts of India, patiently heard, documented and reconstructed their business histories — their entry, sustenance and experience of the markets as owners of capital. The book made use of 90 comprehensive business accounts. I have used the narration of Dalit businesspersons, juxtaposed it against dominant theoretical understanding and tried to build arguments on state, market and civil society from the Dalit standpoint.

In this attempt, there were numerous institutions and individuals who helped me either directly or indirectly. The Centre for Political Studies where I was given the opportunity to pursue my doctorate under the able and benevolent guidance of Professor Sudha Pai. Her political sensitivity to the theme and remarkably insightful understanding of Dalit issues helped me tremendously to build strong arguments. The very fact that she was able to convey her intellectual arguments without imposing her views on me made a big difference to the final output. A sincere thanks to Sudha Pai Ma'am who has not only been my teacher during postgraduation but also a supportive supervisor. Professor Valerian Rodrigues, also at CPS, was always available for discussion and so was G. Ajay who helped me in numerous endeavours. My sincere thanks to both of them. Professor Pralay Kanungo, the then Chairperson of CPS for always pushing me intellectually as well as helping me to finish all the administrative formalities. Thank you, Sir! My special thanks are due to Professor Ashwini Deshpande for the insightful comments provided by her to further improve my doctoral thesis before it could be shaped into a book. My sincere thanks to Niraja Ma'am for encouraging me from my MA days and continuing to support all my academic endeavours till date. Ma'am, I owe you more than words of acknowledgement. Professor C. P. Bhambri, my teacher during MA and Professor Kuldeep Mathur, my M. Phil supervisor always supported me in all my academic endeavours. Thank you Sirs.

It will be essential to mention three institutions, which helped me to carry out this long study. The Social Initiatives Group of ICICI Bank, led by Dr Nachiket Mor, then Deputy Managing Director, provided me generous research funding to carry out my 18 month long field work. Dr Mor, as is evident from all his professional endeavours, has an eye for picking up potentially challenging and innovative projects. Thank you Nachiket for the right support at the right time. The research was funded while I was working as a senior fellow at the Delhi-based research think tank, Institute for Human Development. My heartfelt thanks to all colleagues and especially the research support of Haridwar Rai, Amrita Dutta and Pinaki Joddar. I am indebted to Barbara Harriss-White for inviting me to Oxford on a Fell Fund fellowship at Queen Elizabeth House (also known as Department of International Development), University of Oxford to write up the business histories. It was an experience which I will cherish for the rest of my life. Three chapters of this book were written during the fellowship period. The interactions with Barbara Harriss-White and Judith Heyer were deeply inspiring not only because of their intellectual depth and commitment but also because of their ability to bring out the best in any intellectual pursuit. While trying to make sense of long winding interviews of Dalit entrepreneurs at Oxford, I was fortunate to have the warmth and affection of Maidul, Padmanabh, Sangeeta, Shweta, Solano, Sumeet and Swagato. The acquaintance with them which largely started at the India Institute Library, University of Oxford or at the QEH weekly seminar is going to stay for life. Barbara along with her two gregarious daughters — Kaveri and Eli — always found an excuse to invite me home for a meal and ensured that I never felt homesick.

While on sabbatical leave, during the last stages of the PhD, I received an Indian Council for Social Science Research (ICSSR) Fellowship which helped me to sustain myself for the last six months. I am grateful to the then member secretary of ICSSR, Dr Ranjit Sinha, for considering my application.

The drafts of the doctoral thesis and then the later version of the book were meticulously read by two close friends, Shashikala and Shreemoye. I don't have enough words to thank them except to fondly remember their help for the rest of my life. Navneet, another good friend diligently keyed in the Hindi text of the book. He has always stood by me in all my ups and downs of life. Navneet, I cherish your friendship. Ashish, another great guy who always takes care of any JNU related work, has actually ensured that I submit my work in time. Thank you so much Ashish. There are a set of elders and friends, with whom I have not been in touch lately, but who have always been a source of immense strength. Thank you Anita, Reeta and Mona Bhabhi, Sandeep, Mayank and Manish Da, Archana, Avinash, Anant, Adarsh, Anitha, Chanchal, Geetanjali, Kailash, Kaveri, Rajesh, Sanjay, Sharad, Seema, Shumona and Vandana.

The final draft of the book was completed at the Jindal School of Government and Public Policy where I was working as an Associate Professor. I not only thank the institution, but also a set of friends — Bhuvana, Mohsin, Partha, Geetika, Prashant, Rajeev, Samrat, Sridhar, Shivprasad, Swagato, Upasna, Vikas, Yugank and Suraj for pushing me to finish the book. Thank you friends! You all are a treasure.

Thanks to the wonderful professionals at Routledge India for meticulously editing and polishing the book. Thank you, it has been a very rewarding experience.

I am sure I have missed many people who have been kind and encouraging to me during my stint at Oxford, IHD, JNU and Jindal. Thank you, friends and colleagues!

Nothing could have ever been done by me without the support of my parents and in-laws. Jayati Bhabhi has been a source of immense moral support throughout this period. Last but not the least, my adorable nephew Riju has been a bundle of joy and calmness while I went through the rigors of the doctorate and book writing. Love you all!

All limitations are mine.

ONE

Introduction

◻

The Context

It has been long argued that any socio-economic relationship configured under the organised political power of the upper castes reinforces the 'traditional marginality' of the Dalits. For instance, in the late 19th century, Jotirao Phule, argued that the predominant control of the day-to-day running of all types of government institutions by *Bhat-brahmin*s (due to the unwillingness of top 'white government bureaucrats' to learn the true conditions of the people) resulted in the pauperisation of peasants and farmers. The Bhat-brahmins deceived the ignorant farmers drawing support and legitimacy from the principles of Hinduism which mandated the lower castes to serve the labour interests of the upper castes. This hierarchical relationship between castes legitimised by religious doctrines led the *shudras* and *ati-shudras* to deeply internalise the belief that they are meant to serve the economic interests of the upper castes. This in turn resulted in rampant social discrimination, economic exclusion or exploitative inclusion in the non-farm economy.[1] Further, reacting to the *Swadeshi* movement, Phule noted that economic nationalism had become a smoke screen to conceal and preserve the socio-economic and religious superiority of the upper castes.[2] Likewise, *Namasudra*s in West Bengal refused to align with the dominant economic nationalism of the early 20th century. Bandyopadhyay points out that the Namasudras perceived the colonial state to be the upholder of 'social equality'. They felt that supporting the Swadeshi movement would weaken the power of the state and reinforce the clout of caste Hindus, resulting in further degradation of the social position of the Namasudras.[3] Similarly, Iyothee Thass in Tamil Nadu argued that economic nationalism during the colonial rule was a strategy of the upper caste elites to maintain social and religious superiority over lower castes.[4]

Therefore, the Dalit discourse of the late 19th and early 20th centuries did not abide by either of the two competing nationalist strategies negotiating with the question of caste. Partha Chatterjee points out that the first nationalist strategy was favoured by the nationalist left and the Marxists, who considered caste a feature of the superstructure of the Indian society.[5] For them, the existence and efficacy of caste was the ideological product of specific pre-capitalist formations, bound to disappear under the impact of modernity. The second strategy, according to Chatterjee, is reflected in the thoughts of Gandhi and Radhakrishnan. Gandhi saw the *varna* scheme as a non-competitive functional division of labour that did not imply a hierarchy of privileges; Radhakrishnan described the *varna* scheme as a 'universal form of organic solidarity of the individual and the social order'. Chatterjee further argues that both the Marxist (Left) and nationalist (Gandhi–Radhakrishnan) discourses accepted the premise of modernity. The former argued that caste is inconsistent with modern society while the latter explained that caste in its ideal form is not oppressive and merely serves the purpose of the division of labour in the modern economy. The discourse of Dalits, while contesting these Marxist and nationalist discourses, draws our attention to two kinds of colonialism: Gavaskar explains that the Dalit discourse makes a distinction between British colonialism and 'Brahminical colonialism', the latter preceding the former. The latter has its roots in Hindu scriptures which provide divine justification to caste-based discrimination and domination. Economic exploitation based on extra-economic grounds was part and parcel of the caste-based society. British colonialism, in spite of its negative features, inadvertently, made available certain normative and cognitive tools to fight Brahminical colonialism.[6] The ideas and views flowing from the enlightenment provided a reason to believe that inter- and intra-social group relationships could be configured on a more egalitarian basis.[7] These very ideas also led to the demise of the colonial empire in India, ushering in a constitutional regime supporting political democracy. Political democracy, henceforth, became the basis of political equality through a constitutional guarantee of the bourgeoisie liberal principle of citizenship (one person one vote irrespective of social location) and also galvanised hopes for economic prosperity. However, it is increasingly perceived that

Indian democracy has provided political empowerment to Dalits but has failed to empower them economically. Gail Omvedt opines that the Nehruvian model and state protectionism retained the caste base of society and restricted social mobility and labour-saving innovations which could have reduced demand for drudgerous manual Dalit labour.[8] Panini also argues that even private ancillary industries and accompanying economic opportunities which came up under state protectionism were cornered by the upper castes.[9] In the present context, Omvedt argues that ongoing globalisation has the potential to open a sea of opportunities for the weaker sections, and hence advocates free markets.[10] Similarly, Prasad argues that the principle of the caste system — blood and occupational purity — is dissolving under the impact of the wealth creation endeavours of markets.[11] Ramaiah also opines that the state-led developmental regime has excluded the Dalits. Dalits have nothing to lose in welcoming globalisation since it holds the promise of freeing of upper caste-inspired and controlled socio-economic relationships.[12]

Thus, scholars and activists supporting free markets as a means of eliminating discrimination basically argue that the disjunction between political equality and the vast economic inequality between different upper and lower castes can potentially be bridged by free market policies spearheaded by economic liberalisation; the logic being that the market has the potential to eliminate discrimination and bias, because it represents the interaction of free individuals maximising their gains/utilities.

Nonetheless, the support for free market policies is also accompanied by a call for state action to help Dalits to enter the markets. For instance, it has also been aggressively argued that the present narrow definition of affirmative action — translating into ensuring jobs in the public sector — should be expanded to include reservations in the private sector. This is accompanied by strident calls by Dalit intellectuals and activists for the creation of a Dalit bourgeoisie (please also refer to the discussion on the Bhopal Declaration in Chapter Four). Thus the demand for state action to back-up policies in support of the free-market creates a complex relationship of Dalits with the state. In other words, Dalit scholars and activists who support free markets also simultaneously demand an enabling role of the state to ensure that the Dalits are sufficiently equipped and empowered to enter the markets on an equal footing with the upper castes.

It is against this backdrop, that we attempt to analyse the outcome of the political and economic desire of Dalits to enter the market as owners of capital and trade in various goods and services. This is done on the basis of 90 detailed interviews of Dalit entrepreneurs conducted in 13 districts located in six states of India. Dalits choose to enter the market as owners of capital in anticipation of earning their livelihood without compromising their इज़्ज़त[13] [dignity/honour], अपनी औकात पे[14] [by the dint of their own capabilities], and बिना किसी के एहसान से[15] [without being patronised or obligated]. Markets are expected to provide them social dignity and end the hitherto oppressive socio-economic relationship often variously described as जजमान–सेवक/दास, मालिक–नौकर, हाकिम–नौकर आदि [master–servant relationship].[16] Thus, our interviewees anticipated that a livelihood earned in the market would allow them to overcome their traditional socio-economic marginality. In other words, it is expected that:

- Outcomes in the market are not contingent on caste location but on efficiency and quality.
- Operating as owners of capital brings in material prosperity and social prestige.
- Adverse outcomes experienced in the labour market in the form of low wages, extra-economic compulsions, physical violence, or threat of violence can be mitigated by this route.

The Objective

The objective of this book is to understand the relationship between social identity and outcomes in the markets with the help of business histories of Dalit entrepreneurs. Therefore our concern is not to look at labour market outcomes in terms of wages, or positions held by various individuals belonging to different ethnic/religious/ caste groups in the economic processes (for instance, labour, manager, supervisor, etc.) but to understand and analyse outcomes in the markets when individuals hitherto branded as 'untouchables' in the traditional Hindu social order enter the markets as owners of capital and trade in various goods and services. While doing so, the effort is to understand whether the social identity of the economic agent mediates and influences transactions in the markets, and if it does influence them, what is the nature of the outcomes. We try to explore whether the interaction of economic agents in the market is governed by the secular principles of the markets or is mediated and influenced by the social structure and the social contexts inhabited by the economic agents. In this endeavour, the documentation of business histories explores a few crucial interrelated questions:

- What are the institutional factors which facilitate/constraint a Dalit from entering the markets as an owner of capital (entrepreneurs) and undertaking trade in goods and services?
- What are the institutional factors which (dis)allow Dalits as owners of capital to sustain their economic activities in the market?
- What is the role of institutions, both formal (for instance the state and its various institutions) and informal (institutions in the realm of civil society like social identity of caste, social networks, etc.) in influencing outcomes in the markets?
- What is the nature of the inclusion/participation of Dalit owners of capital in the markets?

Defining Markets and Social Identity

Before elaborating on the research methodology, it would be essential to explain how two important concepts — markets and social identity — are explored.

Markets

We will explain the concept of markets through three interrelated characteristics, that is, the constitutive element, the relational feature and aspects determining market outcomes.

Markets are *constituted* through sustained human interaction where two or more parties engage in exchange of goods and services of various kinds. The exchange is mostly through money and is embedded in a variety of institutions (formal and informal credit, supply and production chain, etc.), norms (informal codes of conduct), formal rules (rules about taxation, goods and services which can be offered and sold), social relations (social networks, capital–labour relationship, etc.) and infrastructure (roads, electricity, physical spaces, etc.). The state often creates and necessarily regulates all types of markets and provides legitimacy to them.

Two or more parties enter into an exchange *relationship* mostly to earn profit. Profit is the hallmark of any transaction(s) and is one the chief reasons for the markets to exist. The exchange relationships are termed as transactions. Therefore, market interaction is a relationship between buyers and sellers. The relationship is born out of the demand (read want) of the buyer (defined as consumer) who enters into a transaction at certain terms and conditions with the seller (supplier of the good or service). The critical point is to understand how the price of goods to be sold or the services to be offered is determined. This brings us to our third important feature of the markets.

As we know, participants in the market consist of all buyers and sellers of goods and services who influence demand, supply, prices, and profit and in turn determine outcomes in the markets. The prices in the markets are expected to be determined at the intersection of availability of goods/services and the demand for the same. From the standpoint of the seller, the profit is determined by what s/he is able to save over and above the cost price and after meeting all types of transaction costs. Generally, it is understood that price and consequent profits are influenced by economic factors like availability of goods, credit, physical infrastructure, rules of taxation, etc. However, this book contends that it is possible for economic transactions and market outcomes to be determined by non-economic factors along with the economic ones. After all, the individuals entering into market transaction are embedded in their social location (caste, gender, ethnicity, religion, etc.) which in turn can influence their worldview and hence their relationships in the markets. In such a context, there is a possibility that that the relationship between the buyer and seller is *not solely* carved out of the intersection of quantum of demand and supply. Instead, the social identity of the person can mediate and influence economic transactions and thereby have a bearing on demand, supply as well as profit.

Social Identity

How do we understand social identity in our present context of examining its role in influencing market outcomes?

Generally speaking social identity is an individual's identification with other members of the society. Among other factors, belongingness to a social group is one of the most important attributes that constitutes the social identity of any individual. In this sense, the individual gets connected to the wider world though his/her location in a particular social group. The social group could be professional (IT workers, bank employees, etc.), social (trekking club, cycling clubs, football clubs) and ascriptive (hereditary in nature such as caste, race, etc.). In this book, we focus on the social identity of individuals emerging from their ascriptive status, that is, caste location. We are taking the specific case of Dalits and exploring the outcomes of their endeavours when they trade in goods and services in 'open' markets.[17] Therefore, this book deals specifically with individuals with 'subordinate' social identities who have decided to go from being providers of labour to becoming owners of capital (entrepreneurs).

In the course of the investigation, we have tried to re-construct their business histories and engage with their outcomes in the market which are affected and influenced by their ascriptive group identity. The focus on social identity in economic transactions takes our work away from the traditional domain of sociology and should situate it in one of the fast growing disciplines in India, that is, economic sociology. However, this is merely one indication of the expanse of this book.

As already pointed out, modern markets are often created by the state and invariably regulated by it. Therefore outcomes in the markets are also shaped by the nature of state intervention. If social identity can (as it does) influence market outcomes, it can necessarily also influence the state and its actions towards influencing market based transactions. If such is the case, the boundaries of this work further expand to situate it in the discipline of political sociology. Accordingly, this research is situated at the intersection of political and economic sociology. While returning to the question of social identity, it should be stressed that the formation and consolidation of social identity is generally in the realm of civil society. Therefore, social identity, which is shaped at the intersection of state, market and civil society, becomes the common variable to understand the economic outcomes experienced by Dalits.

Documentation of Business Histories

As already indicated, the book attempts to understand the role of social identity in influencing outcomes in the markets. Towards, this endeavour, we have documented detailed business histories of

90 Dalit entrepreneurs. The business histories were recorded with the help of a semi-structured open-ended questionnaire. The experience of these entrepreneurs in the market, their interactions with upper caste business peers, their engagement with the formal institutions of the state, their relationship with the various institutions of civil society were all documented in the form of first person narratives. While going through the transcripts, what emerged was a fascinating account of markets, state and civil society. The entrepreneurs described the micro-politics of local markets, local government, caste and business associations and beautifully situated these in their own social context of a low caste person (expected to serve the labour interest of the upper caste) who chooses to deploy her/his agency and claim equal status by becoming an owner of capital. The documentation of these business histories was no doubt challenging. But the bigger challenge was to situate them in the social science discipline and make sense of the fascinating details. It was challenging because the narration of the everyday experience of these entrepreneurs was contesting the dominant theories of state, markets and civil society in their own simple and plain words bereft of the jargon of social science.

Given the rich qualitative data, the narratives were preserved as it is, juxtaposed against available concepts and theories, and the differences and similarities analysed. While it is true that the experiences of respondents were often found to be contradictory to the prevailing macro-theorisation/conceptualisation, we must keep in mind that most of the theories are meta/macro-narratives trying to grapple with the character of the state, market and civil society. Therefore, even when we disagree with the dominant theories and concepts, we cannot make a universal claim but merely interpret the narratives of a subset of the population. This does not imply that there is no possibility of reconciling the particular with the universal. Macro-theorisation also provides us enough flexibility to incorporate and restructure the universal macro-framework and still be sensitive to the particular. We are calling this method 'narrative analysis'[18] and we outline its central features in the following pages.

Narrative Analysis

In this work, the word narrative is ascribed to the self-description by Dalit entrepreneurs about their market entry and sustenance. It refers to the ways in which Dalit entrepreneurs construct their disparate experiences and make meaningful sense of the socio-economic and political context in which their economic activity is embedded. Insofar as these narratives describe their perceptions about relative success and failure in the markets; they also influence their actions in response to or in anticipation of the market-based actions of their upper-caste business competitors. Narratives play a critical role in the construction of the socio-economic and political structures which influence their lives, the world in general and market outcomes in particular. In other words, we use the narratives of Dalit entrepreneurs to interpret and understand the socio-economic and political structures which affect their entry and sustenance in the markets as owners of capital and ultimately their endeavour to earn a living without being dependent on caste-based economic structures where the fruits of their labour were mostly appropriated by the dominant upper castes.[19]

How do we understand the narratives of the Dalit entrepreneurs? Why should these narratives qualify for inclusion into academic research? We argue that narrative analysis possesses attributes that allow us to construct disparate, often theoretically incoherent statements into a recognisable and discernible framework for academic pursuits. It also enables us to capture the social failures and successes, marginalisation and achievements, oppression and empowerment of the Dalits entrepreneurs and situate these in the wider politics of state, market and civil society.

Key Features of the Narratives

The central features of the narratives which emerge from the reading of the business histories of Dalit entrepreneurs are as follows:

First, narratives of Dalits entrepreneurs provided the means to capture their perspectives in the context of a market situation. They were able to organise their thoughts and share their life-stories while placing themselves at the centre of the narrative, creating above all, autobiographical accounts of their experience in the markets dominated by upper-caste businesspersons. In other words, each narrator selected and described the events, explained the social environment and located herself/himself in the events and thereby interpreted the social world that he/she lived and worked in.

Second, the narrator's experiences were invariably in relation to the 'other'. In our case where the narrator is a Dalit, the relationship with the 'other' was invariably mediated and understood through ascriptive identity and the social location of the group to which the narrator and the 'other' belonged. Further, their respective group social location was inherently perceived to be in some sort of conflict (mostly latent) which is shaped historically. In other words, the Dalit entrepreneurs used the past to explain their present and future. This is as true at the individual level as it is on the macro-level, when the historically deprived social groups invoke their oppressive past to interpret their discriminated present and thereby put forth claims of recognition and redistribution.

Third, the narratives allow us to suggest a connection between social identity (understanding of self) and agency (the circumstances for action). As we will discuss in Chapter Two, agency is manifested both as a positive endeavour of the Dalit to stake parity in socio-economic relationships as well as a negative effort on the part of the dominant castes to restrict the participation of Dalits. The narratives provided a rich description of the processes around the use/misuse of socio-economic power (both by dominant and subordinate social groups), how it has been wielded historically and has thus shaped the current context. For instance, there was a clear perception that upper caste business peers had extensive family contacts within the state apparatus that facilitated their economic endeavours.

This discussion brings us to the fourth feature, wherein, though the narrator's experience was discussed and shared as a matter of fact, the data for analysis not only emerged from spoken responses but also in spaces and silences. For instance the 'contacts in high places' mentioned earlier were certainly few and far for Dalit entrepreneurs but nevertheless very important. This fact, though never explicitly stated, underlines the reason why affirmative action policies at the macro-level find such strong support among Dalit groups and government jobs are still aggressively sought by them.

Fifth, each narrative is not merely the experience of the individual(s). It is supplemented by an explanation of why certain socio-economic patterns are produced and reproduced in a particular fashion. All the narratives taken together show a clear pattern of experiences, which provide a strong foundation for engagement with existing theories and concepts.

Sixth, narratives reveal the interconnected behaviour of stakeholders and institutions in a networked environment that determines winners and losers in the market. We can analyse how backward, forward and lateral linkages work across individual entrepreneurs, buyers groups, sellers' lobbies, middlemen, credit institutions, local political bodies, competitors, and partners to finally evolve a market outcome.

Why Narrative Analysis: Implications for Research

We argue that narrative analysis provides distinct advantages in the context of our research. First, narratives lend themselves to a rich analysis of the aspirations of Dalits and their efforts to scale up from serving the labour requirements of the upper castes to becoming autonomous economic agents by investing capital and earning profits. The sequential narration of events from market entry, operation and engagement with the government apparatus to competition and engagement with upper caste peers allows us to tangibly identify those components of the social structure that facilitate upper caste domination in the markets. The attempts of Dalits to take control and shape resistance to the existing power structure are seen in contrasting relief against this backdrop.

Second, the empirical basis of the narrative analysis captures the dynamic nature of ongoing social relationships and dispels preconceived notions about how people belonging to specific social identities behave.

Third, narratives allow us to look at inter-social group relationships in relational terms. The relational terms are seen in two interrelated dimensions. The first is the burden of the caste structure which forges a specific relationship between two or more social groups. Along with it is the relationship of the individual with the formal and informal institutional structures in the market such as credit institutions, sellers' associations or unions which is also mediated by ascriptive identities in the sense that the nature of interaction of the entrepreneur with these institutions also varies with his/her ascriptive status.

Fourth, narratives challenge us to think and go beyond our parent discipline of research. In other words, if one has to make sense of disparate and seemingly unrelated determinants of market processes and outcomes, then one has to necessarily transcend strict disciplinary boundaries in order to fully utilise the rich data available. This is especially important because narratives of Dalit entrepreneurs are situated locally and it becomes essential for the researcher to situate the local narratives in the wider socio-economic and institutional context and critically engage with available macro-theories and concepts from various disciplines.

Having elaborated on the methodology followed for collecting the business histories of Dalit entrepreneurs, we now describe the organisation of this book.

Schematic Map

The book is structured around five chapters, besides the introduction and conclusion.

Chapter Two entitled 'Dalits, Theories of Caste and Transformative Recognition and Redistribution' engages with the question of why Dalits should be analytically as well as politically considered a homogenous group irrespective of their diverse socio-political and economic locations. This is necessary because our Dalit entrepreneurs come from diverse sub-castes and regional locations. In this endeavour, the first chapter examines the diverse perspectives/approaches on caste and subsequently critiques them from the standpoint of Dalits. We have clubbed these approaches under the following heads:

- **Orientalist:** The lens through which the colonial government (represented by jurists, missionaries, revenue surveyors, military recruiters, and innumerable other observers of Indian life) essentialised and stereotyped the 'natives';
- **Hierarchy and Difference:** Sociologists examine and understand the positioning of caste rather than dissecting and analysing the exploitation and subordination of labour efforts which the caste system perpetuates;
- **Caste as a Superstructure:** Caste is studied as a product of specific pre-capitalist formations which would disappear as capitalist rationality develops;
- **Defence of Varna:** Defending the varna system because it is merely a functional division of labour;
- **Organic Social Block:** Attempting to suppress the internal differences between social groups by supporting and advocating a pan-Indian identity of a homogenised Hindu.

We point out that all these approaches, to understand caste, tend to homogenise the different social groups and thereby fail to provide recognition to the Dalits. For Dalits, social homogeneity implies concealment of the structural differences, which translate into multidimensional subordination, also upheld by religious Hindu texts, whereas social heterogeneity attests the acceptance and recognition of unequal power relationships between different social groups. This in turn helps the Dalits to pursue an agenda of redistribution and transformation and seek rectificatory justice. The rejection of the former and acceptance of the latter also means the appreciation of the political agency of Dalits — institutionalised collective endeavours directed towards continuously engaging and contesting the structural power of caste.

Chapter Three entitled 'Dalit Entrepreneurs in Urban Markets of Middle India' primarily points out that social identity is the source of discrimination and unfavourable inclusion of Dalits in the markets. It initiates the discussion by reviewing the existing theories of markets and discrimination. The literature emanating from neo-classical economics and new institutional economics emphasises 'competition' and believes that any form of discrimination in the markets is a source of increased transaction costs. The neo-classical school argues that while discriminatory patterns originate in the realm of civil society, these patterns are manifested in the actions and decisions of the individual who is the flag bearer perpetuating them. The desire to earn more profit and meet the demands of market competition should persuade every economic agent to enter into business contracts with individuals on the basis of the latter's capability sets rather than their social origin. It is pointed out that considering the social origin will suppress efficiency in the markets while focussing purely on capabilities will enhance it.

New institutionalists, on the contrary, lay greater stress upon the importance of institutions, both formal and informal, in shaping outcomes in the markets as opposed to individuals. They retain the cardinal value of competition and undertake a comprehensive review of history to argue that societies that have graduated from informal to impersonal formal institutions have done better in terms of growth and its distribution. On the contrary, the narratives of Dalits explaining their business histories highlight the pre-dominance of informal institutions like caste, which mediate economic transactions and are instrumental in providing a competitive edge to upper caste business peers vis-à-vis Dalits. The chapter uses the detailed narratives of the

Dalit entrepreneurs to analyse their entry, operation and sustenance in the markets. In the process, it documents and analyses the role and nature of discrimination that is experienced by Dalit entrepreneurs. Based on detailed narratives, the chapter argues that the experience of inclusion in the markets of Dalit entrepreneurs is neither characterised by extreme rigidity (where Dalits are denied entry as owners of capital) nor is completely accommodative (where Dalits are able to enter and operate on equal terms). We have described the experience of Dalits in markets as owners of capital as 'unfavourable inclusion'. They experienced rigidity when former employers (most of the Dalit entrepreneurs initiated the same businesses in which they were earlier employed as labourers) created impediments of numerous kinds and thus tried to block their attempts to start their own business, or when Dalits tried to enter into trade of goods and services which, as per dominant social beliefs, can be rendered impure by their mere touch (for instance, food items). However, upper caste ex-employers were not successful in blocking their entry. As per their narratives, the determination of Dalits to quit their labouring jobs and start their own business enabled them to initiate trade in various goods and services, but they experienced varied forms of discrimination during the course of their business operation. They were relatively more successful in integrating themselves in the markets in 'modern businesses' by employing different strategies such as involving upper castes as business partners where the latter only contribute their name but all the actual work is done by the Dalit, or tapping and creating loose social networks for sustaining themselves in the markets. Although in these cases, the degree of discrimination differed, nonetheless the Dalits were invariably included on unfavourable terms. Analytically, these narratives imply that markets mirror the socio-economic hierarchy present in civil society.

The same is cogently argued by the school of social embeddedness which theoretically attests that the ideology of caste creates exclusion not only in society but also in the markets. Unlike the neo-classical and new institutional economics, this school argues that caste does not suppress competition but is dextrously used by the upper castes to face competition from Dalit entrepreneurs. More specifically, caste is able to configure a regime of accumulation in the markets operating in favour of upper castes. This has been aptly described by scholars as a 'social structure of accumulation'.

Chapter Four entitled 'Dalit Entrepreneurs and the Role of the State in the Markets', interprets how Dalit entrepreneurs visualise the role of the state in the markets. State is an extremely important institution in the imagination of Dalits. Normatively, it is seen as an institution that can compensate for the historical wrongs committed against them. However, the chapter, through the narratives, finds that when Dalits operate in the market as owners of capital, what they experience is quite complex and very distinct from the normative construct. They experience the state as an institution which largely helps the upper castes in their accumulative endeavours. In order to understand the narratives of Dalits with regard to the role of the state in markets systematically, we have drawn from Philip Abrams and classified their narratives on state into 'state-system' and the 'state-idea'. The latter implies the state in its ideological abstraction and the former connotes state in its material everyday existence.

The narratives indicate that when Dalits see the state as a state-idea, it is viewed as a source of immense discretionary power, which can affect any number of socio-economic changes and bring their business to a standstill. At times, the state becomes so opaque and abstract that its action cannot be understood or explained. These patterns are especially seen to be even more incomprehensible when the electoral penetration and articulation of Dalits from inside the state fails to translate into tangible development benefits. Where the state is being viewed as a state-system, the narratives tend to focus on structured state action which favours upper castes and works against the economic interests of Dalits in the markets.

We have referred to this structured understanding of Dalit entrepreneurs as 'state simplification', which is constituted of four distinct theses. Each of the theses has to be read along with the other in order to comprehensively understand the Dalit's construct of the role of the state in the markets.

- Thesis I de-links state departments from statecraft and state officials from norms/rules of statecraft and also perceives that state officials are autonomous from the norms, rules and regulations of the state. State and its institutions are seen to be made accessible through informal relationships carved through caste identity. The narratives explain that upper caste peers have regular access to state resources due to their informal contacts and relationships with state officials cultivated through caste-inspired social networks whereas Dalit entrepreneurs lack such social resources.

- The narratives explaining Thesis II detail the nature of the unfavourable inclusion of Dalits in the markets due to discrimination practised by the state against them vis-à-vis upper caste competitors.
- The narratives describing Thesis III highlight that one of the prominent reasons for the unfavourable inclusion of Dalits in the markets is the role of caste in blurring the boundaries between state and civil society. The values dominant in the latter are reflected in the actions of the former.
- The narratives describing Thesis IV further reinforces the narrative analysis of Thesis III by flagging the role of family and its relationship with caste and its ability to carve out social networks and relationships with state officials through family, caste and marriage connections.

In effect these four theses unfold the 'politics of the markets', which implies that, either the state or its institutions withdraw when they are expected to protect the economic interests of Dalits or act in favour of upper castes and help them in their accumulative endeavours.

Chapters Three and Four provide an insight into the structured patterns of market-based accumulation processes to argue that economic relationships in a typical market setting are embedded in social relationships defined through caste relationships. This pattern becomes more pronounced when it comes to the economic relationship between upper castes and Dalits. These relationships, it is argued, are structured and facilitated by caste-inspired social networks. In other words, caste-inspired social networks facilitate the accumulation of surplus in the markets.

Therefore, the primary questions, which Chapter Five, entitled 'Market-Based Profit Accumulation Process and Civil Society' engages with, are: Can caste be considered an inalienable component of/ influence on/institutional basis for the formation and manifestation of civil society in India? What are the implications of doing so? Accordingly, the chapter delineates the role of caste-inspired social networks in the markets and elaborates its four components.

- The *normative component* of caste attempts to maintain hierarchy between different social groups. This becomes the basis of establishing the economic relationship between upper castes and Dalits. Accordingly, caste-inspired social networks of upper caste economic agents establish norms and informally binding rules, and enforce sanctions against violators. These norms and sanctions are perceived by Dalits as detrimental to their economic interests.

- The *structural component* of the social networks originating in the normative component allows the upper castes to develop a wide and dense social network connecting them with various upper castes and Dalit business people alike. Whereas, Dalits see themselves as socially ill-equipped to have such a wide ranging and dense social networks and as a result they are connected on a one to one basis, mostly with individual upper caste business persons with whom they have unfavourable business relations.
- This feature of caste-inspired social networks leads us to discuss the third component — the *resource component*. This very structural component prevents Dalit entrepreneurs from enlisting the extensive help of social networks in the markets, a feature, which is crucial for market entry, sustenance and market-based accumulation. The resource component of social networks helps its members to access relevant resources of the state and markets, which in turn reduces their transaction costs and contributes to their overall profit.
- The last one is the *dynamic component* of caste-inspired social networks. Social networks are inherent to any market competition and are usually invoked by upper castes while competing with each other. However, the social networks operating against Dalits are relatively more permanent in nature since they originate from the normative component discussed earlier. Dalits are allowed access to these social networks on terms set by the upper castes and agreed by the Dalits. This is the dynamic feature where Dalits are allowed entry in the markets against the dominant sociological belief whereby the latter is expected to serve the labour interests of the upper castes.

These four components of caste-inspired social networks translate into conditions which exclude Dalits from trading in goods and services on equal terms with upper caste business peers, aggressively promote the accumulation endeavours of upper castes, set conditions where upper castes are able to manipulate state institutions to threaten Dalits in order to further their own business interests while hurting the economic endeavours of the former; and, provide the basis for collective action in the interests of the accumulative endeavours of the upper castes.

If caste-inspired social networks play such an instrumental role in the markets, can we argue that caste forms a basis for Indian civil society? The chapter argues that caste is indeed embedded firmly in the formation of Indian civil society. It further argues that while contemporary debate on civil society in India views it as a 'site of democratisation' or conceptualises it as a set of 'institutions facilitating the rule of law, impersonal institutions and universal state', it fails to take into account a crucial argument of the traditional theorists such as Adam Smith, John Locke, Friedrich Hegel, Karl Marx, and Antonio Gramsci who also recognised civil society as a 'site of accumulation'. Caste takes an organised form to connect individuals, articulate their economic and political interests, set norms of market behaviour, regulate credit and labour supply in the market, help in procuring market contracts, set prices, regulate the entry of new market players, etc. This role of caste predominantly helps the accumulative endeavours of the upper castes in the markets. Further, while caste as a basis for civil society explicitly helps in the process of accumulation, it unfolds an institutional process of creating conditions of overlap between state, markets and civil society.

This draws us into Chapter Six entitled 'Intersectionality, Discrimination and Unfavourable Inclusion'. It builds on the arguments of earlier chapters, which have shown that the discrimination and unfavourable inclusion of Dalits is at the intersection of state, markets and civil society. In other words, it argues that the unfavourable inclusion and discrimination of Dalits is effected through multiple institutions — state, market and civil society — acting simultaneously. The chapter claims that the conceptual approach of 'intersectionality' can facilitate a better understanding of this complex phenomenon.

The conceptual approach of 'intersectionality' has been borrowed from feminist studies. Feminist insights argue that cultural and biological categories like race, gender, class, ethnicity, and religion interact and create multiple and often simultaneous conditions of subordination of women, discrimination and social inequality between genders. These intersections are referred to as the race — gender — class matrix or the interlocking system of oppression and marginalisation. Unlike feminist theory, which emphasises informal institutions such as religion, etc., we stress on formal institutions that are informalised due to the articulation of the worldview of informal institutions (for instance, the ideology emerging from the institution of caste) within the formal institutions (state and market). The main argument of the approach of intersectionality is that the caste system and its values as present in the realm of civil society are also articulated through the institutions of the state and markets and manifested in the actions of these formal institutions. This leads to the blurring of boundaries between state, markets and civil society. Analytically, this blurring of the boundaries produces a space which is at the intersection of the state, markets and civil society where the discrimination and unfavourable inclusion of Dalit entrepreneurs is practised. Further, the intersectional spaces, though originating in the realm of the state, markets and society, by intersecting and interacting, transcend their original character and assume unique characteristics with their own norms, rules and behavioural patterns, different and contradictory to the assumed rationalities of state planning and markets but mirroring the unequal relationships present in the realm of civil society.

The approach of intersectionality serves several theoretical and practical purposes. First, while contesting the binaries of the state and markets, the state and civil society and markets and the state, it argues for the interconnectedness of these institutions to understand the experience of discrimination against Dalits in the markets. Second, the focus on intersecting spaces helps us to differentiate between exclusion and marginalisation due to class location and discrimination and unfavourable inclusion due to caste location. Third, the focus on the intersecting spaces also helps us to understand the deployment of the agency of Dalits. In other words, their unequal status is accepted by the Dalits not due to the internalisation of unequal power structures but as a strategic means to leave their caste-ordained professions and enter the markets as owners of capital. In this context, their ability to contest and resist the illegitimate demand of their upper caste business peers is limited. Accordingly, they choose to engage with them through an intelligent assessment of the constraints in their specific context. Finally, the chapter argues that the approach of intersectionality which has its basis in multidisciplinarity has an epistemic superiority in understanding the reasons for the unfavourable inclusion of Dalits in the markets which any scholar should consider, if not adapt, when crafting a normative vision of a just society.

The concluding Chapter Seven organically links the different strands of each of the previous chapters to analytically describe the Dalit experience of adverse inclusion in the markets as owners of capital. Finally, we try and suggest a few themes for further research which can help us to understand better the discrimination in different sectors of the economy as well as enable us to design policy interventions for the economic empowerment of Dalits in India.

—

Notes

1. Jotirao Phule, *Shetkaryaca Asud (The Whipcord of the Cultivators)*, transl. Gail Omvedt and Bharat Patankar, p. 66, http://ambedkar.org/ (accessed on 21 May 2009).
2. Ibid.
3. Sekhar Bandyopadhyay, *Caste, Protest and Identity in Colonial India: The Namasudras of Bengal, 1872–1947*, London: Routledge, 1997, pp. 64–98.
4. S. V. Rajadurai and V. Geetha, *Towards a Non-Brahmin Millennium: From Iyothee Thass to Periyar*, Calcutta: Samya, 1998.
5. Partha Chatterjee, 'The Nation and Its Fragments: Colonial and Postcolonial Histories', *The Partha Chatterjee Omnibus*, New Delhi: Oxford University Press, 1999, pp. 173–74.
6. Mahesh Gavaskar, 'Phule's Critique of Brahmin Power', in S. M. Michael (ed.), *Untouchables: Dalits in Modern India*, Boulder CO: Lynne Rienner Publishers, 1999, pp. 43–44.
7. For a good understanding of the causal relationship between enlightenment thoughts and modern social order, refer to Milan Zafirovski, *The Enlightenment and Its Effects on Modern Society*, New York: Springer, 2011.
8. Gail Omvedt, 'Globalisation & Indian Tradition', http://www.ambedkar.org/News/Globalisation.htm (accessed on 21 May 2009).
9. M. K. Panini, 'The Political Economy of Caste', in M. N. Srinivasan (ed.), *Caste: Its Twentieth Century Avatar*, New Delhi: Viking, 1996, pp. 26–68.
10. Omvedt, 'Globalisation & Indian Tradition'.
11. Chandra Bhan Prasad, 'Markets and Manu: Economic Reforms and its Impact on Caste in India', *CASI Working Paper Series*, No. 08-01, Center for the Advanced Study of India, University of Pennsylvania, January 2008.

12. A. Ramaiah, 'Dalits to Accept Globalisation: Lessons from the Past and Present', mimeo., Tata Institute of Social Sciences, Mumbai, 2004, http://ssrn.com/abstract=568582 (accessed on 21 May 2009).
13. As mentioned by a leather manufacturer and retailer in Kanpur.
14. This was narrated by a stationery and software shop-owner in Aurangabad.
15. As described by a labour contractor in Ahmedabad.
16. These terms denote a socio-economic relationship between a master (belonging to the upper caste) and servant (belonging to the lower caste), where the latter is not just economically but also morally and socially bound to serve the former.
17. Chapter Two presents an elaborate justification of why Dalits should be considered a homogeneous social group.
18. For theoretical roots of narrative analysis and the debates surrounding narrative analysis and identity, see Margaret R. Somers and Gloria D. Gibson, 'Reclaiming the Epistemological "Other": Narrative and Social Construction of Identity', CSST *Working Papers No. 94*, Ann Arbor: The University of Michigan, 1993, http://deepblue.lib.umich.edu/bitstream/2027.42/51265/1/499.pdf (accessed on 26 September 2011).
19. To acquire the role of an economic agent seeking to earn profit in the existing production and distribution chain dominated and controlled by upper caste business competitors, raise formal and informal credit, engage with the local state to sustain their business efforts, negotiate with institutions in the realm of civil society, etc.

Two

Dalits, Theories of Caste and Transformative Recognition and Redistribution

◻

Dalits as an Analytical Category

[b]oth in the past and to a significant extent today, the deprived 'untouchable' and the very poor individual of 'clean' caste may appear to be indistinguishable in economic and other material terms. Yet there is still something real and important that divides them, not just in the abstract sense, but in the bitter realities of everyday experience. Similarly, Brahmans and other 'clean' or high-caste groups and individuals may often be found in deprived material circumstances. Yet such people will not lose the intangible but widely recognized quality that defines them as higher in caste terms than those who may be richer, better educated and even more politically influential than they are, but who will still be seen as their inferiors by the standards of 'traditional' caste ideology.[1]

This remark by Bayly indicates an important social divide that exists in India due to the practice of the ideology of caste — a closed system of social stratification where individual position is fixed at birth and cannot be changed, and this, in turn, also becomes the source of a social hierarchy with associated privileges and disadvantages.

Dalits as a social group are potentially fragmented not only by class, location and diverse sub-caste location, but also by place of residence (rural–urban, smaller towns–metros, etc.), political values and educational background. This diversity of socio-economic locations leads them to a differential experience of power structures. Therefore, it is pertinent to explain the reasons for considering

Dalits as a single and homogenous analytical category irrespective of socio-political and economic location. This section explains why Dalits should be considered as a homogenous group for any intellectual analysis as well as political and policy action. The present usage of the term Dalit can be traced back to the 19th century Marathi social reformer and revolutionary, Mahatma Jotirao Phule (1826–90). Phule used the term to describe the 'outcastes' and 'untouchables' who had been oppressed and pushed to the periphery of the social, economic, political, and cultural order.[2] The 'Dalit Panthers' manifesto of 1973 revived the term and extended its scope to include the scheduled tribes, neo-Buddhists, working people, landless and poor peasant women, and all those being exploited politically, economically or in the name of religion.[3] Essentially it came to be accepted as a political identity of the social groups facing multi-dimensional deprivation and who are determined to fight against this inequality and social subordination. In contemporary India, the term has come to signify the political identity of people who have been called scheduled castes in the official vocabulary of the colonial and post-colonial Indian state.[4]

In order to provide analytical arguments for proposing Dalit as a single social category, we will first examine diverse perspectives on caste and then go on to elaborate how 'ex-untouchables' define themselves. Self-perception and self-definition in our understanding become the crucial criteria to understand the experience of a particular social group. In other words, a distinction has to be drawn between how scholars and different schools of thought elaborate on the caste system on the one hand, and how Dalits themselves understand their collective subjective being on the other. The latter will also work as a critique of the former, and will hopefully provide us convincing arguments for considering Dalits as a homogenous group.

In order to examine the construct of caste, we must make it clear at the outset that even after taking into account a generous amount of literature, the body of texts which we have left out is much greater. However, it has been our attempt to focus on the dominant approaches towards studying caste rather than exhaustively covering all the available literature on caste. We have identified five broad approaches, namely: Orientalist, Hierarchy and Difference, Caste as a Superstructure, Defence of *Varna,* and Organic Social Block.

Constructs of Caste

Orientalist

Bayly[5] notes that initially the East India Company and later the British Crown sought information to identify potential allies in Indian society, people who could support their endeavours and thereby help them distinguish friends from foes. This information-gathering exercise, taken up through large-scale ethnographic surveys, decennial censuses and other official and quasi-official writings (writings of jurists, missionaries, revenue surveyors, military recruiters, and innumerable other observers of Indian life) 'essentialised the natives'. In other words, this process of reportage saw Indian society through the lens of religion and caste. Therefore, it divided the population on religious lines (Hindus/non-Hindus, minorities, etc.). Further, within Hindus, *jati* and varna were used as basic units of identification. Viewing Indian society through the lens of caste and religion fit the orientalist picture[6] and provided the British with moral and political 'justification' to rule the 'irrational' men and women supposedly unfit to govern themselves.[7] For instance, Abbe Dubois indignantly remarked:

> [w]e can picture what would become of the Hindus if they were not kept within the bounds of duty by the rules and penalties of caste, by looking at the position of the Pariahs, or outcastes of India, who, checked by no moral restraint, abandon themselves to their natural propensities . . . For my own part, being perfectly familiar with this class, and acquainted with its natural predilections and sentiments, I am persuaded that a nation of Pariahs left to themselves would speedily become worse than the hordes of cannibals who wander in the vast waste of Africa, and would soon take to devouring each other.[8]

Accordingly, Dirks points out that:

> [u]nder colonialism, caste became a specifically Indian form of civil society, the most critical site for the textualisation of social identity but also for the specification of public and private domains, the rights and responsibilities of the colonial state, the legitimating conceits of social freedom and societal control.[9]

In other words, caste was seen as an institution disallowing Indians from forging the bonds of a universally recognised ethical code; and hence the society was not seen as fit to acquire and work towards the principle of modern nationhood.

Hierarchy and Difference

Caste also found analytical expression in the writings of scores of (historical) sociologists. Much of the literature is crowded with attempts to understand the positioning of caste rather than dissecting and analysing the exploitation and subordination of labour efforts which the caste system perpetuates. Ghurye and Bougle both elaborated on the central features of caste.[10] Though they used different conceptual vocabularies to describe the characteristics of caste, they broadly agreed on the important underlying features of the caste system, such as hierarchy among caste groups (unequally divided rights and privileges), endogamy, occupational specialisation, and rigid norms of restrictions on social intercourse between different caste groups.

Bougle makes two important points. First, he argues that theoretically, Brahmins have kept the option open for themselves to pick up any profession, while not allowing the same occupational mobility to other caste groups. Second, he uses the conceptual lens of 'repulsion' to reveal the rigid boundaries between caste groups; the spirit of caste isolates each group and every effort is made to prevent its members from entering into alliances or relationships with other caste groups. In other words, his argument that caste groups are discrete entities was a precursor to the later theorisation of caste by Gupta.[11] As far as Ghurye's analysis is concerned, he sought to understand the social reality of the operational aspect of the caste system through the concept of *jatis*, an approach later reinforced by Srinivas.

Srinivas clarifies the distinction between varna and jati.[12] He opines that the four-tiered varna system does not operate in reality. Instead, it is the jatis specific to region with their norms regarding marriage, commensal taboos and occupation rigidity that regulate the social order. This formulation has led him to propose two important theses. First, there is a lack of clarity in the hierarchy, especially in the middle regions. Second, he puts forth the concept of 'sanskritisation' which basically implies that the social groups that feature lower in the caste hierarchy (jatis) adopt the cultural practices of caste groups higher up the ladder, and gradually claim a higher social status.[13] However, the social mobility associated with sanskritisation only results in positional change and does not lead to any structural change. The caste system remains intact even as different jatis move up and down the ladder.

So far, it is evident that the focus of scholars was limited to a more descriptive analysis of the caste system. The debate took a new turn with the publication of Dumont's *Homo Hierarchicus*.[14] Dumont claimed to theorise about the totality of caste relations as a system, and argued that the essence of caste is hierarchy, that is, different castes are vertically organised in terms of relative purity. Brahmins are supposed to be the purest, and Dalits the most polluted; the other caste groups lie in between. The ruler or the king is indeed important and powerful, and represents the political domain. However, he is inferior to the Brahmin. The various castes are held together with the ideological force of *dharma* or religion, presided over by the Brahmins. Dharma defines the place of each caste and its relationship with other castes. Therefore, in Dumont's framework, Dalits are positioned at the lowest rung of the caste ladder, and are considered polluted because they (are expected to) provide menial services to the members of higher castes. By giving primacy to religion, Dumont regards the politico-economic aspect of castes as relative, secondary and isolated, and in turn reduces the individual to a position of relative unimportance.[15] Gupta disagrees with this neat hierarchical model to describe caste as a social system.[16] According to him the main feature of caste is not one continuous and common hierarchy but its differentiation into separate and discrete endogenous jatis.[17] Even if hierarchy exists, it may not necessarily be along the purity/pollution axes. Further, he points out that there are several caste ideologies, not one, which share some principles and differ on others.

Caste as a Superstructure

The Marxist analysis of caste has certain dominant features. First, they revisit history in order to look at the historical roots of the caste system, and inform the readers about the specific material circumstances that resulted in its development and sustenance. Second, caste has been seen as a superstructure and its main role is to conceal class-based exploitation. The horizontal divide created by caste identities restrains the development of class identity. Third, Marxists view caste as a product of specific pre-capitalist formations which were expected to disappear as capitalist rationality develops.[18]

In other words, the corpus of work looking at caste through the lens of Marxism uncritically accepted:

> [t]he identification of proletariat as vanguard and the peasantry as basically a backward, feudal class designed to disintegrate (or 'differentiate') under capitalism into a basically proletarianised agricultural labourer/poor peasant class and a basically bourgeois rich peasant/capitalist farmer class. They accepted the notion that not only socialism but also capitalism laid a basis in the forces of relations of production for eradicating caste relations. Thus they tend to argue that while caste is an important superstructural feature of capitalist society, its main function is to exercise a retarding role on the development of class struggle (for instance, when rural rich farmers elites from 'dominant caste' use caste ties to split the rural poor).[19]

Defence of Varna

Gandhi used the term *Harijan* (literally meaning Children of God) for Dalits.[20] Guru argues that this is an entirely 'metaphysical connotation — it inculcates an element of resigned fate in the subject and therefore can render him or her inactive'.[21] Gandhi even went ahead to support the varna system (the bedrock of caste-based exploitation) for functional reasons. Gandhi does seem to give an apparent concession by pointing out that 'there is nothing in the varna system which stands in the way of the shudra acquiring learning or studying military art of offence or defence', but quickly adds 'what the varna system enjoins is that a shudra will not make learning a way of earning a living'.[22] In other words, a shudra can acquire knowledge but to earn a living he must stick to his hereditary profession, that is, to serve the upper castes by performing menial services. Therefore, Gandhi also binds Dalits under the overall social division of labour supported by the structure of the caste system vehemently defended in the name of Hindu religious texts for centuries.

Aloysius perceptively remarks that during the course of the nationalist struggle, Dalits were sought to be included by limiting their concerns to:

> [m]oral reform through constructive programme, obedience to the customary law of land relations, social fixity and in general a reversal to the old order, however differentially understood . . . [I]t sought to

divert the masses from its own agenda of economic and social interests
. . . in the name of uniqueness of Hindu/ Indian civilisation.[23]

Put differently, Gandhi attempted to solve the question of varna on
a moral plane by idealising the hierarchy rather than taking political
issue with the discrimination and inequality embedded in it.[24]

Organic Social Block

We also explore the social construction of caste in general and of
Dalits in particular within the praxis of (Hindu) nationalists and
Hindu reformists. To understand this, it is essential to first com-
prehend and critique the nationalist discourse on the idea of Hindu
India, developed during the colonial period, and later consolidated
and effectively deployed by cultural nationalists advocating the
Hindutva cause in post-colonial India.

The common endeavour of all three ideological groups — the
nationalists, the Hindu reformists in the colonial period, and the
cultural nationalists in the post-colonial period — was to eke out a
Hindu version of nationhood, by weaving together an organic social
block of Hindus, disallowing for the internal differences (reflected
in the division of caste and ethnic locations) within Hinduism. The
middle class activists tried to rhetorically present the concept of a
singular imagined Hindu community, even though many of them
tacitly accepted that the notion of a single Hindu community did
not go well with the hierarchical social order. This was particularly
true when they questioned caste hierarchy, which was part and parcel of the Hindu social order.[25] They actively resisted any attempt
by the colonial government to restrict religion to the realm of the
personal; even as they publicly rejected superstitions, devotional
belief, or, to some extent, even caste, they continued to use religious
symbolism for political mobilisation and public/intellectual debates.
We find that, during the early 19th century, a number of high caste,
middle class Hindus across the subcontinent took on the mantle of
reforming Hinduism and its religious practices in order to adapt
to western modernity while retaining the core of Hindu religion.
During the same period, we see the emergence of the Brahmo Samaj
(1828) and the Arya Samaj (1875). Both these reform movements
were initiated because of the perceived threat from Christianity and

were led by western-educated, upper-caste, middle-class Indians, i.e., Ram Mohan Roy and Swami Dayanand respectively. The idea was to reform the religion to make it better tuned to modern realities, while also glorifying the Vedas and Upanishads in order to contest the superiority claim of western religion (Christianity).[26] In other words, in order to consolidate and build a Hindu social block, the reformists attempted to re-invent the 'glorious' Hindu past and, in the process, also defended the hierarchical social order presided over by Brahmins. Within the Congress, two leaders who adopted a similar strategy for socio-political mobilisation against the colonial rulers were Bal Gangadhar Tilak in Maharashtra and Aurobindo Ghosh in Bengal. In Punjab, we find middle class Hindu activists like Lal Chand furthering the cause of the Arya Samaj.[27] In substance, the attempts of middle-class, upper-caste reformists were not only directed towards proving to the colonial rulers the superiority of their native religion and culture, but also to create a sense of homogeneity among the Hindus, irrespective of caste distinctions. Later, this political project was forcefully taken over by the militant Hindu nationalists (a natural by-product of Hindu reform movements) by deliberately constructing a religious 'other' in an attempt to consolidate all Hindus into a single social block. In other words, Hindu nationalists wanted to create a Hindu *rashtra* (state).

Hindu middle class intellectuals like Savarkar and Golwalkar pointed out that the nation-state cannot be conceived in universalistic terms.[28] They argued against the conception of the nation in terms of territory, advocating instead the idea of the nation being conceived and understood in terms of culture — rituals, social rules, religious festivals, common mythology, and language. In other words, Savarkar and Golwalkar's efforts towards conceptualising the basis for a Hindu nation derived its strength from a matrix that consisted of all castes woven into a single organic social block. It is important to note that this organic unity was not to be achieved by challenging the hierarchy from within; in fact, this hierarchy was sought to be preserved and legitimised by invoking the *dharma* (universal law) that governs Hindu social rituals and customs — the bedrock of social hierarchy. These reformist and nationalist movements also laid the foundations of present day right-wing social and political organisations.

A Dalit Critique of these Approaches

The literature quoted in the preceding paragraphs educates us on various dimensions of caste as seen by colonial administrators, historical and contemporary sociologists, political economists, and nationalists. In this section, we attempt to interpret the approaches discussed earlier from the point of view of the Dalits. Therefore, this section has two interrelated aims. First, while discussing the key differences and critical similarities, we delve into the Dalit critique of these approaches and elaborate on their understanding of caste.

While each of these approaches come from a different political perspective, there are also some striking similarities. 'Orientalism' was expected to justify colonial rule and made caste system as an alibi to defend it. The politics embedded in the 'Defence of the Varna' approach and the 'Organic Social Block' approach provides a socio-political framework as well as an epistemological claim to preserve the caste system. In spite of the moral claim of larger social good through their argument that caste is merely a social division of labour, there is an attempt to preserve the status quo in social relationships. The 'Hierarchy and Difference' approach merely informs us about the possibility and processes of mobility within the caste system and changes which the system has seen over the period of time, while not providing any epistemological tools or political framework to understand the oppression and exploitation inherent in the caste system. Any struggle by a jati or set of jatis for upward mobility will be seen as a struggle for movement within the caste system and not necessarily against the caste system.[29] The 'Caste as Superstructure' approach is a political programme. This is not to say that other approaches do not have a certain politics embedded in their operational frameworks. However, this particular approach provides a framework of action for the toiling masses (the lower class — proletariat), irrespective of caste, to liberate themselves from socio-economic oppression.

Critics argue that this approach makes class relations and the class struggle so fundamental to any social change that it renders any other sociological category (for instance caste) irrelevant. Accordingly, the critiques show that caste is also a material reality and does not only exist at the level of superstructure. The material, social, political, and cultural aspects of caste are so tightly woven together that one aspect cannot be separated from the other.[30]

Coming to similarities, all these approaches tend to homogenise the differences within and between social groups. The Orientalist interrogation in general and pertaining to India in particular has sought to impose political domination through knowledge creation. As Said has argued, colonialism is 'supported and perhaps even impelled by impressive ideological formations which include notions that certain territories and people require and beseech domination, as well as forms of knowledge affiliated with that domination'.[31] In the process of facilitating domination, orientalists have homogenised the 'natives' through two interrelated intellectual projects. First, all societies in the east were taken to be essentially similar to each other and fundamentally dissimilar to western societies. Within this framework of 'essentialisation', Indians were constructed as 'unvirile, irrational and socially atomised, thus unfit to govern themselves'.[32] Second, Indians were stereotyped as 'slaves' to rigid Brahmin-centred caste values. This is what Ronald Inden[33] has called the 'imagined India' of false and dehumanising orientalist stereotypes.[34] If homogenisation was the intellectual-cum-political project of the orientalists for political domination, the 'organic social block' school of thought also attempted to suppress all internal differences in Indian society so as to construct a pan-Indian Hindu identity in order to uphold the socio-economic hegemony of the upper castes. Gandhi's 'Defence of Varna' provides a moral twist to the debate with the coining of the term Harijan to refer to Dalits; though in the final analysis, it sought to conserve the social hierarchy embedded in Hindu religion. The 'Caste as Superstructure' standpoint precludes the possibility of internal differences by analytically creating a political identity of 'working class' or 'proletariat'. All poor are clubbed into a single sociological category, thereby ignoring the social contradictions existing within them. The 'Hierarchy and Difference' school does acknowledge the internal diversity but it seems to be satisfied with discovering the rules of mobility within the continuum of 'pure' and 'polluted'. Thus, when caste is viewed through any or all of these lenses, a clear attempt is made to bury any kind of social distinction which may emerge due to caste division.

Second, all these approaches envision only a negative role for human agency, that is, the political domination imposed by the colonial power (orientalists); varnas or the hierarchical social order (defence of varnas/ organic social block) is defended and sought to be preserved; lower castes are compelled to practice the norms and rules of the Brahminical social order in order to gain any mobility within the system (hierarchy and difference). The Marxist interpretation of caste as superstructure does provide a positive role to human agency which can potentially re-order social relationships, but it limits this role by subsuming all conflicting social identities within the single sociological category of class. While trying to understand the caste system, the historical and contemporary sociologists discussed above are silent on the role of Dalits in the production processes, and as a result, also deny them any positive political agency to engage, protest and possibly change the oppressive structures responsible for their subordination.

Finally, these approaches do not provide us with any epistemological tools for defining an institutional framework required for social change that can overcome the multi-dimensional historical subordination of Dalits. If historical injustice meted out to a particular social group has to be mitigated, especially in a socio-political, cultural and economic milieu where social infrastructure sustaining discrimination and deprivation may have weakened in some respects but has also acquired new forms as a consequence of the attempts by the privileged castes to retain *status quo* vis-à-vis the deprived, then there is enough normative ground for supporting a universal institution which can provide a framework for engaging with and removing the institutional source of such discrimination. In this sense, mitigation of discrimination and deprivation of any one or more individual due to his/her group identity is also a larger question of social justice. Social justice, in turn is about defining the framework of the relationship between different social groups on the one hand and the relationship of various social groups with various formal and informal institutions on the other.

This discussion explains that Dalits do not sit comfortably with the dominant theories of caste, because their particularistic identity is subsumed under the universal identity, thereby making them part of the large Hindu social order under which their political agency to oppose the causes of their subordination is denied at worst and is considerably muted at best. Further, the support of homogeneity and denial of political agency to Dalits contributes to an institutional framework for social injustice. Having critiqued the theories of caste from the standpoint of Dalits, we shall now discuss the position of Dalits on three crucial issues — *social homogeneity and difference, political agency and social justice*. This will help us conclude our section on why Dalits should be considered a homogenous group.

Social Homogeneity versus Recognition and Redistribution

For Dalits, social homogeneity is about masking the structural differences, which translate into multi-dimensional subordination sanctioned by the caste system and legitimised by Hindu religious texts, whereas acknowledgement of differences or social heterogeneity is about the acceptance and recognition of unequal power relationships between different social groups. In the case of Dalits, it is the overarching framework of caste society that is understood to be the cause of this immense structural disparity between social groups that are considered 'pure' vis-à-vis those perceived to be 'polluted'. Therefore, the adverse experience of social relationships embedded in caste-structures forces Dalits to articulate their social presence through a common identity, irrespective of other axes of difference and inequality — class, region, religion, gender, etc. — to engage in possible emancipatory programmes and actions. An individual cannot rescue himself/herself from the upper-caste-endorsed social stigma of being considered a polluted being; the whole social group has to fight the political battle to contest and overcome the power embedded in the praxis of the caste system. Therefore, the social identity of Dalits has to be fiercely preserved and deployed in the public domain to fight injustice.

Second, the Dalit standpoint of opposing the integration of their social identity and existence into the larger Hindu fold is driven by their political aspiration for recognition and redistribution, which therefore forms the core of the political articulation of all Dalits. It is necessary to pause briefly and understand the Dalit standpoint on these important social principles around recognition and redistribution. In existing literature, recognition and non-recognition have been viewed through more than one lens.[35] In the liberal tradition, there are broadly two approaches. The first is described as the 'politics of equal recognition', which entails equal dignity of citizens, equal rights and entitlements, and the principle of equal citizenship. This approach has been rejected by Dalits because it is 'difference blind' and translates into negating their identity by forcing people into a homogenous mould. The supposedly neutral set of difference blind principles of the politics of equal recognition is in fact a reflection of one hegemonic culture. The second approach is articulated through the 'politics of difference'. It emphasises the distinctness and particularities of each individual and therefore, unlike the politics of the equal recognition approach, argues for non-assimilation of group/individual identity. This approach thus advocates non-discrimination by acknowledging differences and making them the basis for differential treatment.[36] From a Dalit standpoint, the 'politics of difference' approach is necessary but not sufficient. Nancy Fraser argues that politics of difference (she calls it the identity model) is based on a Hegelian premise that identity is constructed dialogically.[37] One becomes an individual subject only by virtue of recognising, and being recognised by another subject. Recognition from others is thus essential to the development of a sense of self. To be denied recognition — or to be 'misrecognised' — is to suffer both a distortion of one's relation to one's self and an injury to one's identity.[38] Viewed through this Hegelian lens, the politics of difference transposes the framework of Hegelian recognition onto cultural and political terrains. For Fraser, this is an important step whereby initiatives springing forth from the politics of recognition will lead to upward re-evaluation of disrespected identities, recognising and positively valourising cultural diversity, and the transformation of societal patterns of representation, interpretation and communication in ways that would change everybody's sense of self. However, she argues in favour of going beyond the politics of recognition towards the politics of redistribution. The politics of marginalisation demands initiatives for redistributing income, reorganising the division of labour, subjecting investment to democratic decision-making, and transforming other basic economic structures.[39] In the real world, to be sure, political economy and culture are mutually intertwined, as are the injustices of distribution and recognition. 'Even the most material economic institutions have a constitutive, irreducible cultural dimension; they are shot through with significations and norms. Conversely, even the most discursive cultural practices have a constitutive, irreducible political-economic dimension; they are underpinned by material supports'.[40] In the case of Dalits, the most celebrated articulation of this intertwining was elaborated by Ambedkar, way before the social sciences started engaging with the interrelated properties of recognition and redistribution. Gail Omvedt, while reviewing Ambedkar's rich corpus of writings, underlines the major themes in his thought. Ambedkar advocated total annihilation of the caste system and the Brahmanic superiority it embodied, contesting the Brahmanic historical cultural interpretations in order to rescue the socio-cultural history of Dalits from getting submerged in a homogenous Hindu identity. Besides a fierce rationalism against any kind of religious superstitions, he sought to repudiate Hinduism and advocated Buddhism as an alternative religion. He proposed an economic programme with a strategic mix of state socialism and democratic liberalism, and donned a political orientation which linked a firmly autonomous Dalit movement with other socially and economically exploited social groups.[41] Besides Ambedkar, a considerable amount of literature also exists which has documented and analysed numerous social movements and socio-political, economic and cultural articulations of Dalits seeking to claim an identity, culture and history of their own, as well as demanding a restructuring of the redistributive framework of Indian polity and economy.[42] The rich corpus of literature indicates the collective socio-political assertion of Dalits for claiming what Fraser calls 'transformative recognition' and 'transformative redistribution'.[43] The former refers to the carving out of a new self-representation by fiercely contesting negative identities (for instance, untouchability) imposed on them by the caste system, while also collectively producing and disseminating a self-affirming culture of their own (for instance, taking pride in their literature, language, dress, food), in the hope that their socio-cultural existence and achievements will be socially recognised and respected by society at large. Along with this, there have been aggressive socio-political claims to address the historical and material injustice perpetuated against the Dalits. In recent years, remedy has been sought by asking the state to provide job reservations in the private sector in the face of dwindling state sector employment.[44] Also, pressure has been mounted on the state to provide Dalits with capital and other facilities to enter the markets as owners of capital.[45] For Dalits, as already pointed out, recognition and redistribution are closely intertwined and dialectically influence each other, though each requires different actions and programmes. As a social group, Dalits have seen varying degrees of success in their quest for transformative recognition and redistribution. The experience has been still better in the political domain, though the political space they occupy in terms of numbers hugely differs across regions and states.[46] In states like Punjab, West Bengal, Odisha, and Haryana, among others, where Dalits constitute a significant proportion of the population, they are still not able to articulate their political presence and continue to survive under the patronage and domination of upper castes.[47] In the socio-cultural domain, there has been considerable effort towards self-recognition and public assertion.[48] However, their assertion has also resulted in a backlash which is often manifested in physical violence inflicted on them by members of the upper castes.[49] In the realm of the economy — work, employment and wages, and quality of work — Dalits along with other historically deprived social groups and minorities, especially Muslims, continue to subsist at the margins.[50] Dalits perceive that their current socio-cultural and political assertion and consequent political empowerment has not erased the damage of centuries of caste oppression. The social group as a whole still seems to be caught between newer forms of social repulsion (experience of humiliation as untouchables which is constantly acquiring newer forms), their new-found political assertion and self-belief in the domain of culture and electoral politics, and a sense of disappointment that socio-political empowerment is not sufficient for economic well-being.[51] It is in this context that the politics of transformative recognition and redistribution calls for collective assertion as a community, a sense of solidarity within, and alliances with similar marginalised groups. The Dalit identity, then, is not merely a cosmetic social identity but also a means through which deprived social groups deploy political agency to seek transformative recognition and redistribution.

This leads us to the next discussion on the crucial issue of agency, a notion on which dominant theories of caste are conspicuous by their silence.

Political Agency and Dalits

The endeavours for transformative recognition and redistribution bring forth the question of the political agency of Dalits, which is crucial to socio-political and economic change. Why do Dalits privilege collective political agency of the whole group over the political agency of an individual?

Here, we use the term 'political agency' instead of 'human agency' because the present efforts of Dalits for transformative recognition are invariably inspired by a long democratic struggle and are currently located in the wider framework of a democratic state. It is their collective political agency which has brought them to a crucial historical juncture, where they are politically challenging the structures that have perpetuated their subordination and exploitation.[52] Therefore, it is essential to conceptually understand and contextualise the meaning of political agency in such a way that not only explains the importance of a collective Dalit identity but also allows them to further consolidate this identity, as well as to build alliances with similarly situated groups in order to engage and challenge the structures of domination and exploitation. Therefore, political agency has to be necessarily seen in relation to the structure.

Following Layder, we understand a structure as having four important and interrelated properties. First, structures are an 'ongoing set of reproduced relations which have an ongoing, organised and relatively enduring quality to them'. Second, in spite of possessing some semblance of stability, 'structures are historically variable and just as subject to the forces of development and change as other social phenomena'. Third, 'structure, in the sense defined above, integrally involves the notion of power, since the power of social groupings relative to one another defines the pattern of ongoing reproduced relations'. Fourth, structural power provides resources which the social groups collectively possess, that in turn situate them in some pre-established unequal relations to other groups.[53]

In this sense, the institution of caste will be inevitably understood as a structure reproducing unequal relationships between social groups for centuries. Throughout its history, caste has shown the dual properties of stability and change. It has changed in terms of content but has retained amazing stability in terms of form, thereby helping retain what Krekel, in a different context, calls 'primary asymmetry' between social groups.[54] This primary asymmetry acquires strength from the dextrous use of social power by the upper castes. The structural power of the upper castes is acquired through their superior status as sanctioned by religious texts and is effected through moral, religious and social sanctions, control over means of production and means of violence, and near-monopoly over skills and information, besides their social ability to draw on the vast resources of the state. This structural power of the upper castes is often described as what Béteille in a different context calls the 'zero-sum' approach to power.[55] In other words, the social power of the upper castes derived from caste location can only be protected, enhanced and operationalised by curtailing or denying the power of Dalits. It is in this sense that privileges and disrespect or humiliation are different sides of the same coin. The framework of social power derived through caste identity necessarily draws its sustenance from group identities. A good illustration of this kind of social power is the praxis of untouchability that Ambedkar defined as 'graded inequality'.[56] Untouchability alienates Dalits from the products of their own creation as well as from their labouring body. Further, the stigma of alienation continues to persist even if they change their vocation. 'The logic of lowness and labour exists in contrast to counter logic of highness and intellect. Brahmins born into an exalted status are meant to perform only acts of mind, and these, in turn, become them, sanctified as it were their bodily purity'.[57] These arguments reflect a specific nature of social power translating into an unequal power relationship. 'Born to labour, Dalits cannot claim the right of knowing; and being denied the right, they cannot know of or escape their condition of being labourers' and thereby cannot claim a social position equivalent to a Brahmin's.[58] In case the Dalit acquires the privilege of knowledge and learning, the power relationship is altered and Brahmins (or, more generally, upper castes) stand to lose their privileged status.

Against this backdrop, how do we understand the political agency of Dalits in the face of the structural power of caste? As already discussed, we have to bring in the notion of power not only to understand the durability of the structure but also to comprehend how it mediates between structure and political agency. Before we elaborate on the praxis of power embedded in the political agency of Dalits, it is essential to take into account the notion of power in the context of the structure–agency debate found in existing literature.

Broadly, there are two dominant notions of power found in the structure–agency debate. The first is represented in the writing of Lukes who understands power as involving a situation where A has power over B to the extent that he or she prevails over B not only through one-dimensional decision-making (to prevail over B while making the decision) and two-dimensional restriction of issues (power to decide what the issue is and thereby restrict the issue for discussion), but also by preventing B from realising what his or her 'real' interests are, thereby influencing, shaping or determining his/ her very wants.[59] Lukes' conception mirrors Bourdieu and Passeron's concept of symbolic violence, which basically implies an unconscious absorption of the dominant worldview by those in a subordinate position.[60] Giddens' writings can be taken as representative of the second notion of power. He challenges the structure–agency dualism and argues that there is an ongoing relationship between human agency and social structure; they are interactive and reciprocal.

Giddens introduces the concept of 'structuration' which implies that structures are produced and reproduced simultaneously. Every act which contributes to the reproduction of structure is also an act of production, and therefore could potentially initiate change by altering the structure at the same time as it produces it. The agency is both autonomous of as well as dependent on the structure since it draws upon and reproduces structural properties of domination while also being capable of altering the structure. Expressing the same argument differently, Giddens argues that social structures (rules and resources) are produced by human agency, yet at the same time they reproduce conditions of human agency. Therefore, analytical attention ought to focus on the mutuality of the processes of social development and human interaction. Power, while mediating between structure and agency, is never held as a form of totality, but is involved in the dialectic of control. Dialectics refer to the shifts that take place in power relations as a result of attempts by subordinate groups to alter the power balance.[61]

From a Dalit standpoint, the outcome of the conception of power reflected in Lukes' work will be similar to the operations of caste discussed in the 'defence of varna' and 'organic social block' approaches, which will mandate that Dalits accept their deprivation and discrimination as natural, consensual and justified. There will be little scope for any resistance leading to social change. Further, as Layder points out, Lukes' analysis of power seems to lie between two or more actors and he does not 'concern himself with the group possession of resources [as in the case of caste] and in the way in which these affect exercises of power through prior relations of domination and subordination'.[62] Giddens' analysis can be considered an important step forward since it provides some agency to the socially underprivileged to overcome structural determinism. However, it is argued that the framework put forth by Giddens does not take into account the historical roots affecting the production and reproduction of the structure, since he seems to emphasise that the structures are created and recreated in every encounter.[63]

> Contrary to Giddens' formulation, the notion of 'reproduced relations' must convey the idea that not only are actors in specific encounters actively engaged in the reproduction of social relations, but that these relations have already been produced in an historical sense, in order that agents are able to reproduce them.[64]

The existing inequalities of power derived from historically constituted relationships of domination and subordination between social
groups constrain and determine the relative negotiating strengths of
the actors prior to their social encounters.

Given the fact that Dalits refuse to abide by the historically-
shaped structural power of caste which is overwhelmingly biased
in favour of dominant castes, they envision their political agency
in the form of an institutionalised collective socio-political protest,
continuously engaging and contesting the structural power of caste.
Hence it is not calculated actions of individuals but collective agency,
based on a shared knowledge and experience of historically-shaped
subordination, which in turn constitutes and cements their group
identity. On the other hand, the structural power of caste is also
actualised through what we may call the negative political agency of
the upper castes deployed towards upholding the caste system. Once
the structural power of caste develops a coherent form, it acquires
relative autonomy from agency and it tends to be reproduced until
fundamentally questioned, contested and negated. The latter implies
that neither is the structure permanent nor is the power invariably
top-down. In other words, in the face of socio-political contesta-
tions, the attempt of the dominant group is to preserve the original
structures of authority, albeit admitting changes in content to suit
the emergent realities. Theoretically, both form and content can also
alter if the dominant structure is socially and politically delegitimised
through sustained and aggressive protest. Hence, power in a certain
sense is an integral part of agency as well as structure. 'Power as
agency and power as structure are analytically separable, although
empirically related phenomena'.[65] Therefore the political agency of
Dalits continuously evolves with changing socio-economic requirements and is not unanimous on the structural power of castes as
Lukes seems to have suggested. Rafannell and Gorringe argue that

> rules, norms, laws and beliefs exist because individuals repeatedly
> adopt them but acts of repetition are open to challenge and open
> up choice, action, and resistance . . . Therefore, [the political agency
> of Dalits sees] resistance and change, not as possible but, rather
> inevitable.[66]

It is in this context that Dalits invoke a group identity, because
it facilitates the development of somewhat coordinated action and

deployment of collective political agency towards rectifying the institutionalised patterns privileging certain groups and in turn oppressing them.

Social Justice and the Question of Institutions

As we have seen in the earlier discussion, the social objective of Dalits is to assert, advocate and uphold transformative recognition and redistribution by the deployment of political agency. Such transformation is not only a question of social justice but also has serious implications on the kind of institutions which are required for addressing the question of social justice. This further begs an answer to two interrelated questions: Why is a Dalit identity necessary for seeking a claim to a transformative social justice agenda? And what are the institutional requirements for the same? The first part of the question acquires a degree of complexity because social justice is seen to be a universal value while the invocation of Dalit identity is particularistic in nature. Is there a contradiction in the demand for social justice by promoting a particularistic identity? We grapple with these issues in the following pages while also outlining the complexities inherent in discussing the institutional arrangements supporting the agenda of transformative justice. The latter is also a larger question that will be elucidated in subsequent chapters.

The normative framework of social justice from the Dalit perspective has been elaborated by Guru.[67] Drawing on Ambedkar, Guru argues that any modern notion of justice has to be defined in terms of comparative worth in place of relative worth. The notion of relative worth seems to be grounded in the 'defence of varna' and organic 'social block approach' which we have discussed earlier. Guru points out that relative worth demands mutual respect and by this criterion, every form of labour/work including scavenging has worth. Thus the notion of relative worth keeps the hierarchical arrangement of worth intact. Unlike relative worth, comparative worth is deeply political in nature and goes against the hierarchical arrangement since it demands substantive equality. This notion of social justice is therefore also conflictual in nature since it questions the status quo favouring the powerful. Accordingly,

> conceptions of justice are to be articulated through struggle. The idea of struggle was premised on the possibility that society could

in fact be shaped by the agency of marginalised . . . [who are] not only interrogat[ing] the system of hierarchical social relations, but more fundamentally seek[ing] to alter these social relations along egalitarian lines.[68]

This demand for a comparative notion of social justice has a few interrelated objectives which in turn are also claims to universality. First and foremost, as already discussed, its claims include the recognition and redistribution of resources in favour of a group of people suffering from both socio-economic maldistribution and cultural misrecognition, where neither can be reduced to an effect of the other. The injustice that such a collective faces arises in the economic sphere and in the cultural sphere simultaneously.[69] Arguing differently, social justice demands socio-political, economic and cultural parity between all sections of the society rather than facilitating some and ignoring others under the pretext of 'larger good'. Thus, this notion of comparative justice is antagonistic, and rightly so, to utilitarian approaches which propound that utilities of different people should be simply summed together and the higher the sum of utilities the better the state of affairs or choice.[70] A utilitarian view can, in essence, result in the idea that there is nothing wrong if some human beings are treated as instruments for fulfilling the objectives of others, as long as it serves the aggregate good. Therefore, utilitarianism as a normative framework will invariably strengthen the hold of the ascriptive majority.[71] Second, the comparative notion of social justice sits immeasurably uneasy with the distributional notion of justice that restricts justice to morally appropriate distribution of benefits and burdens among all members of society.[72] The uneasiness does not emanate from the notion of distribution *per se*, but emerges from the framework of such distribution. Like the dominant theories of agency and power that we discussed earlier, the distributional theories of social justice are also ahistorical in nature. They either construct an ideal state and then try and explore a just institution which can produce a just and fair society, as in the case of Rawls, or seek to advocate a redressal mechanism in the existing situation, as Sen seems to suggest. Against these normative frameworks, Mills[73] argues that the crucial task of any normative theory is not merely to focus on moral wrongs in the non-ideal world or the ideal right in a well-ordered society, but also to provide a normative framework for rectificatory justice, so as to compensate the injustices of the past. Extending Mills' arguments in the context of racial segregation, one can suggest that a society without a caste system is more just than a society with caste, and that a society without caste-inspired segregation is more just than a society where caste-based domination is unquestioned. But this does not offer any solution for those whose ancestors were oppressed and exploited, and who are now morally entitled to make up for the historic wrongs. 'An explicit recognition of the peculiar features of rectificatory justice, which takes into account how the privileges have been moulded by deep social injustice, would have to be part of the theoretical agenda'.[74] Therefore, any framework of social justice has to necessarily take into account the historical factors which have shaped the present pattern of injustices. However, the comparative notion of justice which Guru proposes is in agreement with Sen on his discomfort with the Rawlsian proposal of equity in the distribution of primary goods[75] for a socially just society. For Sen, equitable access to primary goods is a necessary condition for justice but it is not sufficient, since injustice can still persist because of the inability of the people to convert primary goods into good living.[76] For instance, Dalits may have the right to move freely and by virtue of this right, should have physical access to all religious places including temples. It is a possibility that they are unable to convert this right into actual practice and temple entry may be denied to them through physical violence or social reprimands/ humiliation. Sen's intervention is an important step forward in the literature on social justice as it helps us to recognise the social processes which may cause the gap between intent (acknowledging and granting rights) and practice (outcomes) leading to injustice. Mills, while writing about race-based discrimination, points out that 'we need to work towards a more global — doubly — re-theorization of justice that would be centrally based on the recognition of the actual white evasiveness of this nominally colour-blind transcendence and ideality'.[77] In this context, what would be the characteristic feature of social justice which acknowledges transformative recognition and redistribution from the standpoint of a historically deprived social group(s)? Young elaborates on a 'family of concepts and conditions' relevant to any conception of social justice which, if understood in the context of socio-cultural and economic subordination of Dalit labour, will read as follows.[78]

a. Mitigating Exploitation: Institutionalised efforts to restrain transfer of the fruits of labour of Dalits to the dominant caste group(s) which are actualised through the use of legal and extra-legal means.

b. Tackling Marginalisation: Ensuring the active participation of Dalits in social life so that they are not 'potentially subjected to severe material deprivation and even extermination'.

c. Powerlessness: Enabling Dalits to overcome lack of authority, acquire status and pride in self.

d. Cultural Empowerment: Overcoming a situation where their experience and interpretation of social life finds its own expression, and dominant cultures and experiences are not imposed on them.

e. Freedom from Violence: Freedom from attacks 'which have no motive except to damage, humiliate, or destroy the person'.

In the absence of enabling institutionalised conditions to meet the demands of the 'family of concepts and conditions', the experience of Dalits forms a distinct pattern where multiple forms of oppression coalesce, leading to specific dominant–subordinate social relationships. The historical longevity of socially depressing, economically dependent, politically incapacitating, and culturally debilitating experiences gives them the moral and legitimate right to invoke their particularistic identity to pursue the politics of transformative recognition and redistribution in the interest of social justice. The particular in this case becomes universal, because the demand is to mitigate historical injustices, which by itself is not only a political claim but also a moral claim.

In the face of this multi-dimensional oppression of Dalits, there is universal consensus on the need for an institutionalised endeavour to correct these wrongs and promote social justice. In contemporary India, 'the state has acquired a huge role in determining social justice both as a concept as well as policy' argues Guru.[79] The state as a vehicle for social transformation (and therefore, social justice) is invariably invoked since it is normatively considered to be an agency which upholds universal values of democracy, equality, participation, and economic justice. Further, the framework of the liberal democratic state in India is seen to be sensitive to the issue of social justice. Thus the Indian state seems to have 'adopted compensation as the dominant mode of responding to justice concerns'. Compensation is a sort of co-responsibility which the state shares for the historical and contemporary wrongs perpetuated by dominant social forces.[80] Second, the Dalit voice in the domain of the state is expected to be articulated through democratic politics. Therefore, it is also believed that the disjunction between the norms and practice of social justice is due to the domination and control of upper castes over the political and administrative apparatus of the state. This has led to aggressive political assertion which on many occasions has translated into the entry of Dalits into the state as political executive. Accordingly, it is expected that the historical disadvantages and injustice perpetuated can be redressed through the apparatus of the democratic state once Dalits have also acquired political control or influence over the bureaucratic apparatus.

We argue that the faith in the apparatus of the democratic state is well-intentioned and justified. However, we also realise that the various kinds of oppression which we have noted earlier do not necessarily acquire roots in the domain of the state or cannot necessarily be rectified only by the intervention of a democratic state. The structures of oppression are also embedded in the norms, habits and symbols, in the assumptions underlying institutional rules, and the collective consequences of following those rules.[81] Exploitation, marginalisation, powerlessness, cultural subordination, and violence also exist in the realm of the markets as well as the civil society, though one can argue that the state has an over-determining role in addressing the factors responsible for various forms of oppression. In other words, we are going to pursue this line of argument further and explore how exploitation, marginalisation and discrimination are perpetuated as well as contested at the intersection of the state, market and civil society. The blurred boundaries between these formal institutions make it difficult to acknowledge or assign one of them the primary role in promoting the social justice agenda. This is the large aim of the present work.

To sum up, we have discussed the reasons for the discomfort of Dalits with dominant theories of caste. We have pointed out that these theories do not critically discern and flag the specificities of their multi-dimensional subordination and subsume their identity in the larger Hindu community, thereby retaining the hierarchical socio-cultural and economic order. Second, Dalits stake a powerful socio-political claim for transformative recognition and redistribution. This is precisely the reason that they have faith in collective political agency as the vehicle to carry forward their political struggle against the dominant power structures, thereby pushing forth the agenda of social justice. Third, any social justice agenda has to explicitly take into account the 'family of concepts and conditions' — exploitation, marginalisation, powerlessness, cultural subordination, and violence. Fourth, all our discussions so far point towards the fact that transformative recognition and redistribution leading to social justice must consider Dalits as a homogeneous analytical category in order to understand their historical subordination. Fifth, Dalits have placed their faith in the state because it is normatively perceived as an institution which can uphold the social justice agenda. Finally, we conclude our discussion by indicating the need to situate the systematic subordination and exploitation of Dalits at the intersection of the state, market and civil society, and hence, the social justice agenda has to be similarly explored, understood and analysed at the juncture of all these institutions.

—

Notes

1. Susan Bayly, *Caste, Society and Politics in India from the Eighteenth Century to the Modern Age*, Cambridge: Cambridge University Press, 2008, p. 11.
2. This social group was given certain names that were associated with expressions of contempt. They include: Dasa, Dasysa, Raksasa, Asura, Avarna, Nisada, Panchama, Chandala, Harijan, and Untouchable. Each of these terms has a history and background. Many of them are region specific. For example, Chura in Punjab (North West India), Bhangi or Lal Beghi in Hindi (North India), Mahar in Marathi (Central India), Mala in Telugu, Paraiya in Tamil, and Pulayan in Malayalam (South India).
3. Gail Omvedt, *Dalit Visions: The Anti-Caste Movement and the Construction of an Indian Identity*, New Delhi: Orient Longman, 1995, p. 72.
4. See C. B. Webster, 'Who is a Dalit', in S. M. Michael (ed.), *Dalits in Modern India: Vision and Values*, New Delhi: Sage, 1999, p. 76.
5. Bayly, *Caste, Society and Politics in India*, pp. 99–100.
6. The term Orientalism signifies a system of representation in the writings, vision and studies dominated by imperatives, perspectives, and ideological biases of western thinkers constructing stereotypical images

of non-white people as culturally backward, irrational and violent, with a tendency towards despotism and away from progress. See Edward W. Said, *Orientalism*, New Delhi: Penguin, 1995.

7. In the Indian context, Inden examines how the orientalist discourse — the history of religion, anthropology, economics, and political philosophy — produced and reproduced a stereotypical image of India and its people. See Ronald B. Inden, *Imagining India*, Oxford: Blackwell Publishers, 1990. Also refer to n. 6.

8. Abbe J. A. Dubois, *Description of the Character, Manners, and Customs of the People of India; and of Their Institutions, Religious and Civil*, 1817, transl. Henry K. Beauchamp, London, p. 29, quoted in Nicholas B. Dirks, 'Caste of Minds', *Representations*, 1992, 37: 56.

9. Dirks, 'Caste of Minds', p. 76.

10. G. S. Ghurye, *Caste and Race in India*, Mumbai: Popular Prakashan, 1969, pp. 1–30; C. Bougle, 'The Essence and Reality of Caste System', *Contributions to Indian Sociology*, 1958, 2(1): 17–30.

11. Dipankar Gupta, *Interrogating Caste: Understanding Hierarchy and Difference in Indian Society*, New Delhi: Penguin, 2000, pp. 15–85.

12. M. N. Srinivas, 'Varna and Caste', *Caste in Modern India and Other Essays*, Bombay: Asia Publishing House, 1962, pp. 63–69.

13. M. N. Srinivas, *Social Change in Modern India*, Hyderabad: Orient Longman, 1966, pp. 1–48.

14. Louis Dumont, *Homo Hierarchicus: An Essay on the Caste System*, Chicago: University of Chicago Press, 1970.

15. Dirks, 'Caste of Minds', pp. 56–57.

16. See Gupta, *Interrogating Caste*.

17. According to R. S. Khare, the concept of *jati* implies the existence of caste in its 'concrete and factual' forms in everyday social life, as opposed to the 'ideal and symbolic archetypes' reflected in the varna. See R. S. Khare, *Normative Culture and Kinship: Essays on Hindu Categories, Processes and Perspectives*, New Delhi: Vikas Publishing House, 1983, p. 85.

18. For instance, see E. M. S. Namboodiripad, 'Caste Conflicts and Growing Unity of Popular Democratic Process', *Economic and Political Weekly*, Annual Number, 1979, 7/8: 329–36; Ajit Roy, 'Caste and Class: An Interlinked View', *Economic and Political Weekly*, Annual Number, 1979, 7/8: 297–312; Sharad Patil, 'Dialectics of Caste and Class Conflicts', *Economic and Political Weekly*, 1979, Annual Number, XIV(7/8): 287–96; Joan P. Mencher, 'The Caste System Upside Down, or The Not-So-Mysterious East', *Current Anthropology*, 1974, 15(4): 469–93.

19. Gail Omvedt, *Dalits and the Democratic Revolution: Dr Ambedkar and the Dalit Movement in Colonial India*, New Delhi: Sage, 1994, p. 26.

20. Mendelsohn and Vicziany point out that the term Harijan was adopted by Gandhi in 1933 from a winning entry in a national competition for a suitable name. Gandhi's object was to invent a name which identified the relevant people without fixing them with an inferior status. See Oliver Mendelsohn and Marika Vicziany, *The Untouchables: Subordination Poverty and the State in India*, New Delhi: Cambridge University Press–Foundation Books, 2000, p. 3.

21. Gopal Guru, 'The Language of Dalit-Bahujan Political Discourse', in Manoranjan Mohanty (ed.), *Class, Caste, Gender*, New Delhi: Sage, 2004, p. 261.

22. The extracts are taken from an article by Gandhi from the book entitled *Varna Vyavastha*, written in Gujarati and translated by B. R. Ambedkar. Relevant extracts are quoted in B. R. Ambedkar, *What Congress and Gandhi Have Done to Untouchables*, New Delhi: Gautam Book Centre, first published in 1945, reprinted in 2009, p. 266.

23. G. Aloysius, *Nationalism without a Nation in India*, New Delhi: Oxford University Press, 1997, p. 225.

24. Bhikhu Parekh, *Colonialism, Tradition and Reform: An Analysis of Gandhi's Political Discourse*, New Delhi: Sage, 1989, pp. 228–71.

25. Sanjay Joshi, 'Republicizing Religiosity: Modernity, Religion and the Middle Class', in Derek R. Peterson and Daren R. Walhof (eds), *The Invention of Religion: Rethinking Belief in Politics and History*, New Jersey: Rutgers University Press, 2002, pp. 79–87.

26. The colonial state was making inroads in the religious domain of Hindus by abolishing several social customs like child marriage, *sati*, etc. These very practices made the colonial government and its sympathisers as well as western-educated middle-class Indians brand the Hindu religion as archaic and amodern.

27. Christophe Jaffrelot, 'Hindu Nationalism: Strategic Syncretism in Ideology Building', *Economic and Political Weekly*, 20–27 March 1993, XXVIII(12/13): 517–24; and Christophe Jaffrelot, *The Hindu Nationalist Movement and Indian Politics: 1925–1990s*, New Delhi: Penguin, 1996, pp. 11–22.

28. V. D. Savarkar, *Who is a Hindu?*, Bombay: S. S. Savarkar, 1969; M. S. Golwalkar, *We are Nationhood Defined*, Nagpur: Bharat Prakashan, 1934.

29. Omvedt, *Dalits and the Democratic Revolution*.

30. Ibid., pp. 1–31.

31. Edward Said, *Culture and Imperialism*, London: Chatto and Windus, 1993, p. 8.

32. Bayly, *Caste, Society and Politics in India*, p. 99.

33. Inden, *Imagining India*.

34. Bayly, *Caste, Society and Politics in India*, p. 99.

35. According to Charles Taylor, the demand for recognition acquires salience because it is also linked to identity, which provides an understanding of who we are, our fundamental defining characteristics as human beings. Recognition can also take the form of non-recognition. 'Non-recognition or misrecognition can inflict harm; can be a form of oppression, imprisoning someone [for instance, a particular social group] in a false, distorted, and reduced mode of being.' See Charles Taylor, 'The Politics of Recognition', in Ajay Heble, Dona Palmateer Pennee and J. R. Tim Struthers (eds), *New Contexts of Canadian Criticism*, Ontario: Broadview Press, 1997, pp. 89–131.

36. Taylor, 'The Politics of Recognition'.

37. Nancy Fraser, 'From Redistribution to Recognition? Dilemmas of Justice in a "Post-Socialist Age"', *New Left Review*, 1995, 212: 68–93; Nancy Fraser, 'Rethinking Redistribution', *New Left Review*, May–June 2000, 3: 107–20.

38. See G. W. F. Hegel, *Hegel's Philosophy of Right*, transl. T. M. Knox, Oxford: Clarendon Press, 1967.

39. Fraser, 'From Redistribution to Recognition?', p. 73.

40. Ibid., p. 72.

41. Omvedt, *Dalits and the Democratic Revolution*, pp. 223–24.

42. Barbara R. Joshi (ed.), *Untouchables: Voice of Dalit Liberation Movement*, London: Zed Books, 1986; Eleanor Zelliot, 'Perspectives on the Dalit Cultural Movement: Editor's Introduction', *Comparative Studies of South Asia, Africa and the Middle East Fall*, 1987, 7(1&2): 2–64; Gail Omvedt, 'Dalit Literature in Maharashtra: Literature of Social Protest and Revolt in Western India', *Comparative Studies of South Asia, Africa and the Middle East Fall*, 1987, 1&2: 78–85; Eleanor Zelliot, *From Untouchable to Dalit: Essays on the Ambedkar Movement*, New Delhi: Manohar, 1992; Gail Omvedt, 'Peasants, Dalits and Women: Democracy and India's New Social Movements', *Journal of Contemporary Asia*, 1994, 1: 34–48; Anand Teltumbde, *Ambedkar in and for the Post-Ambedkar Dalit Movement*, Pune: Sugawa Prakashan, 1997; Sekhar Bandyopadhyay, *Caste, Protest and Identity in Colonial India*, New Delhi: Oxford University Press, 2011; G. Aloysius, *Nationalism without a Nation in India*, New Delhi: Oxford University Press, 1997; Sudha Pai, *Dalit Assertion and the Unfinished Democratic Revolution: The Bahujan Samaj Party in Uttar Pradesh*, New Delhi: Sage, 2002; Aditya Nigam, 'In Search of a Bourgeoisie: Dalit Politics Enters a New Phase', *Economic and Political Weekly*, 2002, XXXVII(13): 1190–93; Ramaswami Mahalingam, 'Essentialism, Culture, and Power: Representations of Social Class', *Journal of Social Issues*, 2003, 59(4): 733–49; Ronki Ram, 'Untouchability, Dalit Consciousness, and the Ad Dharm Movement in Punjab', *Contributions to Indian Sociology*, 2004, 33(3): 323–49; Ajay Gudavarthy, 'Dalit and Naxalite Movements in

AP: Solidarity or Hegemony?' *Economic and Political Weekly*, 2005, XL (51): 5410–18; Gopal Guru and Anuradha Chakravarty, 'Who are the Country's Poor: Social Movement Politics and Dalit Poverty', in Raka Ray and Fainsod Katzenstein (eds), *Social Movements in India: Poverty, Power and Politics*, Oxford: Rowman and Littelfield Publishers, 2005, pp. 135–60; Hugo Gorringe, *Untouchable Citizens: Dalit Movement and Democratisation in Tamil Nadu*, New Delhi: Sage, 2005; S. K. Thorat, Aryama and Prashant Negi (eds), *Reservation and Private Sector: Quest for Equal Opportunity and Growth*, New Delhi: Indian Institute of Dalit Studies and Rawat Publication, 2005; Badri Narayan, *Women Heroes and Dalit Assertion in North India: Culture, Identity and Politics*, New Delhi: Sage, 2006; Amar Nath Prasad and M. B. Gaijan (eds), *Dalit Literature: A Critical Exploration*, New Delhi: Sarup and Sons, 2007; Manu Bhagwan and Anne Feldhaus, *Speaking the Truth: Religion, Caste and Subaltern Question in India*, New Delhi: Oxford University Press, 2007; Gail Omvedt, *Seeking Begumpura: The Social Vision of Anti Caste Intellectuals*, New Delhi: Navayana, 2008; Eleanor Zelliot, 'Dalit Literature, Language and Identity', in Braj Kachru, Yamuna Kachru and S. N. Sridhar (eds), *Language in South Asia*, Cambridge: Cambridge University Press, 2008; Milind Wakankar, *Subalternity and Religion: The Pre-History of Dalit Empowerment in South Asia*, New York: Routledge, 2010; Imtiaz Ahmad and Shashi Bhushan Upadhyay (eds), *Dalit Assertion in Society, Literature and History*, Delhi: New Orient Black Swan, 2010; Anupama Rao, *The Caste Question: Dalits and Politics of Modern India*, Ranikhet: Permanent Black, 2011.

43. Fraser, 'From Redistribution to Recognition?' pp. 68–93.

44. S. K. Thorat, Aryama and Prashant Negi (eds), *Reservation and Private Sector*.

45. Government of Madhya Pradesh, *The Bhopal Conference: Charting a New Course For Dalits For The 21st Century*, Bhopal, 2002.

46. See Christophe Jaffrelot, *India's Silent Revolution: The Rise of Lower Caste in North India*, London: C. Hurst and Company, 2003; Pai, *Dalit Assertion*; M. S. Pandian, 'Dalit Assertion in Tamil Nadu', *Journal of Indian School of Political Economy*, 2000, 3&4: 501–17.

47. For a macro overview see Suhas Palshikar, 'Caste Politics through the Prism of Region', in Rajendra Vora and Anne Feldhaus, *Region, Culture and Politics in India*, New Delhi: Manohar, 2006, pp. 271–90. For a few state-specific commentaries, see Surinder Singh Jodhka, 'Caste in the Periphery', *Seminar*, 508, 2001, http://www.india-seminar. com/ 2001/508/508%20surinder%20s.%20jodhka.htm (accessed on 16 July 2011); Surinder Singh Jodhka, 'Prejudice Without Pollution? Scheduled Castes in Contemporary Punjab', *Journal of Indian School of Political Economy*, 2000, 3–4: 381–404; Surinder Singh Jodhka

and Murli Dhar, 'Cow, Caste and Communal Politics: Dalit Killings in Jhajjar', *Economic and Political Weekly*, 2003, XXXVIII(3): 174–76; Dip Kapoor, 'Gendered-Caste Violations and the Cultural Politics of Voice in Rural Orissa, India', *Gender, Place & Culture*, 2007, 14 (5): 609–16; Achyut Yagnik and Anil Bhatt, 'The Anti-Dalit Agitation in Gujarat', *Comparative Studies of South Asia, Africa and the Middle*, 1984, 4 (1): 45–60.

48. See Zelliot, 'Perspectives on the Dalit Cultural Movement; Omvedt, 'Dalit Literature in Maharashtra'; Zelliot, *From Untouchable to Dalit: Essays on the Ambedkar Movement*, New Delhi: Manohar, 1992.

49. Smita Narula, *Broken People: Caste Violence Against India's 'Untouchables'*, India: Human Rights Watch, 1999; S. George Vincentnathan, 'Caste Politics, Violence, and the Panchayat in a South Indian Community', *Comparative Studies in Society and History*, 1996, 31(3): 484–509; Gopal Guru, 'Understanding Violence against Dalits in Marathwada', *Economic and Political Weekly*, 1994, XXIX(9): 469–72; Chad M. Bauman, 'Identity, Conversion, and Violence: Dalits, Adivasis, and the 2007–08 Riots in Orissa', in Joseph Marianus Kujur and Rowena Robinson (eds), *Margins of Faith: Dalit and Tribal Christianity in India*, Thousand Oaks, CA: Sage, 2010, pp. 263–90; Prashant Kumar Trivedi, 'Violence and Atrocities Against Dalit Women in Rural Uttar Pradesh', *Journal of Indian School of Political Economy*, 2007, 19 (1&2): 65–92; Jodhka and Dhar, 'Cow, Caste and Communal Politics'.

50. These groups emerge as a sort of a coalition of the socially discriminated, educationally deprived and economically destitute, so that less than one-fourth of the Indian population enjoys a high rate of growth in their purchasing power (see Institute of Human Development India Labour and Employment Report 2014: Workers in the Era of Globalisation, Academic Foundation, 2014). Although the complete report is valuable, the third chapter on 'Access to and Exclusion from Employment: Social and Regional Dimensions' is especially important to understand the social roots of exclusion and marginalisation.

51. V. Geetha, 'Bereft of Being: The Humiliations of Untouchability', in Gopal Guru (ed.), *Humiliation: Claims and Context*, New Delhi: Oxford University Press, 2009, pp. 95–107; Ghanshyam Shah, Harsh Mander, S. K. Thorat, Satish Deshpande, and Amita Baviskar (eds), *Untouchability in Rural India*, New Delhi: Sage, 2006; Pallavi Polanki, 'Untouchability Declassified', *Open*, 2010, 2(11): 43–51.

52. For a good account of the socio-political struggle facilitating their discarding of the 'identity of untouchables and consciously acquiring the identity of Dalits', see Zelliot, *From Untouchable to Dalit*.

53. Derek Layder, 'Power, Structure and Agency', *Journal for the Theory of Social Behaviour*, 1985, 15 (2): 132–33.
54. R. Krekel, 'Unequal Opportunity Structure and Labour Market Segmentation', *Sociology*, 1980, 4: 525–49, quoted in Derek Layder, 'Power, Structure and Agency', *Journal for the Theory of Social Behaviour*, 1985, 15 (2): 132.
55. Andre Béteille, 'Empowerment', *Economic and Political Weekly*, 1999, XXXIV(10&11): 589–97.
56. B. R. Ambedkar, *Dr. Babasaheb Ambedkar Writing and Speeches*, Section IV, Kalaram Temple Entry Satyagraha, Nasik and Temple Entry Movement, Volume XVII, Government of Maharashtra.
57. V. Geetha, 'Bereft of Being', pp. 97–105. Further, much documentation shows that untouchability is not an archaic practice which has been socially discarded by modern India. In a survey conducted in 60 villages in 11 states, it was found that untouchability continues to be widely prevalent and practiced in several forms in almost 80 per cent of the villages. See Ghanshyam Shah et al., *Untouchability in Rural India*. Also, a report which is as recent as 2010, documents 80 different forms of untouchability and discrimination practiced in the country. See Pallavi Polanki, 'Untouchability Declassified', *Open*, 2010, 2 (11): 43–51.
58. V. Geetha, 'Bereft of Being', p. 98.
59. S. Lukes, *Power a Radical View*, London: Macmillan, 1974.
60. Pierre Bourdieu and Jean Claude Passeron, *Reproduction in Education, Society and Culture*, California: Sage, 1977, pp. 1–68.
61. Anthony Giddens, *The Constitution of Society: Outline of the Theory of Structuration*, Cambridge: Polity Press, 1984, pp. 5–25.
62. Layder, 'Power, Structure and Agency', p. 136.
63. Ibid., p. 144.
64. Ibid.
65. Ibid., p. 133.
66. Iren Rafanell and Hugo Gorringe, 'Consenting to Domination? Theorising Power, Agency and Embodiment with Reference to Caste', *The Sociological Review*, 2010, 58(4): 604–22.
67. Gopal Guru, 'Social Justice', in Niraja Jayal and Pratap Bhanu Mehta (eds), *The Oxford Companion to Politics in India*, New Delhi: Oxford University Press, 2010, pp. 363–64.
68. Ibid., pp. 364–65.
69. Ingrid Robeyns, 'Is Nancy Fraser's Critique of Theories of Distributive Justice Justified?', *Constellations*, 2003, 10 (4): 538–54.
70. For a comprehensive discussion on the philosophy of Utilitarianism, see Amartya Sen and Bernard Williams (eds), *Utilitarianism and Beyond*, Cambridge: Cambridge University Press, 1982.

71. Valerian Rodrigues, 'Justice as the Lens: Interrogating Rawls through Sen and Ambedkar', *Indian Journal of Human Development*, 2011, 5 (1): 155–57.

72. For Rawls, the first criterion of justice is to provide a benchmark that can assess the distributive aspect present in the basic structure of society. The distributive framework has to be assessed in terms of whether there is just distribution of basic liberties, whether offices and positions are open to all, and whether social and economic inequalities are arranged so that they are to everyone's advantage. Inequalities are only permitted if they are to the advantage of the worst-off. Inequalities are to be judged in terms of social primary goods — goods that every rational person is assumed to want, such as rights, liberties, opportunities, income, wealth, and self-respect (See John Rawls, *A Theory of Justice*, Cambridge: Harvard University Press, 1971). Runciman too wants an ethical criterion as a reference point for measuring the distribution of social goods in society (W. G. Runciman, 'Processes, End States and Social Justice', *Philosophical Quarterly*, 1978, 28: 37). Dworkin is concerned about the distribution of impersonal resources (for instance, financial resources) in a manner that people are compensated for less personal resources. Inequalities in impersonal resources due to differences in people's ambitions are justified, whereas inequalities in impersonal resources resulting from causes that are beyond people's control are not (see Ronald Dworkin, 'What is Equality? Part 2: Equality of Resources,' *Philosophy and Public Affairs*, 1981, 10 (4): 284–345). Sen emphasises on the distribution of basic capabilities and argues that 'social realisations are [to be] assessed in terms of capabilities' without the need to know what constitutes perfectly just social arrangements or perfectly just institutions (see Amartya Sen, *The Idea of Justice*, Cambridge: Harvard University Press, 2009, p. 19, and detailed arguments on pp. 225–90). This emphasis on distribution is by and large also true for the Marxist and Socialist notions of justice. We have already noted while discussing the 'caste as superstructure' approach, that caste tends to mask class-based exploitation which will eventually disappear with the development of capitalist rationality, and the emergent labour/proletariat will be at the vanguard of a socialist/communist revolution. 'For Marx justice refers only to superstructural juridical relations of distribution, which are constrained by the underlying mode of production.' (Allen Wood, 'The Marxian Critique of Justice', *Philosophy and Public Affairs*, Spring 1972, 1 (3): 244–82, quoted in Iris Marion Young, *Justice and the Politics of Difference*, Princeton: Princeton University Press, 1990, p. 22). Implicit in this argument is the idea that a socialist/communist society will have a different and just distributional pattern. See Edward Nell and Onora O' Neill, 'Justice under Socialism', in James Sterba (ed.),

Justice: Alternative Political Perspective, Belmont: Wadsworth, 1980, pp. 196–217.

73. Charles W. Mills, 'Re-Theorizing Justice: Some Comments on Amartya Sen's *The Idea of Justice*', *Indian Journal of Human Development,* 2011, 5 (1): 148–49.

74. Ibid.

75. For Rawls, primary goods include 'rights, liberties and opportunities, income and wealth, and the social bases of self-respect (see Rawls, *A Theory of Justice,* pp. 60–65).

76. Sen, *The Idea of Justice,* p. 66.

77. Mills, *Re-Theorizing Justice,* 151.

78. Iris Marion Young, *Justice and the Politics of Difference,* New Jersey: Princeton University Press, 1990, pp. 48–62.

79. Guru, 'Social Justice', p. 361.

80. Ibid., p. 369.

81. Young, *Justice and the Politics of Difference,* p. 41.

THREE

Dalit Entrepreneurs in Urban Markets of Middle India

◘

The Context

As economic boundaries open up and India responds to the momentous forces of globalisation, every individual and organisation has to stand purely on its own strength and merit. With employment opportunities with the Government waning, Dalit youth must strive to stand on their own feet and to create opportunities of self employment. The spirit of enterprise and ' knowledge' are the crucial resources which would help them grow. It is with this perspective that the Dalit Indian Chamber of Commerce and Industry (DICCI) works to empower Dalit youth and harness the potential to accomplish their own progress.

— Dalit Chamber of Commerce and Industry (DICCI)

The Dalit Chamber of Commerce and Industry (DICCI) was established in 2005 with the aim to 'instil the spirit of entrepreneurship among Dalit youth and to empower them to walk along with the rest'.[1] DICCI encourages Dalit youth to start business enterprises through various support services.[2] DICCI emphatically claims that the 'market' is the new mantra for Dalits' economic mobility, especially in the context of waning jobs in the public sector. Some aggressive pro-market voices in DICCI view reservation as an outdated concept. For instance, Milind Kamble, an important voice of DICCI, says:

I believe reservations are an outdated concept. Earlier, the public sector was the biggest source of job opportunities for Dalits, but this is a sector that is shrinking. However, the answer to the jobs shortfall cannot be reservations in the private sector. We at DICCI want Dalits to turn to trade and industry; entrepreneurship should be the new mantra.[3]

Others point out that affirmative action policies in education have helped a critical mass of Dalit youth venture into trade and commerce.[4] In spite of the apparently contradictory views on the role of the state, there is no contesting the fact that economic growth in India over the last two decades has not significantly benefited Dalits and other historically deprived groups.[5] Kannan's viewpoint is that irrespective of the political regime or the levels of economic development in a region/state, the poor are more likely to be from the historically deprived categories.[6] His argument, based on available empirical information, is that, for socially advantaged groups, regional location is 'less of a constraint, if not irrelevant'. Other indicators pointed out are:

a. Dalits are seen to be systematically excluded from various state-promoted developmental schemes and services;[7]
b. Dalit wages are universally low in comparison to upper-castes performing similar jobs;[8]
c. Dalits' demand for equal wages or social status often results in further exclusion or physical violence against them.[9]

In short, Dalits suffer from poverty and systematic marginalisation because of the regimes of discrimination structurally embedded in the socio-political structure of the country.[10]

Against this backdrop, there is a growing perception among Dalits that 'markets' have the potential to mitigate and remove discrimination as in a competitive market, the opportunity to engage is based on skills and goods offered, *not* on social identity.[11]

To understand the scope and potential of markets in removing discrimination, it is necessary to first analyse the business histories of Dalit entrepreneurs and their views on market potential. Given this framework, we need to first examine the existing theories of discrimination that have developed in the context of labour and markets.

What Do Existing Theories Tell Us and What Do They Not?

Theories on discrimination in the market, in both international and Indian academic literature, are particularly developed in the context of labour market discrimination. The key premise of these crucial analyses is that workers who have the same endowments — skills, education, experience, etc. — but, who do not belong to the 'dominant' race, caste, gender, religion etc., will command substantially less income. This has been broadly termed as 'labour market discrimination'. Most of these theories were explicitly developed for understanding differential and discriminatory practices in labour market transactions, especially in relation to the wages of 'subordinate' social groups. On the face of it, these analyses do not directly relate to our own inquiry, as our quest is not to evaluate economic discriminatory practices in terms of wage employment, but to understand market outcomes from the standpoint of owners of capital who belong to a historically ostracised social group — the Dalits. Nevertheless, the analyses provide crucial insights for our inquiry, as economic discrimination in the labour market is a result of the same social processes that Dalits experience when they enter the market as owners of capital.

Several economists adhering to the neo-classical school have attempted to capture the discrimination inherent in market operations. Although

> the bulk of economic theory is built on the assumption that social identities of agents do not matter in the market, there are powerful exceptions that show how social identities of economic agents can be central to the determination of their economic outcomes.[12]

Two broad frameworks of inquiry can be taken up to understand the existing work on the role of identity in influencing market outcomes.

First, the crucial work of Gary Becker,[13] which has inspired scores of scholars, and explains discrimination in terms of a 'taste for discrimination'. An individual is a discriminator because he has a taste for it and 'must act *as if* he were willing to pay something, either directly or in the form of a reduced income, to be associated with some person instead of others'.[14] Deshpande argues that Becker's theory addresses prejudice directly since for him, the taste of discrimination originates from a set of beliefs or values that sit in contradiction to objective facts.[15] Becker's work, though it does not deal with caste discrimination, has influenced the work of numerous authors, in areas of discrimination in general, and caste discrimination in particular.

Second, the framework of statistical discrimination has also been employed to understand the role of caste (identity) in influencing market outcomes. Deshpande explains that the statistical discrimination approach

> treats discrimination as a consequence of lack of information, and prima facie does not allow for individual prejudice. In other words, under statistical discrimination, employers simply inherit dominant stereotypes about various groups and individuals; it is possible for them to discriminate without necessarily having a taste for discrimination.[16]

Akerlof,[17] while approaching the issue through the statistical discrimination lens,[18] puts forth the argument that the social identity of an economic agent mediates any economic transaction. Given the perception that economic transactions with lower castes are against widely accepted social norms, Akerlof, with the help of economic modelling, demonstrates the possibility that an economic agent who transacts with lower castes may

> suffer the stigma of the outcastes [and hence economic loss]. If the punishment of becoming an outcaste is predicted to be sufficiently severe, the system of caste is held in equilibrium, irrespective of individual tastes, by economic incentives; the predictions of the caste system become a self-fulfilling prophecy.

'The idea here is that the identity of an agent, as perceived by other agents is seen as an indicator of merit or worth and that, in turn determines their labour market outcomes'.[19] Akerlof shows how the sanction of caste can render the market less competitive, as a successful arbitrageur in a discriminatory transaction will not be a winner but a social outcaste. Lal's[20] argument, similar to Akerlof's, is that the caste system, by mandating occupational division of labour, ensures segmentation. If social norms are broken, the penalties are greater than the benefits. Building on Akerlof's insights, Scoville's[21] model further elucidates on segmentation of the labour market through caste identities, which, according to him, essentially means 'suppression of competition' and 'absence of institutional change'. He highlights the three characteristics of the caste system that promote such segmentation, namely a. *Impermeability:* preventing labour market competition so that workers cannot easily leave the mandated occupation of their caste and enter another;[22] b. *Inevitability:*

preventing product market competition by reinforcing a system of hereditary occupation, so that buyers who seek particular goods or services have no choice of an alternative source; c. *Permanence*: historical social acceptance of caste system as the basis for division of labour.

The common threads emerging from these analyses are as follows:

a. The caste system is hereditary and endogenous; it segments the labour market, and the values inherent to the caste system shape collective consciousness. But it is the *individual* who refuses to go against dominant beliefs because of the fear of possible adverse outcomes. For instance, Deshpande notes that in the Akerlofian model, there is a theoretical possibility of an anti-caste coalition succeeding in breaking free of the caste code, but possibly fails to do so due to the free rider problem.[23]

b. Discrimination, in the long run, translates into suppression of competition and results in imperfect/inefficient market outcomes; it is the *individual* who affects discriminatory practices like inefficient allocation of labour, diminished profits and low wages.

Thus, according to the neo-classical school, discrimination practised by individuals in the market has a non-economic origin, and, in all likelihood, will wane in the long run since it breeds inefficiency and prevents competition.

Deshpande, in her critique, questions the silence of the following issues in the above discussed approaches. She argues that this model fails to answer why the attitudes of the upper-castes towards the Dalits are derogatory. Why is it that some social groups are considered inferior while others are seen as superior? Is there a role played by social institutions in maintaining the privileges of certain social groups and meting out unfavourable treatment to Dalits? If the latter is the case, then the practice of discrimination has nothing do with the presumed or actual characteristics of Dalits. Banerjee and Knight[24] argue that the models talk about discrimination but do not examine the economic basis for this discrimination, and they do not grapple with the question of production of surplus and who (more specifically, which castes) it is appropriated by.[25] Thus these critiques point to the lack of an institutional explanation in the neo-classical account that allows discrimination in the name of caste to be sustained in the economic domain.

Drawing on neo-classical theory, an important thesis has been proposed by the new institutional economics, that brings to the fore the role of institutions[26] in determining market outcomes. In the words of Douglas North,[27]

> [t]he new institutional economics builds on, modifies and extends neo-classical theory to permit it to come to grips with an entire range of issues . . . What it retains and builds on is the fundamental assumption of scarcity and, hence, competition — the basis of choice and the theoretical approach that underlies micro-economics . . . What it abandons is instrumental rationality — the assumption of neo classical economics that has made it an institution-free theory.

Baldly stated, new institutional economics is primarily concerned with increasing market efficiency by lowering transaction costs with the help of impersonal institutions that are perceived to be legitimate.[28] Stiglitz argues that the introduction of a competitive market backed by secular regulatory institutions will produce superior outcomes, and will replace particularistic and discriminatory transactions propelled by groups within the market.[29] In order to support this claim, the proponents of this school revisit history and reveal that trade gains have been best achieved in societies that successfully evolved towards impersonal contract enforcement, because personal ties, voluntaristic constraints and ostracism are not as economically effective as impersonal forms of exchange. Accordingly, evidence has been collated to show that an *institutional environment* (i.e. formal rules of the game, secure rights to property, effective legal structure and a court system to enforce contracts) and *corresponding political and bureaucratic institutions* that align with the institutional requirements, are necessary for superior market outcomes.[30]

Thus, new institutional economics, like its predecessor (neo-classical economics), retains the need for competition, but highlights the role of institutions in shaping market outcomes. It emphasises the important part played by the state[31] in structuring the institutional environment for reducing transaction costs and enhancing competitiveness.

However, within the worldview of new institutional economics, the question that raises its head is whether caste (being a robust institution with an ideology drawing its philosophical justification from

Hindu religion) can be an institutional factor influencing a market outcome. New institutional economics, to the best of our knowledge, does not have a specific theoretical model for the institutional role of caste in the market, though it does recognise informal institutions such as religion, norms, customs, tradition, etc. North raises pertinent questions: 'What is it about informal constraints that give them such a pervasive influence upon the long run character of economies? What is the relationship between formal and informal constraints?'[32] He has not, however, proposed answers to these questions. Williamson points out that new institutional economics considers informal institutions as a given.[33] But the historical evidence generated in this context seems to suggest that impersonal/formal institutions are imperative for lowering transaction costs and, hence, promoting competition, which in turn can lead to growth.[34] Thus, the source of strength of new institutional economics — factoring in institutions to understand market outcomes — also becomes a cause of weakness, because of its apparent stress on formal institutions. In the Indian context, Harriss-White reminds us that 'market exchange does not always lead to "contracts" replacing "customs"'.[35] She emphasises that there is no contradiction between caste and corporatist capitalist development[36] (also refer to the next chapter on state). This crucial insight becomes the springboard to probe several questions that remain unanswered by the new institutional economics account:

a. How do we understand the nature of competition in a market that, on the one hand ensures a positive outcome for the dominant players who also belong to dominant social groups, and an adverse outcome for marginalised social groups?

b. How do we factor in the presence, and at times domination, of informal institutions (caste, religion, etc.) within formal institutions (state), especially where the latter significantly influences market outcomes in favour of dominant social groups?

c. How do we understand the motives of an apparently impersonal institution (i.e. credit agencies) when it blatantly mirrors the values of discrimination and exclusion by making credit available to the dominant group whilst constraining liquidity for marginalised social groups, thereby drastically affecting outcomes in the market?

In order to answer these questions, we need to understand the factors which contribute to the blurring of boundaries between informal and formal institutions governing markets. The answers are perhaps best provided by authors belonging to the 'school of social embeddedness'.

The most important contribution of the social embeddedness school is to flag the failure of 'mainstream' economists to incorporate social structure into their analyses. According to this approach, social relations are fundamental to those of the market, and these relationships are configured to mitigate the effects of market competition and protect the market space. It was Polanyi who pointed out that the economy is an instituted process of interaction, and that this process is embedded in both economic and non-economic institutions.[37] Within this school, there are three sets of scholars with similar ideological roots but crucial internal differences. These differences do not work against each other but contribute to make the approach more vibrant.

The first set of scholars whom we discuss work primarily in the United States. These scholars question the anonymity of individuals in the market and help us understand the crucial role of social networks therein. Harrison C. White suggests that stable production markets can only exist if economic actors are able to take into account each other's behaviour through the medium of what he calls, 'joint social construction — the schedule of terms of trade'.[38] Granovetter states that economic actions, like all other actions, are socially situated. They are embedded in social networks, built on kinship or friendship and trust or goodwill that not only sustain economic relations and institutions, but also govern economic rewards and punishments.[39] Similarly, Burt holds the view that networks stand in for resource dependence,[40] while Podolny believes it is the primacy of the status and hierarchy of producers that propels the configuration of networks in markets.[41] In substance, the analyses of these authors lead us to the understanding that economic activities in the market require co-operative action, which finds its basis in social networks. In other words, it helps us recognise the importance of strong ties of kinship (with both immediate and extended family), community, and culture, in mobilising resources — both economic and non-economic — in the course of market operations.

The second set of scholars, originating from the CEPREMAP[42] research centre in Paris, argues that market forces, though very important, are only one of the contributing factors for capitalist development. Capitalist economies inevitably include economic and extra economic structures. The latter include, inter alia, institutions, collective identities, shared visions, common rules, norms and conventions, networks, procedures, and modes of calculation, and these play a critical role in the processes of capitalist accumulation. The French scholars not only highlight the social embeddedness of the market relationship, but also flag the vital role of civil society in nurturing and sustaining the norms and conventions practiced and observed in market transactions.[43]

Both these sets of scholars from the 'social embeddedness' school enrich our understanding by questioning the main assumptions of neo-classical economics and new institutional economics. They disagree with the possibility of a 'socially disembedded' sphere of market exchange that is entirely driven by the actions of rational individuals oriented to the forces of demand and supply, with a tendency towards optimal equilibrium. Their argument is that economic rationality cannot be understood solely in terms of pure market exchange, and therefore emphasise the existence of a socially structured capitalist economy. These arguments, when analysed in the Indian context, put forth reasons why marginalised social groups like Dalits are faced with adverse inclusion in the market — when social networks in the market are formed on the basis of caste location, it can lead to negative intent and purposeful creation of unfavourable conditions for businesspersons from the lower castes. This introduces a high degree of informality, and raises questions about the possibility of the market being regulated by both formal rules and impersonal institutions. However, we still feel that we do not have a convincing answer as to why caste-like groups endure and continue to shape economic transactions.[44] Moreover, this explanation of the socio-economic factors that sustain social networks will also contribute to our understanding of the informalisation of formal institutions and differential credit access. In other words, we need to have an explanation for the informalisation of state and quasi-state institutions which are supposed to be governed by secular and impersonal rules and procedures. Unlike markets, they have written rules and procedures which do not evolve with social practice but are arrived at through reasoned deliberation. Here we draw on the works of a third set of scholars belonging to the school of 'social embeddedness' who work primarily on India.

Drawing from B. R. Ambedkar's work, Thorat states that the caste system is a coherent ideology that is rooted in the Hindu religion. Caste ideology states that the privileges and rights of individuals are determined by virtue of their being members of a particular caste, and it does not recognise the individual as the 'centre of social purpose'. Hence, Dalits find themselves excluded, or at best included on adverse terms in the market.[45]

> Exclusion and discrimination in civil, cultural and particularly in economic spheres such as occupation and labour employment is therefore internal to the system, and a necessary outcome of its governing principles . . . In the market economy framework, the occupational immobility would operate through restrictions in various markets such as capital, land, labour, credit, other inputs, and services necessary for any economic activity.[46]

The emphasis on caste as an ideology helps us make the critical link between exclusion and discrimination. Individuals are excluded or adversely included not for any economic reasons but because of deep-rooted social values. Thorat underlines the fact that the social value of discrimination has a material basis since exclusion or adverse inclusion always works in favour of the material interests of dominant castes.

Yet, if caste is still a robust ideology, how do we explain the fundamental changes that have occurred in India under the official ideology of the Indian state, namely, *modernisation*? Some of the writings on caste and modernisation point to the ever-dissolving socio-economic relationships based on caste.[47] Harriss-White, while not denying the enormous changes within the caste system, introduces dynamism into the arguments of caste as ideology. She remarks that 'elements of the caste system are often rearranged leaving the principles intact'.[48] This implies:

a. The ideology of caste still forms the basis of various corporatist projects. In this sense, the ideology of caste is a social structure of accumulation.[49]
b. It provides the basis for building networks in the market, thwarts competition, mobilises resources, and regulates labour, all with the objective of regulating the market.[50]

   c. Caste helps to support the politics of the market.[51] The politics of the market essentially governs the operations of the market, and in the process, blurs the boundaries between state, market and civil society. In short, caste forms the basis of contacts for informal or illegal dealings, within both formal and informal institutions.[52]

As a result, economic transactions in the market are invariably mediated through social structures which, in turn, ensure that contracts in the market are enforced through social rules, and the secular state machinery either abstains or provides tacit consent, as the latter can be ideologically driven or bought at a price.

Summing up

The three schools of thought discussed above give us several convergent and divergent insights into the practice of discrimination during the course of market transactions. The key areas where there is convergence of thought are:

   a. All of them agree that caste is a material reality, and a source of discrimination in the market.
   b. All of them locate such discrimination in the realm of civil society.
   c. All of them perceive the state as an important institution; albeit the role of the state is understood differently.

The divergence of thought between the schools can be summarised as follows:

According to the neo-classical school, though the source of discrimination lies in the realm of civil society, what is ultimately at work is the rationale of the autonomous, individual and economic agent. It is the individual who adheres to the dictates of dominant values of civil society, for fear of penalties. Adherence to discriminatory practices leads to thwarting of free competition which, in turn, results in imperfect market outcomes. However, the neo-classical school fails to explain the factors responsible for the survival of exclusion or discrimination in the economy.

New institutional economics emphasises that it is institutions — both formal and informal — that influence and determine market outcomes. Caste can be considered as an institution that operates in and regulates the market. This school of thought considers informal institutions to be a given and collates historical evidence to show that competition in the market will lead to the demise of informal institutions, and the birth and sustenance of institutions driven by impersonal codes. It believes that the values of exclusion and discrimination practiced in the realm of civil society can only be mitigated by impersonal institutions, and like the neo-classical school, lays stress on the role of the state in setting up institutional requirements — political, legal and economic — necessary for ushering in impersonal institutions.

The school of 'social embeddedness' exposes the fragility of the above two discourses. The radically different approach of this school of thought informs us that, fundamentally, the market functions with the help of social networks created through social and personal ties. In the Indian context, scholars point to the importance of caste in carving out social networks. These social networks, formed on the basis of caste, are not merely social collectives bound by common social origin, but collective identities sustained by a well-developed ideology. They are used as 'institutions' to protect socio-economic interests and, in this sense, mirror the socio-economic hierarchy present in civil society. Caste and caste-based networks do not suppress competition, as assumed by the neo-classical and new institutional schools, but are used as institutions to meet the demands of market competition by regulating credit and labour, thus influencing outcomes in the market. More crucially, caste in its regulative capacity helps to configure a regime of accumulation in the market which has been aptly described as a 'social structure of accumulation'.

With this backdrop, we will analyse the attempts made by Dalits in middle India to enter the market as owners of capital and earn their living as well as surplus through trade and commerce. Through this study, our goal is demonstrate that the market is mediated and influenced by the social structures and social contexts in which the economic agents live.

General Profile

Towards the goal stated above, we look at the experience of Dalit businesspersons who have managed to enter the market, sustain themselves and have earned investible surpluses through trade and commerce in towns in middle India. The base material is collated from detailed interviews — structured and unstructured — of 90 Dalit businesspersons in six states and 13 districts in middle India[53] (Table 3.1). These businesspeople were perceived by their immediate community to be successful, though many of them consider themselves at the periphery of the class of peers among whom they work, earn their living and survive.

**Table 3.1 Location and Number of
Dalit Businesspersons Interviewed**

State	City	Number of Interviewees
Gujarat	Ahmedabad	8
Madhya Pradesh	Bhopal	10
	Hoshangabad	1
	Raisen	3
	Vidisha	1
Maharashtra	Aurangabad	9
	Mumbai	1
	Pune	10
Rajasthan	Jaipur	10
Uttar Pradesh	Agra	5
	Kanpur	13
	Lucknow	9
West Bengal	Hoogly/24 Parganas	10

Source: Compiled by the author.

The sample of 'successful' business-people was derived through a. the community's perception; b. references given by other businesspersons during the course of their interviews and c. information given by organisations working for the Dalit cause. Sample identification was a difficult process as there were not many individuals who were perceived to be successful in the economic endeavours that they owned and controlled. An interesting first observation of the identified samples is that there is a vertical division (along the axis of class) of people trading their goods, skills and capital, in a market segmented by caste, class and religion.

Table 3.2 shows the classification of businesses by a. general economic type, and b. size, as measured by annual turnover. An analysis of the total numbers in each size group shows that the majority are 'small' and 'average'-sized businesses, together accounting for nearly 65 per cent of the sample. If we include 'petty'-sized businesses as

Table 3.2 Type and Size of Economic Ventures (percentages in parentheses)

	Very Big (More than 5 crore)	Big (₹1–4.99 crore)	Middle Range (₹50–99 lakh)	Average Range (₹5–50 lakh)	Small (₹4.9–2 lakhs)	Petty (less than ₹2 lakhs)	Total
Caste Related	2	1	2	12	6	3	26 (29)
Earlier Restricted and Considered Taboo	0	0	2	2	4	4	12 (13)
General	1	2	6	13	10	4	36 (40)
Liberalised market	0	2	0	5	2	0	11 (12)
Specialised	0	1	0	3	1	0	5 (6)
Total	3 (4)	6 (7)	10 (11)	35 (39)	23 (26)	13 (14)	90 (100)

Source: Compiled by the author.

well, the proportion rises to nearly 80 per cent. Only 20 per cent of the sample operates 'very big', 'big' and 'middle'-sized businesses. The strength of the sample tapers sharply as we go up the ladder.

The businesses in the sample have been further classified into five categories (Table 3.2):

a. Economic ventures inspired by caste location: These include trade in sanitary ware, bulk washing of clothes, washing clothes for the garment industry, sanitary labour and house-keeping contractors, leather work, hair-cutting salons, etc. Nearly 30 per cent of the respondents traded in the market for goods and services that were associated with their sub-castes.

b. Trade in goods and services earlier disallowed to Dalits by the Hindu social order: Only 13 per cent of businesspersons entered the market for such goods and services which include educational coaching, trade in food and food products, priesthood, etc.

c. General economic ventures: Nearly 40 per cent of the sample belonged to this category, which included smaller economic ventures like trade in wood and fuel wood, handloom material, grocery shops, etc., as well as big businesses like mining, construction and real estate, production and sale of ceramic ware, etc.

d. Liberalised market: The fourth category comprises the many newer avenues for business that have been created by the opening of markets and the ongoing integration of the Indian economy with the global economy. These include trade in communication, electronics and computers, real estate, etc. Only 13 per cent of the total interviewees were trading in this particular category.

e. Specialised businesses: Less than 6 per cent of the total Dalit businesspersons interviewed belonged to this category, the participation in which is contingent on higher education, specialised training and professional degrees. The category includes economic activities related to medicine and hospital services.

In the corpus of our interviewees, we observed that Dalits are fairly well represented in caste-related trade and commerce (trade in sanitary ware, leather goods, cleaning services, clothes washing, etc.).

It was also noted during field work that Dalits, as workers and owners (of varying size) still constitute the majority in these sectors. However, their control over these businesses is through labour-intensive rather than capital-intensive work. It is perceived that, in the last decade, Dalits have become increasingly marginalised in sectors where they had previously held a near monopoly. They have been gradually reduced to the position of contract suppliers, supervisors or workers (depending on the size of business and capital they hold), replaced by big capital-intensive operations managed by upper-caste Hindus. A leather goods manufacturer in Agra told us:

आगरा में हजारों की संख्या में चमड़े के छोटे छोटे कारखाने हैं, पिछले कुछ सालों में पंजाबी, गुजराती और बनिया ने, कई तो आगरा से बाहर से आए हैं और छोटे कारखानों को खरीद लिए हैं। पुराने मालिक या तो वहां काम देखते हैं या खुद महीने की तनख्वाह पर हैं। मेरा कारखाना भी अब धारावी के एक सेठ के लिए काम करता है। सारा माल उसे सप्लाई करता हूँ। माल वही देते हैं और हमको हर एक सामान पर बंधा बंधाया पैसा मिलता है।

Agra has thousands of small leather workshops. In the last few years, these small workshops have been taken over by Punjabis, Gujaratis and Baniyas. Several of these businessmen are located outside Agra. The original owners of the workshop have been relegated to the position of supervisors or workers in their own workshop. My workshop also supplies all leather goods to a businessman from Dharavi, Mumbai. He gives us raw material and we make leather products. We are paid per piece for all the leather goods we supply to him.

A Dalit woman who owns a beauty parlour in 24 Parganas, West Bengal, shared a similar experience:

Nowadays, people are very conscious about hygiene, beauty and health. Beauty parlours are mushrooming all over. Most of the investment in the beauty parlours in our district is by petty Marwari traders of Kolkata. Instead of having his own shop, the traditional barber is an employee. I have somehow managed to sustain myself because of my goodwill and hard work, but I don't have money to invest in a modern beauty parlour-cum-health club.[54]

These two testimonies reflect a crucial trend over the last decade in India, in all levels of the economy — the centralisation of capital and decentralisation of production processes. As suggested in the testimony of the salon owner, the surplus controlled by the upper-castes is increasingly being invested in all sectors, including those vocations hitherto considered 'polluting'. The Agra entrepreneur's views reflect the recent changes in economic policies that have resulted in massive investment in the leather sector by big capitalists. A direct result of these shifting trends is that many of the manufacturers, who could earlier be considered big in terms of their annual turnover, have slid down to the status of average or small-size businesses. Further, numerous small manufacturers have closed shop and now work as wage labourers in big production units that have come up after the deregulation of the leather sector.[55] It appears that, even in the face of pervasive social change, Dalits are finding it increasingly difficult to compete with upper caste peers, who wield control over relatively scarce capital. Even where markets are becoming delinked from caste, that is choice of vocation seems open, the capital required to pursue it appears to be controlled by specific caste groups. Consequently, Dalits continue to be relegated to the lower rung of the market.

A small proportion of the Dalits we interviewed have entered into trade and commerce in areas that were earlier restricted to their castes. Some of them have managed to raise the required initial capital, and are trading in 'mid'-sized wholesale food and beverages businesses. These entrepreneurs, we were told, supply to their customers at a slightly lower profit margin than their upper-caste business rivals, thereby keeping trade lines open to them. As explained by a wholesale supplier of beverages in Jaipur:

बड़ी मुश्किल से धंधा जमा पाया हूँ। पहले मैं सेठ की दुकान का सामान साइकिल से ग्राहक के घर पहुंचाता था। मेरे दिमाग में आया कि क्यों नहीं अपना धंधा किया जाए। अब मेरी बीवी और दोनों लड़कियां घर में नाश्ते का सामान बनाती हैं और मैं दुकान पर उसे सप्लाई करता हूँ। नये धंधे को बैठाना बहुत मुश्किल था। कोई भी बनिया सामान नहीं खरीदता था। किसी ने बोला नहीं पर मैं जानता हूँ कि दलित के हाथ का बना सामान बनिया नहीं खरीदना चाहता है। पर पैसा बड़ी चीज है . . . मैंने बाजार से सस्ते पर बेचना शुरू कर दिया। कई लोग सामान खरीदने लगे। पर अब भी मैं बाजार के भाव पर सामान बेचूं तो कोई नहीं खरीदेगा।

It is with great difficulty that I have managed to set up my own business. Earlier, I used to work for a local trader. My duty was to supply goods from his shops to the homes of different customers. I thought of starting my own business. My wife and two daughters prepare various food items at home and I supply them to different shops in the city. It was really difficult to get established in the market. None of the baniya traders would buy my products. Nobody said so explicitly but I perceived that they were not buying from me because of my low caste origin. But money has great power. I started selling my goods at a price lower than the market price. Several shop owners started buying my goods. Still, if I sell my goods at the market price, nobody will buy them.

Further, in the case of Dalits who own hotels and are in direct interaction with consumers, the size of their operation seems to be constrained by their caste and the location of the business. Our field evidence indicates that their hotels are generally found in localities inhabited by Dalits. In other areas, successful food entrepreneurs may be 'tolerated' as long as they are not a threat to their rivals. If the latter perceive that their profits are being threatened by these Dalit rivals, the upper-caste food traders leverage their caste. This is exemplified in our case studies of Dalit food entrepreneurs in Pune and Jaipur, whose successful average-range businesses fell into the category of small businesses because of similar adverse publicity by upper-caste rivals. A Dalit woman who supplies lunch boxes to offices, and has experienced the wrath of upper-castes told us:

मेरे खाने की बहुत डिमांड थी। जब मांजरेकर का प्राफिट कम होने लगा तो उसने सब को बता दिया कि मैं छोटी जात की हूँ, उसके बाद मेरे रोज का आर्डर आधे से भी कम हो गया।

There used to be huge demand for the food I prepared. However, when the popularity of my food affected the business interests of Manjrekar[56] [an upper-caste], he went and told everybody that I belong to a lower caste. Thereafter, the demand for my food reduced by more than half.

Similarly, in our documentation of an educational coaching institute managed and controlled by Dalits, our interviewee felt that upper-caste children and their parents stayed away from his institute on the assumption that his educational qualifications were a result of the state's affirmative action, and he did not have the intellectual ability to train others. This is what he shared with us:

सब समझते हैं कि जो खुद कोटा की वजह से पढ़ाई किया है वो दूसरों को क्या पढ़ाएगा।

Everybody thinks that I cannot teach because I have acquired my educational qualifications due to reservation policies.

The interviewee, in response to these allegations, and also because of his ideological inclination, started coaching Dalit students at concessional rates.

Even in the general economic ventures category where there is a proportionately high presence of Dalits as owners of capital, the interviewees spoke about how caste continues to determine business practices. In an interview, a 'very big business' owner and manager of a ceramic manufacturing unit informed us that her business reached its scale because of sustained supply of goods at a much lower price than her upper-caste counterparts.[57]

The ongoing process of globalisation in India is expected to open up newer economic opportunities for Dalits. However, our field evidence indicates that the majority (many of whose cases are not documented here), with access to minimal capital, still fall in low-return sectors of the liberalised market, such as telephone booths, internet kiosks, photocopy shops, etc. A telephone booth owner in Hoogly told us about his inability to exploit available opportunities in the 'new' market due to lack of capital:

> I want to expand my business and sell mobile phones, computers, and also start computer-related services like internet and printing. However, I don't have any capital to start the business and I don't have any avenues to raise money from the market.

There are a couple of cases where the respondents had the requisite skills and education, as well as the ability to raise capital, and managed to make decent earnings, which enabled them to rise above the status of petty to mid-range business by trading in computer hardware and software, electronics, and graphic printing. But such examples are, to the best of our knowledge, the exception rather than the rule.

Dalits have, generally, fared poorly in sectors which require specialised skills and education, and their presence in these sectors is minimal, as can be evinced from our sample — only one of them operates a 'big' business, three have 'average'-sized businesses, and another one has a 'small' business. As the owner of a nursing home at Aurangabad explained:

> बहुत कम लोग हमारी कम्युनिटी में बहुत ज्यादा पढ़े लिखे हैं। जो थोड़े बहुत हैं उनके पास पैसा नहीं है, इस तरह का बिजनेस करने का। हम लोगों के घर में ज्यादातर लोग रोज जीने

की लडाई लड़ते हैं, कैसे कोई सालों पढ़ाई कर सकता है। पैसा कहां से लाएंगे बिजनेस करने का, और जो छोटा मोटा बिजनेस शुरू करते हैं उसमें ज्यादा प्राफिट नहीं कमाते हैं। मार्केट से पैसे का सपोर्ट नहीं है जो बड़ा बिजनेस कर सके।

There are very few in our community who can invest big money to start their own business. The few who have such specialised skills do not have sufficient capital to start a business. Moreover, most of our community members struggle everyday to survive. How can they study for years? Even if they have such education, how can they raise money for starting such business? Many Dalits, after completing their education, start their own business but they fail to grow in size because of lack of profit. Neither do they manage to raise money from the market.

Acquiring higher education in the face of persistent poverty is an arduous project for Dalits. The respondent, a doctor, thinks that even if a Dalit has the relevant education, it is difficult for him/her to engage in profitable economic activity related to his/her acquired professional skills. As a result, Dalits are stuck in small businesses where the returns are too low to permit up-scaling. This is further reinforced by the lack of availability of capital from the market.

The above testimonies have already suggested that caste matters. To delve into this further, in light of the theory developed earlier, we move on to examine how Dalit businesspeople gain entry in the market as owners of capital and trade their goods and services. How and from where do they source their initial capital? What are the constraints they face while sourcing credit and other essential requirements such as human resource and physical space for their business operations? How do they try and overcome these constraints? What is their source of credit once they start operating in the market? How is competition structured in the market? It is by exploring these issues that we attempt to understand the nature of markets, from the standpoint of Dalit entrepreneurs. To do this we make use of evidence collected during the course of the interviews.

Market Entry and Market Operations

As is true for most business-people, Dalits' attempts to enter the market as entrepreneurs requires raising capital through multiple means, both formal and informal, besides investing their savings and funds raised through the sale of assets. In addition to initial credit, new market entrants have to arrange human resources from the labour market, if their own labour or labour contributed by their family members is not sufficient. They need to set up physical space to carry out their business, and procure official permissions from concerned government offices. Once they succeed in entering the market, they then have to engage with market processes and carve out a space for their economic endeavours. Their attempt to enter the market and operate as 'free' economic agents gives them a distinct experience of market processes. In the following pages we document the range of experiences among Dalits of these processes.

Initial Credit for Market Entry

The Reported Facts

Institutional credit in India is extended by banks (public as well as private), various development schemes of the union government and state governments, and various co-operative financial institutions.

A majority of our interviewees reported that their attempts to approach government institutions and banks for credit largely involved repeated visits, many of them unsuccessful, constant harassment, rent-seeking and rejections. Nearly 80 per cent of our respondents (70 businesspersons) applied for credit from various nationalised banks, of which nearly 65 per cent were rejected. Similarly, more than 85 per cent (78 businesspersons) applied for credit from government agencies, over 50 per cent (40 businesspersons) of which were rejected; this despite the fact that several of the government agencies approached by our respondents have been exclusively created to fund Dalit economic ventures. In some cases, the state government (for instance, Madhya Pradesh) had launched explicit initiatives to encourage Dalit entrepreneurs by providing credit as well as an assured market for goods. More than 50 per cent of the Dalit interviewees in this category had their applications rejected.

The percentage of denials was more or less the same for all sizes of economic ventures, ranging between 60 to 70 per cent, with the exception of mid-sized businesses, where the denial rate was more than 75 per cent. A little over half of the applications from average and small-sized businesses were rejected, and three-fourths of those from the petty business class category had their loan requests declined. Conversely, the rate of acceptance of business proposals for credit was higher for the bigger businesses. Only one-third of the applicants in our top three size categories had their applications rejected.

Given the limited availability of credit from formal sources, almost all our Dalit interviewees obtained credit from informal sources. This often meant a very high interest rate, ranging from 3 to 6 per cent per month, and also the mortgaging of their assets. In a few cases, like for leather goods, credit was made available by some big businesspersons in the same sector. In such cases, the credit was tied to a commitment to supply goods at lower-than-market prices, in addition to high, non-negotiable interest rates. Some also managed to raise capital through their social networks. Surprisingly, most of the interviewees who sourced money from people of their own caste (27 businesspersons) did not pay any interest for it or paid very low interest (2 per cent on average). Of the sample, 79 businesspersons also raised money through their social networks outside of their own castes, and 57 of these paid relatively high interest rates (between 10 and 12 per cent per month) on the money borrowed.

The above narration overwhelmingly points to the following conclusions:

a. A majority of Dalit applicants sought loans from institutional credit agencies (banks and other institutions of the central and state government[58]) and were denied these.

b. All our Dalit entrepreneurs raised whole or part of their capital through their social network or informal credit. However, if the required capital was sourced from outside their own caste, high rates of interest were often paid. This was not true when the required capital was raised from within their caste.

These reported facts indicate that the attempts of Dalit entrepreneurs to trade in goods and services are severely hampered by the denial of institutional credit. To understand their near exclusion from institutional credit, we discuss and analyse two sets of arguments. The first set of arguments comes from organisations and academics adhering to the neo-classical school of thought. The second set of arguments is built on the perception of Dalit entrepreneurs with regard to the denial of credit to them.

Why the Poor are Denied Credit: A Neo-Classical Explanation and its Critique

In the Indian context, the neo-classical argument is put forward by bankers, credit rating agencies and academics who proximate the neo-classical school of thought.[59] The arguments identify three different types of shortcomings in the present credit regime which restrict market competition and, in turn, impede the flow of credit to poorer sections of the population. These are:

a. Shortcomings in the criterion for extending credit:

Credit decisions by institutional credit agencies, especially banks, are made on the basis of loan applications. The loan application consolidates many different pieces of information (income, ratio of expenses to present income, ratio of debt/liability to present income, employment history, credit history, prospects of the proposed economic venture, projected turnover[60]) into a single credit score. If the credit score is positive, the loan is approved, otherwise it is denied. Joshi,[61] while studying the access to credit among hawkers in Mumbai, elaborates on the problem faced by banks and other formal credit institutions in procuring relevant information, that is, the difficulties experienced by banks in preparing the credit ratings of individual clients. In her work, she identifies two sets of problems:

a. The first is related to information required for screening applications: Borrowers differ in their risk type and lenders do not possess complete and symmetric information to perfectly distinguish among loan applicants.

b. The second can be understood in terms of perceived transaction cost. Credit denial may occur when the lender perceives a higher cost of preventing loan defaults. Loan defaults could occur due to i) Incentive problems: Given asymmetric information, borrowers may engage in opportunistic behaviour. Lenders, in their efforts to overcome this, find it costly to ensure that borrowers take actions that make repayment more likely; ii) Monitoring problems: After the loan is granted, many circumstances may change the borrower's ability and/or willingness to repay. The lender has to incur costs on actions taken to observe these changes in the probability of default, and to induce borrowers to take corrective action; iii) Enforcement problems: It is difficult to compel repayment, particularly when the institutional and legal infrastructure is not efficient, and court procedures are too expensive. Transaction costs are also high because the amounts are small — the bank spends the same amount of money managing small amounts as it does big amounts. Hence, for the bank, it is more cost effective to manage larger amounts.

Since, the process of calculating credit ratings is based on the construction of a scientific index of credit worthiness, the denial of credit is understood as a rational decision, wherein a loan is denied because the borrower has failed to score a sufficiently high credit rating.

A bank manager in Lucknow candidly admitted that poor people are often bypassed by formal financial services.[62] He blames it on interest rate ceilings imposed on banks for loans below ₹2 lakh.[63] Such a ceiling is expected to allow the poor to access loans at a cheaper rate. In his view, however, this measure is counterproductive as the ceiling on interest rates prevents the bank from factoring in additional risks and other transaction costs.[64] Consequently, banks extend credit only to those who, in their perception, offer lower risks and better security. The default outcome of such decision-making is the extension of credit 'to him/her that has'.[65] In other words, rich borrowers with established businesses are always treated as credit worthy, simply because they have sufficient assets and capabilities to *formally* prove that they can reproduce the capital they have invested in their economic ventures, and return the loaned amount.

The Credit Rating Information Services of India Limited (CRISIL)[66] and Investment Information and Credit Rating Agency (ICRA),[67] two leading credit rating agencies in India, mirror the arguments put forth by the Lucknow bankers by elaborating on the kind of institutions required for de-capping interest rates. In their view, de-capping of interest rates will allow credit to reach even the poorest. They argue that Indian banks do not follow the principles of 'risk based pricing' (RBP), that is, high risk loans are not priced according to the risk involved; therefore, banks are not able to discriminate against the low rated borrowers. The rationale behind this is to charge high risk borrowers higher interest rates in order to potentially cover the losses caused by loan defaulters. Moreover, a uniform rate of interest is generally preferred due to the high degree of competition in the loan market which, in turn, makes banks extra careful while judging the borrower's ability to repay. This extra care (denying loans where they perceive risk) is an attempt to keep the banks' transaction costs at the minimum possible level. An unintended outcome of this is that even the obligation of priority sector lending is not fulfilled.[68] CRISIL and ICRA's recommendation to banks is to charge interest rates as per risk-based pricing, thereby allowing them to raise risk premiums commensurate to the risk which the bank intends to undertake. This will also enable them to reach the lowest economic segment of borrowers, hitherto excluded because of the traditional credit rating exercise.

b. Shortcomings in the Bank's Governance Regime

According to studies by Banerjee, Cole and Duflo,[69] small-scale firms suffer from severe credit constraints. They pose the following question: 'if firms are willing to absorb more credit, and more credit means more sales, more profits and no more defaults, why is the bank not willing to give them more credit?' They examine the loan data from a particular public sector bank, and point out that the decision to extend loans by banks is based on the current sales and liquidity position of the firms. According to this criterion, there is no emphasis on profits, either current or projected, except in as much as profits are related to turnover or current assets. In their view, the misplaced emphasis on current sales and liquidity results in similar treatment of two firms with very different costs, but the same turnover and current assets. They suggest that another reason for the refusal of credit to borrowers who are perceived to be potential defaulters emerges from what they call the 'culture of fear'. Public sector bank officials are liable for prosecution on charges of corruption if numerous loans in their portfolio go bad. The 'culture of fear' created by this provision either discourages them from extending a loan if they have the slightest doubt about the borrower, or makes them extend only an amount that has been borrowed by a client and successfully returned earlier. The history of timely repayment does not seem to become the basis for extending a higher loan amount. Thus, the misplaced emphasis on current assets and the unwarranted apprehension of the assessors, result in the denial of credit.

c) 'Faulty' Regulatory Regime

Another set of influential bankers, Ananth and Mor,[70] state that the present regulatory policies aimed at universalising access to credit are unable to deliver results. This, they argue, is because regulatory instruments like the 'service area approach'[71] (the service area norm also reveals a bias for a branch-based approach[72]), restrict competition among banks, and raise the price of credit. Similarly, re-financing (through self-help groups) to increase access to credit for certain segments, 'discourages banks from making pricing decisions based on risk estimation, and undermines the scope for innovation by providing a direct subsidy'. Likewise, restrictions placed on financial institutions (other than banks and approved non-bank finance companies) against collecting deposits prevents people from saving and, consequently, seeking credit. The banks, too, cannot provide saving bank accounts to all small clients because of huge transaction costs, especially when returns to deposits are universal across all accounts. Further, subsidising financial services through interest rate caps or premium caps discourages providers from innovating product designs. Based on this understanding, Ananth and Mor conclude that the current flaws in regulations have restricted rapid growth in outreach. Hence, they advocate *domestic de-regulation* (emphasis added) which incentivises existing players to expand access through market-based mechanisms. Such restructuring, in their view, holds more potential than *entry of further players* (emphasis added).[73]

The above arguments, from three different sources, are embedded in the neo-classical school. In this view, state intervention is seen to inhibit market-based competition. Further, it is stressed that any external regulatory measures to suppress competition, though taken apparently in favour of the poor, become counterproductive and in turn disenfranchise them from credit markets. Adherents of this school of thought advocate allowing market competition to determine interest rates, yet, at the same time, disapprove of the entry of newer market players. The critique of this school of thought takes the following line:

i) Most of the time, credit default is a rational decision. Therefore, if defaulting on a loan payment is made on rational grounds, risk-based pricing of the loan would not help in disciplining the defaulter and ensuring repayment. At the same time, if the rationale behind a higher interest rate through risk-based pricing is to cover the cost of a few defaults with higher returns from many, this results in gross economic injustice to disciplined borrowers.

ii) This nature of credit either excludes low-income families and first time borrowers, or includes them only at high interest rates (unfavourable inclusion). In other words, the present credit regime, by interlocking credit with assets, reproduces the existing inequality of access in the credit markets.

iii) The emphasis placed on current assets (property rights) and liquidity, and de-emphasis on the market potential of the individual(s), depends significantly on the discretion of the assessor. Even if one managed to establish the market potential of the individual, one would still need to rely on an assessor. This absolute mandate of the assessor completely ignores the fact that socio-economic relationships are mostly configured on the lines of existing social structures, where interactions between individuals (assessor and the client) are not always secular in nature, and can be mediated by personal values and beliefs.

The neo-classical school also considers two non-complementary points, which do not stress on 'rational' and 'scientific' credit index-based decisions. These include: i) the development of mutual trust between bankers and borrowers over a period of time, which in turn facilitates fresh credit to borrowers; and ii) the 'culture of fear' that may fog the mind of assessors and prevent them from complying with the demands of scientifically derived credit indices. However, according to this school of thought, financial transactions that are facilitated either in terms of 'trust' or the 'culture of fear', thwart competition and the expansion of credit. In effect, the finely carved theoretical logic emphasising market competition as a remedy refuses to acknowledge the possibility that trust can find its roots in social relationships which might not necessarily be based on secular pro-fessional credentials, and may not be created only by professional interests. As for 'culture of fear', while it accepts the possibility of individuals restricting the supply of credit, it may not acknowledge that such restrictions may be exercised by individuals (assessors) due to their bias against certain individuals/social groups, or based on values of discrimination dominant in civil society. Further, restriction of credit may not always constitute thwarting of competition but could, in fact, be an instrument to meet the demands of competition, in this case between Dalits and other social/caste groups. In this sense, the denial of credit is also perceived by Dalit entrepreneurs as a means of systematic discrimination against them. This is further discussed in the subsequent sections.

Why was Initial Formal Credit Denied? The Perception of Dalit Entrepreneurs

In this section, we outline the attempts made by our Dalit entrepreneurs to understand their near exclusion, or adverse inclusion, in the formal credit market. This effort will not only help us understand the processes affecting their entry into the market as owners of capital, but will also enable us to critique dominant theories (discussed in the first section) from the standpoint of Dalits.

A fundamental assumption in the neo-classical economics-inspired, credit index-based lending is that secure property rights will encourage lenders to extend credit, by using property as collateral. It is argued that institutionalised property rights help to address three crucial problems of the market: measurement of assets, monitoring of activities and enforcement of agreements,[74] while weak property rights reduce access to external financing.[75] Bardhan reviewed the recent spate of literature from new institutional economics that emphasises contract law and the security of property rights, and noted that all of this literature points to the importance of predictability of these property rights for economic performance and investment.[76] It also emphasises the 'rule of law' variable (one standard measure that combines indices of effectiveness and predictability of judiciary, enforceability of contracts, and incidence of crime) which is imperative to create secure property rights. The World Bank's World Development Report of 2002, which was inspired by new institutional economics, delineates the institutions required for market-led economic growth, and places critical importance on secure property rights.[77]

Thus, we see that both the neo-classical school and new institutional economics, despite their internal differences, converge on the point that that secure property rights promote efficiency in markets. Once these rights are in place, they form the basis for the efficient execution of other associated administrative and legal structures.[78]

On the other hand, in refutation of our understanding of these two schools of thoughts, an owner of a sanitary ware shop at Pune told us:

मेरे सारे कागज पूरे थे। मेरे पास अपना घर भी था जिसकी कीमत 3 लाख से ऊपर थी जिसको मैंने गिरवीं रखा था, पर मुझे 40 हजार का कर्ज बैंक ने नहीं दिया।

My loan papers were complete. I owned a house market value of which was more than ₹3 lakh and which I was willing to mortgage, but the bank did not give me a loan of ₹40,000.

As per his testimony, this particular entrepreneur was unable to procure a loan from the bank, despite his willingness to hypothecate his house which was five times the value of the loan. In fact, collation of data from all our interviews overwhelmingly indicates that, in the case of Dalits, secure property rights do not always translate into access to formal credit. Out of 45 entrepreneurs who were denied credit by banks, only six reported that they did not possess clear titles to any kind of property; more than half (23 entrepreneurs) reported that they had clear titles to property which they had proposed to hypothecate; and nearly one-third (16 entrepreneurs) held the property rights as joint owners, with clear permission from the co-owner(s) for hypothecation. Around 40 of the Dalit entrepreneurs we interviewed were denied credit by institutions of the state like the Scheduled Caste Development Finance Corporation, Department of Urban Development, Department of Industry/Industrial Development Corporation, etc., and by various development schemes of the government specifically designed to promote entrepreneurial activities among Dalits. Of these, nearly three-fifth (22 entrepreneurs) reported that they were denied credit even though they possessed clear titles to property; more than one-tenth (five entrepreneurs) held property in joint ownership and had a 'no objection certificate' from the co-owner, and the remaining two-sixth (13 entrepreneurs) were denied credit by the government because they did not have secure titles to property which they could have hypothecated.

Our Dalit entrepreneurs do not perceive this large-scale denial of loans as an outcome of credit-based indices seeking to maximise returns to the banks while minimising the transaction cost. They also do not consider the denial as an attempt by formal institutions to channelise available resources to the most viable economic activity, which they might not have opted for, thus disqualifying from accessing credit. Instead, they see it as systematic attempts of discrimination against them.

A laundry owner from Lucknow pointed out that the geographical segregation of their community also translates into their exclusion from credit. His community, also called Dhobis, resides in Dhobi Katra (a ghetto of the community that has traditionally washed clothes, primarily of upper-castes) in the Mehmoodabad area of Lucknow, an area where they have stayed over many generations. Our interviewee revealed that the very mention of Dhobi Katra invokes condescension as well as contempt in the minds of credit officials:

जैसे ही साहिब लोग धोबी कटरा का नाम सुनते हैं उनका व्यवहार बदल जाता है। मुझे समझाए कि मैं धंधा नहीं कर पाऊंगा। सारा पैसा डुबो दूंगा। मुझसे बोला कि मैं प्रेस का ठेला लगाऊं और घाट पर ही कपड़े धोऊं। यहां तक ये भी बोला कि मैं अपने लड़के को एक नया प्रेस ठेला दिला दूं जिससे कि आमदनी बढ़ जाए। वाशिंग मशीन लगाके मैं धंधा नहीं कर पाऊंगा। आप ही बताइए कि अगर बाप दादे ने गोमती घाट पर कपड़े धोए हैं तो क्या मैं भी और मेरा लडके को भी कपड़े धोने पड़ेंगे . . . मैंने तय कर लिया था कि मैं घाट पर कपड़े नहीं धोऊंगा। जिसको कपड़े धुलाना हो उसको मेरे पास आना ही होगा और मैं घर घर नहीं जाऊंगा।

As soon as the officer [person dealing with my loan request] learnt that I reside in Dhobi Katra, his behaviour changed. He explained to me that I would be unsuccessful in managing a modern laundry and will lose all my money in the market. He further told me to continue with my washing activities on the river bank, along with ironing clothes. He went to the extent of suggesting that I should buy my son a new cart to iron clothes so as to augment my family income. You tell me, if my father and grandfather have washed clothes on the banks of the Gomti river, does it mean both I and my son also have to wash clothes there? . . . I had decided that I would not wash clothes any more on the banks of the river and whoever wants to get their clothes washed and starched has to come to my shop. I will not go door to door collecting clothes for washing and then delivering them back.

It is obvious from this narrative that the loan officer touched many sensitive chords, bringing to the fore many gloomy and cynical emotions and perceptions: hurt at the worldview of the official who thinks that he is incapable of entering and managing a business in the modern market; dismay and anger at his advice that the son should also be locked into old methods; agitation, at the assumption that they are expected to always remain in the same caste profession.

Yet, it will not be out of place to state that the laundry owner does not perceive the lender as somebody who is practising, what Becker calls, a 'taste for discrimination',[79] because he belongs to a specific low caste. The Dalit entrepreneur perceives this denial primarily as an attempt to consign him and his family back to their traditional caste occupation and thereby maintain status quo. In other words, it is a line of reasoning which suggests that certain social groups from lower castes should keep on performing the required manual labour in the society, while other non-manual and better-paying labour can be exclusively taken up by individuals belonging to the upper-castes. In this sense, discrimination also emanates from material logic. Moreover, this particular narration tells us about the increasing social assertion of Dalits, and their refusal to accept the social position as ordained by the Hindu social order.

The other face of this social assertion is reflected in the aggressive political mobilisation and assertion of Dalits in most parts of the country, particularly in the state of Maharashtra. In Maharashtra, such assertion by the Dalits has been historically spearheaded by Mahars (a sub-caste among Dalits).[80] It seems that this growing assertiveness and claim to equality in all domains of socio-political and economic existence, is resisted by the upper-castes, as indicated in the testimony of a medical doctor who approached the Maharashtra State Financial Corporation (MSFC) for a loan in order to start a nursing home. He informed us that his loan application was rejected and the MSFC official said:

महाराष्ट्र में तुम सब महार लोग सारा सरकारी पैसा ले लोगे। कोई भी पार्टी तुम्हारे विरूद्ध नहीं बोलती हैं, सबको वोट जो चाहिए।

You Mahars[81] in Maharashtra are cornering all the government's re-sources. All political parties support you because you are an important vote bank for them.

Cloaked within the accusation that the narrator's community is pampered as a social group because of its political clout, there seems to be an implicit assumption that members of this community do not deserve resources; it is the political imperative of various political parties that ensures diversion of resources. Hence, the denial of loans perhaps indicates an administrative measure taken by upper-castes to 'rectify' the mistakes emanating from the electoral compulsions of the political process. Also evident from this episode is the fierce contempt, not against a particular individual, but against the assertive lower caste community as a whole, which can also be termed an ideology of caste. In contemporary articulation, this ideology does not adhere to pure sociological principles which segment society based on notions of purity and pollution, but works skilfully to maintain a power relationship between the upper and lower castes. This power play is well articulated in the above two narratives: in the first, the attempt of a lower caste to enter the market as an entrepreneur in defiance of his 'divinely ordained' traditional occupation is questioned, and in the second, by restricting credit to the Dalit entrepreneur, the upper-caste official also seems to question the political process of the country, which has given lower-castes an institutionalised medium to claim equality with upper-castes.

Another instance of how the ideology of caste can colour and shape official decisions was shared by a woman entrepreneur who owns a large ceramic factory in Ahmedabad. In her efforts to use the surplus she had earned through trading in retail coal to start a ceramic factory, she approached a public sector bank for a loan of ₹5 lakh, with a proposal to hypothecate her land worth ₹12 lakh. This is what she said of her experience with the bank manager:

उसका कहना था कि हरिजनों को कर्ज देने का मतलब है पैसा डूबना। ज्यादातर लोग धंधा करना जानते ही नहीं हैं उसने ये भी बोला कि अगर सारा पैसा वो ऐसे ही देता रहा तो, बैंक भी बंद हो जाएगा और उसकी नौकरी भी चली जाएगी।

He was of the opinion that extending loans to Harijans[82] means losing the money, since most of them don't know how to do business. He also told me that if he kept giving money to Harijans, the bank would shut down and he would also lose his job.

The bank manager seemed to believe that Dalits (whom he calls Harijans) as a community cannot engage in business and are perpetual defaulters; hence extending loans to them is a grave risk for the bank.

The above narratives seem to emphasise the robustness of the informal institution of caste that sustains, mediates and influences outcomes, even in engagements with formal institutions. Dalit entrepreneurs explain to us that the denial of initial credit for entering the market has less to do with the 'misplaced' regulatory policies of the government, and more to do with systemic discrimination practised against them by the upper-castes. Their perception is that such discrimination is shaped by the ideology of caste which, in its modern incarnation, works to prevent them from entering the market, and, in doing so, maintains the power relationship between upper and lower castes.

In spite of the barriers to credit placed by formal credit institutions, our Dalit entrepreneurs have still managed to enter the market as owners of capital and thus pursued their desire for accumulation in the market.

Social Structure of Accumulation: Markets Seen Through the Lens of Dalit Entrepreneurs

Markets, as institutions, essentially enable the production and distribution of goods and services and involve buyers and sellers. The buyer enters into a transaction with the seller to procure goods and services, in order to satisfy varied wants. The seller supplies goods and services in order to earn a surplus over the capital investment. The earning of surplus through the market can also be described as capital accumulation. Capital accumulation, then, refers to the processes whereby a certain sum of capital is invested and transformed into a larger sum of capital. In the following section we attempt to understand the constraints experienced by Dalit owners of capital and the strategies they employ in their attempt to accumulate capital by participating in markets.

As discussed earlier, according to new institutional economics, the process of capital accumulation is based not on the instrumental rationality of the individual (the assumption of neo-classical economics that enables it to be an institution-free theory), but is shaped by a wide range of institutions. The school of social embeddedness goes further and demonstrates that economic actions are rooted in social relations and hence, informal institutions are also crucial for understanding the outcomes of market processes.

Market outcomes can be considered to find their basis in an array of institutions which are not necessarily governed by the impersonal norms and regulations of the state, but are contingent on informal institutions organised around the ideological inclinations — values, beliefs and dominantly accepted norms — of its leading players. Therefore, it can, perhaps, be safely argued that existing social relationships (relationships between members of different castes, religion, ethnicity, language, age, region, gender, etc.) and the associated power structures (privileges/rewards, as well as disadvantages/punishments) mediate almost all market transactions and influence their outcomes.

How do existing social relationships produce a relatively stable pattern of economic relationships shaping capital accumulation processes?

Levi Strauss has argued that social relations are the raw materials out of which models making up social structures are built, but the social structure can, by no means, be reduced to an ensemble of social relationships to be described in a given society.[83] Hence, capital accumulation affected through social relationships (constructed through caste, religion, ethnicity, gender, age, region, etc.) can also be described as a social structure of accumulation. While it may not be the only factor configuring economic relationships, it would, nevertheless, be a very crucial enabler shaping the actions of economic agents in the market.

In the Indian context, relationships configured through caste identity provide an important basis for the structuring of economic relationships between individuals and social groups. Thus, in line with Harriss-White,[84] the influence of caste ideology on market outcomes can also be described as a social structure of accumulation (refer to the earlier discussion). In other words, the social/ideological institution of caste can be deployed in the market in the interest of market-based accumulation, by the dominant owners of capital belonging to the upper-caste. Indeed, this is what our Dalit entrepreneurs seem to believe. In the following sections, in order to understand how caste operates in the market as a social structure of accumulation, we will elaborate on the experiences of Dalit entrepreneurs with regard to markets and market-based transactions.

Accommodation and Rigidity: Relations with Non-Dalits

A building contractor from Ahmedabad who supplies construction and building material explained to us:

पटेल और बनिया फ्लैट में पैसा लगा सकते हैं पर लेबर का इंतजाम हम जैसे लोग करते हैं। अपने गांव से और दूसरे राज्य से लेबर लाते हैं और पटेल और बनिया को सप्लाई करते हैं। गुजरात में कोई जात को लेकर लड़ाई नहीं है। सब लड़ाई पैसे की है। पटेल और बनिया

कभी मेरी जात नहीं पूछते हैं। पर अगर मैं अपना धंधा शुरू कर दूं तो मेरी जात पर सवाल खड़े हो जाएंगे और मेरा धंधा चौपट हो जाएगा।

The money for the construction of the flats is invested by Patels and Baniyas but people like me supply construction labour. I bring labour from my village and even from other states. There is no caste conflict in Gujarat. All conflict is over money. [Patels and Baniyas] never question my caste but if I try and step in their shoes and set up my own small business, they will question my caste and ensure that my business doesn't survive.

The testimony of the labour contractor illuminates two aspects of market operations: First, the apparently inclusive nature of market processes, where neither caste is questioned nor are sociological norms of the caste system adhered to, by the upper-caste economic 'masters'. The inclusion of a lower caste labour contractor as a junior partner is taken to indicate the accommodative character of the market-based system of accumulation in the emerging 'new' economy, where sociological rules governing economic effort appear to be changing. The second characteristic of the market, highlighted in this narrative, is its rigidity — the interviewee is included, yet, at the same time, is not allowed the opportunity to step into the shoes of his 'masters' in the market. He feels that if he tried to emulate his 'masters', the sociological norms of caste would be re-invoked, which in turn would go against his accumulation strategy. How do we understand this apparently contradictory nature of market processes?

Existing market players will always try to maintain status quo that is the nature of the market processes is inherently rigid. This rigidity implies a greater degree of hostility toward Dalits; accordingly, Dalits perceive that institutionalised attempts are made by the upper-castes to block them from staking accumulation claims in the market. At the same time, the market may also be flexible enough to accommodate the economic interests of Dalits — the dominant market players may permit their entry and operations though only under certain conditions.

A model of pure rigidity implies that all economic actors in the market are assigned fixed places in a given structure, with defined economic roles, responsibilities and duties, which are determined by a. the structural principles of capital (capability to invest), and b. the logic of divinely ordained division of labour (upper-caste will control and invest capital, and Dalits and other marginalised social groups will labour towards the ends envisaged by capital). Any attempt by labour in general, and social groups historically equated to labour in particular, to enter the market as owners of capital is mostly resisted. The model of rigidity, hence, portrays the classic case, where caste overlaps with class. On the other hand, an accommodative model of market-based accumulation, in its ideal form, will permit anybody to acquire capital, invest, and earn surplus, irrespective of social location. In its not-so-pure form, it indicates the possibility where Dalits, as owners of capital, are integrated into economic processes in varying degrees. Hence, caste may not necessarily overlap with class.

Our evidence suggests that market-based accumulation does not complement either of the models in their ideal forms, but operates between the continuum of absolute rigidity at one end and accommodativeness on the other. The move towards rigidity will mean extreme adverse inclusion while a shift towards accommodation will still imply moderate adverse inclusion. Hence, Dalit owners of capital experience adverse inclusion in market processes, though the degree of adversity varies. In other words, access to market spaces for Dalits as owners of capital is neither entirely blocked, nor are avenues provided for complete integration as equal players. Further, the leanings of market processes towards either end of the continuum are decided not only by the market, but also by the balance of forces in the wider socio-economic and political realm. In the following section, we will discuss the processes that *lean* towards maintaining rigidity, followed by practices that are *disposed* towards accommodation. In order to further understand the contradictory aspects of markets — rigidity and accommodation — we turn to ethnographic evidence.

Experiencing Rigidity

a. Impediments Created by Former Employers

The last two decades have witnessed a growing political consciousness amongst Dalits with regards to their socially sanctioned marginalisation. This is also evinced by their increasing attempts and strategies to challenge the status quo. However, their socio-political assertions have not translated into benefits in the economic domain. On one hand, they find newer forms of discrimination scuttling the policy processes avowedly drafted and executed for their benefit;[85] on the other hand, they witness newer forms of control and discrimination within the economic domain.[86] Our fieldwork informs us that our respondents entered the market as businesspersons because they perceived urban markets as being less discriminatory, and driven more by the quality of goods and services offered. Out of the 90 businesspersons interviewed, 57 (nearly 64 per cent) were engaged in the same economic activity as when they were wage workers. In other words, they had acquired the skills and basic capabilities to earn and manage the present business while working in economic units controlled by upper-castes. The interviewees reported that their movement from 'worker' to 'manager/owner' was seen both by their upper-caste masters and by their caste peers, as a step that did not suit their 'stature'. For instance, a former sweeper who is now a general merchant in Lucknow testifies to having been subjected to adverse remarks from a labour supervisor. He narrates this experience:

जब मेरी दुकान का एलाटमेंट हो रहा था तो ठेकेदार ने बोला कि मेरा दिमाग खराब हो गया है, बड़े बनने के सपने देख रहे हो, सारा पैसा डुबो दोगे। कोई तुम्हारी दुकान से सामान नहीं खरीदेगा।

While I was taking charge of the shop that was allotted to me, the labour supervisor told me that I had gone insane; I was dreaming of becoming rich, I would lose all my savings since nobody would buy things from my shop.

Similarly, while trying to raise finances to run a sanitary shop in Pune, the owner was dissuaded by his former employer. This is what he narrates:

मेरे पुराने मालिक ने बोला कि हम लोगों की बस की बात नहीं है, हम लोगों को मेहनत से काम करना चाहिए और मजदूरी करके पैसा कमाना चाहिए, दुकान खोलने से कोई फायदा नहीं है।

My old employer told me that we are not capable of doing business; we should be doing hard labour and putting in extra effort to earn more money instead of starting our own business.

As suggested in these two testimonies, the former employers expressed their prejudices regarding the kind of economic activity members of the Dalit community can possibly undertake. While upper-caste employers seem to think that their lower caste employees do not have the capacity to undertake economic activities directed towards accumulation in the markets, our Dalit entrepreneurs perceive that the worldview of their upper-caste employers is shaped by their belief that the lower castes can only be efficient labourers and not astute entrepreneurs. Accordingly, the employers were seen to create multiple impediments to hinder the Dalit entrepreneurs' entry into the market (Table 3.3). Of the base of 57 respondents, almost 80 per cent[87] (44) said that their respective employers thought that they would lose a worker trained by them. This was considered a hindrance as it constituted a loss of time and resources which would have to be reinvested in a new worker. Around 36 per cent (21) felt that the registration of their ventures was delayed because of the influence of their former employers.

Table 3.3 Market Impediments Created by Former Employers

Nature of Impediment	No. of Interviewees
Registration of their Enterprises	21
Credit Related	33
Physical Space of Location of Economic Unit	27
Getting Workers	51
Procuring Initial Orders	53

Source: Compiled by the author.

Nearly 60 per cent (33) faced considerable difficulty in accessing the private capital market; even when they managed to do so, it was at relatively higher interest rates. Almost 50 per cent (27) were refused tenancy at least once in their search for physical space to carry out their economic activities. This denial was perceived as discrimination by the prospective tenant because they belonged to a lower caste, or because the owner was influenced by the former employer, or both. An overwhelming 90 per cent (51) had tremendous difficulty in recruiting workers. Even in cases where the workers belonged to the same caste, there was the fear of a backlash from their powerful upper-caste employers. An even higher number of them (53) reported that they faced problems in procuring initial orders. Several respondents felt that their former employers actively hindered their business in the initial stages; others felt that the lack of capital (further accentuated by market/credit impediments,[88] forcing them to take high interest loans and also pay rent-seekers to operationalise their business) made their business propositions less competitive. Many of them, particularly those in retail, felt that the wider society was also unwilling to accept them as independent economic agents.

b. 'Pure' Goods and 'Impure' Caste

There are certain economic activities in our sample that were traditionally disallowed to Dalits (education and profession of teaching), or where it was believed that their touch would 'pollute' the goods and render them unfit for human touch or consumption (food and related items). The credit market is certainly most unfriendly to those who enter the retail trade in food. For instance, a Dalit entrepreneur operating a small food joint in a general locality is, mostly, refused credit, but the same entrepreneur, when operating from a Dalit locality in the same city, is extended credit. A small joint owner serving tea and refreshments at Kanpur explained:

मैं आर्य नगर में नाली सफाई का काम करता था। मुझे नगर महापालिका दलित कोटे से एक दुकान आर्यनगर में मिली, बड़ी मुश्किल थी। होलसेलर से कभी तेल, घी, चाय का उधार नहीं मिलता था। उन लोगों को पूरा विश्वास था कि आर्यनगर में होने की वजह से मेरी दुकान डूब जाएगी और पैसा मैं वापस नहीं कर पाऊंगा। उसका सोचना भी ठीक था क्योंकि वहां सिर्फ सुबह मेरे पुराने साथी सफाई करने के बाद आते और चाय और ब्रेड पकौड़े खरीदते थे। आमदनी ज्यादा नहीं थी। मैंने उस दुकान को किराए पर उठाके अब यहां पर (खटीक मुहल्ला में) दुकान खोली है। मेरी जात का सवाल नहीं है। मेरे कस्टमर भी ज्यादा हैं। मुझे पहले से ज्यादा उधार मिलता है पर बाकी लोग को 14 दिन का उधार मिलता है मुझे 7 दिन का, और नहीं देने पर 6 प्रतिशत ब्याज।

I used to work at Arya Nagar as a sweeper. My job was to clean public drains. I was allotted a shop at Arya Nagar by the Municipal Corporation under the Dalit quota. The biggest constraint in my business operation was that I never got credit from the wholesaler while purchasing cooking oil, cooking butter and tea. The wholesalers would think that my business will not be profitable because I am a sweeper by caste and the shop was in a predominantly upper-caste area. Now, it seems, they were right. Most of my customers were my sweeper friends who would come and buy tea and bread pakora [a kind of vegetable burger] after finishing their work in the morning. There was not much profit. I rented out that shop, and now I have opened the shop here [Khatik[89] colony]. Here, my caste is not an issue and I get more customers . . . I do get some credit from the wholesaler. However, others get credit for 14 days and I am given credit for 7 days. If I default, I have to pay an interest of 6 per cent.

In the above narrative, the Dalit entrepreneur highlights the nature of rigidity in the market that he has experienced: by taking advantage of the secular norms of the state, he is able to get a shop allotment in an upper-caste area; however, this deemed benefit is mitigated by the discriminatory processes dominant in the realm of civil society. First, the wholesaler refuses to advance credit because he believes that a tea stall owned by a lower caste member will not attract business in a predominantly upper-caste area. These dominant discriminatory values force the tea stall owner to rework his accumulation strategy and shift his business to a mainly lower caste area where, as he anticipated, his economic efforts attract more consumers. Now, the same wholesaler is ready to extend credit to him, yet the rate is higher than the prevailing market rate. It can be argued from the process detailed above that the wholesaler's initial refusal to extend credit was linked primarily to his anticipation of loss. However, the narrator appears unconvinced by this explanation, as he experiences inequitable treatment even when his business becomes economically viable, as well as socially acceptable.

Further, when it comes to wholesale trade in food items, it is perceived that the Dalit businessperson has the lowest bargaining power in the market, and this is demonstrated in our interviews in Ahmedabad and Jaipur. We have already narrated the experience of the Jaipur entrepreneur on page 71. Similar to this, the wholesaler in food items in Ahmedabad shares his experiences:

हमें कम दिन की मोहलत मिलती है और जो माल मैं सप्लाई करता हूँ उसका पेमेंट भी देर से होता है। बाजार का उसूल है एक हफ्ता से दस दिन, मेरा पैसा लेने के लिए दस बार जाना पड़ता है . . . कौन लड़ाई करे, धंधा खतरे में पड़ सकता है।

I get fewer days to pay and other entrepreneurs take more time than usual to pay me for the goods I supply. The rule of the market is that the wholesaler gets his money within one week or ten days, but I don't. I have to visit them at least 10 times to get my payment released . . . Why should I fight? It might jeopardise my business.

In this case, the nature of the upper-caste businesspersons' rigidity is quite different from the previous experience, though it results in a similar outcome, that is, adverse inclusion in the market processes. Here, the practice of late payment enhances the availability of operational capital to the upper-caste business colleague who withholds the payment but, at the same time, restricts capital availability for the Dalit entrepreneur. The latter's decision not to protest and instead, to ignore the discriminatory practices of his upper-caste business colleagues, reveals yet another accumulation strategy. In other words, he realises that traditional social norms, according to which the mere touch of a lower caste would pollute food, could possibly be invoked to completely exclude him from the market.

c. Network Closure: The Role of Social Networks in Restricting Business Resources

The social embeddedness school, discussed earlier, emphasises the centrality of social networks in controlling resources and, in turn, affecting outcomes in the market. Social networks operate in the market primarily as informal, loose coalitions, formed by existing market players to maintain their position in the market against non-network member(s). As delineated by Podolny and Page, we also understand that network members pursue exchange relations with one another, but at the same time, lack a legitimate institutional authority to arbitrate and resolve disputes that may arise during the exchange.[90] Market players turn towards network resources for help or support during their operations in the market; such support ranges from providing market information for newer businesses, getting more business, fulfilling credit needs, arranging labour supply, resisting competition by blocking credit and labour supply, influencing price, influencing regulatory institutions, etc. In practice, therefore, the resources raised through social networks are used to negotiate the constraints present in the markets, through interpersonal relationships that operate outside the regulatory framework of the state.[91]

How do social networks operate in the markets of urban middle India, which is where we have collected the business histories of Dalit entrepreneurs? Our interviewees seem to believe that networks find their basis in religion, caste, family and kinship ties, regional identity, etc., and are further strengthened by class location. Network resources are, mostly, not available for new entrants or historically deprived social groups, because of the prevalence of the ideology of discrimination. Thus, the entrepreneurs feel that social networks constitute an important factor in determining the nature of inclusion in the market. In the following pages, we will discuss some of the important aspects of social networks that influence accumulation processes in the market, and also show how they are embedded in the caste identities of the dominant market players.

It has been reported that every sub-sector of the market is normally controlled by specific groups of businesspeople who are mostly, though not always, identified with particular castes or communities.

For instance, the leather trade in Lucknow, Agra and Kanpur is perceived to be primarily controlled by Baniyas, Marwaris and Punjabis. Similarly, the sanitary ware trade in Pune is considered to be dominated by Marathas, and the Patels are seen to be controlling a significant space in the real estate market of Ahmedabad.

Each of these dominant social groups is mostly seen to constitute a closed network, whose members work towards each other's advantage, and Dalit entrepreneurs feel that it is almost impossible for them to become members of these social networks that have been configured by their upper-caste peers. According to a general merchant in Lucknow:

> धंधे में मेरी कोई माँ बाप नहीं है। हमें उधार पर माल नहीं मिलता है॰॰॰ सब चाचा ताऊ मौसी, मामा को उधार मिलता है। समाज में औकात होनी चाहिए, रहने के लिए, दोस्ती करने के लिए, और खासकर धंधा करने के लिए।

> In my business, there is no godfather. I don't get any material for my shop on credit . . . only people who have their uncles and other relatives as wholesalers get material on credit. One should have some kind of status in society, to live, make friends and especially to do business.

The merchant seems to equate social status with a higher caste location, and feels that only people with a particular social status (read those belonging to upper-castes) can do profitable business. In other words, powerful social networks in the market are necessary for business, and such social networks find their basis in upper-caste identity, from which he is automatically excluded.

How do social networks affect business outcomes?

Resource raising networks are a great asset for procuring orders, especially bulk orders, from government departments and big industries. They also facilitate the procurement of immediate soft loans from the open, informal credit market.[92] Many of our interviewees expressed that the lack of resource networks has prevented them from getting bulk orders. It also restricts their access to credit on the same terms (time, quantity and rate of interest) as those enjoyed by their peers. The following testimonies — of a courier company owner and a brick kiln owner in Pune — further elaborate this point. First, the courier company owner:

> सबसे बड़ा डिस्पैच का काम प्राइवेट कंपनी से मिलता है, यहीं पर मैं मात खा जाता हूँ, मेरा काम बहुत अच्छा है, सभी कस्टमर खुश हैं, लेकिन मैं बड़ा काम दो कारण से नहीं ले

पाता हूँ। पहला, मेरी कोई जान पहचान नहीं है . . . दूसरा, अगर जान पहचान हो भी तो भी बड़ी कम्पनी का काम नहीं कर पाऊंगा, वो लोग मंथली पेमेंट करते हैं, मेरे पास इतना पैसा नहीं है कि एक महीने इंतजार कर पाऊं। मार्केट से पैसा नहीं मिलता है। दूसरे डीटीडीसी की फ्रेंचाइज़ी गुजराती और मराठा की है, उनकी मार्केट में बहुत जान पहचान हैं।

The real big orders for letter despatch are given by big private companies. This is where I lose out in the market. My work is much appreciated by my existing customers. However, I am not able to get big business orders due to two reasons. First, I don't have any contacts in the big companies... second, even if I develop some contacts, I am not in a position to do business with them as they release payments on a monthly basis and I don't have enough capital to wait for a month. I don't get credit from the market. Other franchises of DTDC[93] are controlled by Marathas and Gujaratis.[94] They have enough contacts in the market to avail credit and are able to do business with big companies.

The interviewee seems to distinguish between the normative construct of the market and its operating principles. The former connotes that any individual can enter the market and pursue accumulative endeavours (for instance, our interviewee feels that his services keep his customers happy and, hence, his business should grow), while the latter refers to the hindrances experienced by individuals not belonging to the 'right' social networks (our interviewee fails to raise sufficient credit). This is why, as he explains, social networks inspired by caste location and regional identity are crucial, not only for procuring orders, but also for accessing various resources to meet the requirements of big orders. In the same vein, the brick kiln owner feels that his inability to earn a relatively large surplus from his business operations hindered his business expansion plans:

मेरा एक ही भट्टा है, दूसरा भट्टा लगाने का पैसा नहीं है। सब भट्टा मालिक को बड़ा आर्डर मिलता है तो एक दूसरे की मदद करते हैं। मुझे खडकवासला में एक फार्म हाउस का एक बड़ा आर्डर मिला था। मुझे 50,000 ईंट चाहिए थी। किसी ने नहीं दिया। मार्केट से पैसा उठाया 6 प्रतिशत पर। भट्टा मालिक एक दूसरे को पैसा 2-3 प्रतिशत पर देते हैं। ज्यादातर बड़े आर्डर पर पैसा मार्केट से उठाना पड़ता है, इसलिए मुनाफा कम हो जाता है और दूसरा भट्टा नहीं लगा पाता हूँ।

I own one brick kiln. I don't have resources to invest in a second one. All kiln-owners usually help each other. I once got a very big order from a farm house at Khadakwasla. I was short by 50,000 bricks. None of the kiln-owners helped me. I had to take credit from the open market at an interest rate of 6 per cent. Usually, brick kiln owners give credit to each other at 2–3 per cent . . . Mostly, I have to take credit from the open market for any big order I get. This lowers my profit and hence I am not able to invest in the second kiln.

The brick kiln owner details how his accumulation attempts, as well his ambition to invest in the expansion of his business, have both been thwarted by the business practices of his upper-caste peers. For instance, their refusal to share resources with him (he perceives that sharing of resources is a normal practice in this particular sector of trade) and an unfriendly credit market. However, regulation of credit by the upper-caste network is not the only factor constraining the accumulation endeavours of the Dalits. As a handloom business and boutique owner in Vidisha observes:

बाजार का उसूल हैं की हिसाब से जब लेबर की जरूरत होती है तो सब कारखाने एक दूसरे की मदद करते हैं। मार्च में मुझे दिल्ली से बड़ा आर्डर मिला था, सबके पास गया। किसी कारखाने ने लेबर नहीं दिया। ज्यादा पैसे पर होशंगाबाद और भोपाल से माल तैयार करवाया।

As per business principles, all handloom workshops release their labour for each other as and when required. Last March, I got a big order from Delhi. None of the workshops released their labour, and I had to get my order prepared from Hoshangabad and Bhopal at a higher cost.

The handloom workshop owner seems perturbed by the fact that his accumulation strategies were impaired by the strict regulation and control over labour supply by the social networks of upper-caste peers. He also thinks that such labour regulation practices work to his disadvantage, while facilitating the accumulation of upper-caste peers. This forced him to rework his accumulation strategy and structure a different supply chain of workforce. As he points out, this did not produce the best market results, but it was the only option available to him.

The last four testimonies seem to indicate that the Dalit entrepreneurs' accumulation endeavours in the market were impeded by their lack of network resources. They perceive that such networks are not merely economic interest groups (market players with common economic interests by virtue of common trade or profession), but are configured on the basis of one (caste), or more than one (caste and family/caste and region) social identity. Consequently, they also feel that this lack prevents them from competing on equal terms with their upper-caste business peers. In this sense, network resources inspired by specific social location are seen as part of an institutionalised attempt to mitigate competition from relatively new entrants, who also happen to belong to the lower caste. In other words, caste and regional identity are seen to be deployed by upper-castes to marginalise Dalits in the market.

d. Absence of Credit to Dalit Petty Business

In our interviews, we found a complete lack of institutional and informal credit for Dalit-operated petty business. Petty business, as defined in our study, includes businesspersons engaged in leather work (cobblers), general economic activities (grocery and general merchant stores), salons (barber shops), home care services (supplier of maids and domestic help), and communication centres (phone booths and photocopying services). Low caste, in combination with low class, ensures that the credibility of these businesspersons who seek to enter the market as owners of capital is either held in doubt or contempt. A payphone booth owner, also a son of a cobbler, shared his despair at being denied credit by a state government-controlled co-operative society that was meant to extend loans to micro-enterprises:

ऊपर वाले ने गरीब पैदा किया, लेकिन चमार जात में क्यों पैदा किया, गरीब भी सर उठाकर जीते हैं, लेकिन चमार को हर जगह बेइज्जती मिलती है।

God made me poor, but why did he give me birth in a Chamar family? A poor person can still survive with dignity, but Chamars are always disrespected and ridiculed.

His assertion that belonging to a low class is better than belonging to a low caste suggests that he finds exclusion caused by low class tolerable, whereas that engendered by caste discrimination agonising. Likewise, a supplier of domestic help and cleaning staff to offices in Ahmedabad observes:

मेरा मन था कि मैं एक रजिस्टर्ड ऑफिस बना के सारे ऑफिसेज़ को काम करने वाले सप्लाई करूं। उसके लिए एक आफिस चाहिए था। 1.5 लाख लोन के लिए एप्लाइ किया, अपने घर के कागज लेकर गया था। उसकी कीमत बाजार में करीब 5 लाख रुपये है। बैंक के अफसर ने बोला कि हम लोगों के गांव और घर में सब लेबर ही हैं, इसके लिए पैसे

की क्या जरूरत है। हमसे बोला कि जा के काम करो और हमें रोज रोज परेशान मत करो।
उसने ये भी कहा कि मैं कहां से लोन वापस करूंगा। मेरे पास खाने को है नहीं एकदम
नये धंधे की बात कर रहा हूँ। अब मैं अपना धंधा एक वस्त्रापुर की चाय की दुकान से
करता हूँ।

I had a dream of having a registered office and supplying workforce
to offices and homes. For this, I required an office. I applied for a loan
of ₹1.5 lakh. I wanted the loan against the security of my house, the
present market value of which is nearly ₹5 lakh. The bank officer
rejected my application and told me that we people don't need money
for this kind of business, as everyone in my community is already a
labourer. He told me to go away and not disturb him everyday. He
asked me why I was trying to raise a loan when I did not even have
the resources to feed myself. He did not even have the patience to
understand that I was proposing a new kind of venture. Now I operate from a small tea stall at Vastrapur.

And so, a new business idea that seems compatible with the needs
of the 'new' economy,[95] especially in the state capital of Gujarat, is
denied credit by the bank officer. The quality of the Dalit entrepreneur's interaction with the bank official leads him to believe that the
loan assessor did not pay attention to the kind of business venture
he was proposing and, hence, he infers that the denial of credit was
based more on contempt for his class and caste rather than his failure
to achieve a certain credit rating.

Experiencing Accommodation

a. Alliance with Upper-Castes

There are certain sectors of trade and services in our sample where
Dalits hold relative advantage over others. This advantage arises
from two specific reasons: The first, an initiative of one of the federal
units of the Indian state (Madhya Pradesh), to provide an assured
market to Dalit entrepreneurs, through government procurement of
the goods supplied by them, along with ensuring loan facilities (also
refer to discussion on Bhopal Declaration in Chapter Four). The
second relates to their involvement in the economic activities permitted to their respective sub-castes. In our sample, this includes
caste-related economic activities like leather work, trade in sanitary
ware, carpentry, washing of clothes (laundry services), hair-cutting
salons, beauty parlours, and iron-work. This relative advantage,

however, does not mean that Dalit entrepreneurs are able to successfully accumulate capital in the market. The shortage of capital, and their inability to raise credit allows upper-caste traders with sufficient capital to enter into business alliances with them. Thus, we find more than half a dozen case studies from Madhya Pradesh where an alliance with an upper-caste member has enabled a Dalit businessperson to 'overcome' the lack of capital and other resources, towards their mutual interest, that is, capital accumulation. In a few cases, the upper-caste partner's capital and social contacts resulted in the sanction of larger government contracts, and the Dalit was reduced to the status of a junior partner (legally the government contract has to be in the name of the Dalit businessperson). In other instances, the Dalit businesspersons were relegated to the position of supervisor/manager of the economic activity that was legally carried out in their name. A few of the interviewees claimed that they have to abide by the structural logic of the market, that is, maximum returns come to those who can invest a corresponding amount of capital. A supplier of stationery to state government offices working in Bhopal told us:

> अपनी औकात पर तो छोटा मोटा काम करते थे। कई धंधे ट्राई किए, कुछ बात नहीं बनी। फिर सरकार ने हम लोगों को मौका दिया, लोन भी देती है, पर हम लोगों के काम में बड़े पैसे की जरूरत है। मेरे बाप दादों के पास पैसा था नहीं, इसलिए टण्डन को पार्टनर बनाया है। उसने काफी पैसा लगाया है इसलिए उसकी 70 प्रतिशत भागीदारी है और बाकी मेरी . . . टण्डन का ट्रांसपोर्ट का बिजनेस है, इसलिए सारा काम मैं ही करता हूँ।

> Before starting this business, I tried my hand at several activities but was not successful. The state government gave us an opportunity and an assured market, and also provided loans to us. However, we need huge investment in this computer business. My father and forefathers do not have any accumulated wealth. Therefore, I took Tandon[96] as my business partner. He invested a lot of money and so his share in the business amounts to 70 per cent . . . Tandon also has a transport business and hence I have to do all the work in this business.

Further, some feel they are still better off in such alliances, in comparison to their earlier attempts to conduct business with the government independently (when the size of the business was much smaller and delays in payments almost forced them to shut down their businesses). A similar structural logic for the market was also documented in several other caste-related activities, especially in the leather goods, sanitary ware, iron-work, and carpentry sectors.

The influx of cheap machine-made leather goods (both imported and domestically produced), and the entry of big firms in the market, have together almost marginalised the traditional communities specialising in leather related trade. The lower caste traders are unable to compete on economies of scale or produce in bulk, because of the unavailability of the required credit. The problem has been aggravated by the downscaling of Leather Boards by state governments (in this case, our respondents belonged to the states of Gujarat and Uttar Pradesh) which used to support lower caste producers and manufacturers of leather goods. The result is that a minority of them now work as contract producers for big upper-caste traders, and the majority are reduced to supervisors or workers in large factories controlled by dominant castes (also refer to discussion on pp. 70–71). In some other cases, our interviewees related how, the boom in the real estate sector increased the demand for sanitary products, iron works and carpentry, yet their inability to raise credit from the market in order to produce larger quantities and overcome large payment delays had forced them to take the help of an upper-caste partner who could raise and invest money. In such cases, the profit was shared in proportion to the capital investment, even though the business was managed by the Dalit. However, in one of our case studies of a 'very big' business in sanitary ware, the same strategy was used to raise capital, but in due course of time, the capital accumulation was deemed sufficient to enable our Dalit entrepreneur to move into an independent venture.

b. Weak Social Network

The emphasis on weak social networks also enables us to recognise the agency of the weaker players in the market, who negotiate and try to overcome the constraints imposed by the dominant social structures of accumulation.[97] In this context, the crucial question is: What is the relationship between weak social networks of Dalits and the social structure of accumulation in the market?

Our evidence indicates two aspects of the relationship: the first is the use of networks, both economic as well as non-economic, to enter and operate in the markets; the second aspect is the consistent effort to find ways to overcome the constraints imposed by the dominant social network controlled by upper-castes.

The weak social networks of our Dalit entrepreneurs can be broadly classified as social networks based on ascriptive ties, business ties with upper-castes, and market relationships. A caveat is in order: this is not to argue that such networks affecting market outcomes are only configured by Dalits. The dominant social networks of upper-castes also configure networks of a similar nature. However, unlike upper-caste networks that usually build repeat-exchange relationships, the socio-economic relationships inspired by weak networks do not follow a repeat-exchange relationship. Further, even if there is recurring exchange (for instance, in the case of an upper-caste partner, or being in a market relationship with an upper-caste businessperson), the outcomes generally favour the upper-castes. We discuss each of these weak networks in detail in the following pages:

a. Social networks based on ascriptive ties: Such ties are con-figured through family, sub-caste/caste relationships and can blur the boundaries between state institutions (banks and other institutional finance agencies, licensing authorities, etc.) and markets. For instance, almost all respondents informed us that they borrowed some money from family members and friends from their own caste to meet the shortfall in their initial investment in the markets. Irrespective of the amount borrowed (ranging from ₹3,000 to ₹35,000), this help was crucial, especially for the Dalit interviewees classified as small and petty entrepreneurs. Our interviews revealed that around 35 per cent (25) of those who approached banks for credit were successful. Similarly, various government institutions granted credit to nearly 50 per cent of the (38) respondents who applied for it. However, the key factors that seem to be enabling access to formal credit markets are based on ascrip-tive ties — the presence of family members (kith or kin) in lending institutions, people who can influence the process of loan sanction, rent-giving and local political contacts, access to local political leaders through the informal network of friends and relatives belonging to one's own caste (Table 3.4). In a minority of the cases, NGOs working for the cause of Dalits facilitated access to credit, both from the government as well as banks.

b. Social networks based on business alliances with upper-castes: These ties are configured for exploiting each other's strength in the market, and have been discussed earlier in the section titled 'Experiencing Accommodation'. We have shown that

Table 3.4 Factors Facilitating Access to Initial Capital

| | Number of Respondents | |
Loan Facilitated by	Bank	Government
Official Procedural Outcome	NA	2
NGO	2	3
Family Person in Lending Institutions	7	11
Local Political Contacts	4	7
Upper-Caste Business Partner's Influence	NA	5
Bribery	12	8
Govt Servant — Business Controlled and Managed through Proxy	0	2
Total	25	38

Source: Compiled by the author.

an alliance with the upper-castes enables Dalit entrepreneurs to get access to dominant social networks, and also how such alliances may provide the Dalit entrepreneur relatively better outcomes in the markets in comparison to their own efforts. However, in such alliances, the Dalit entrepreneurs are relegated to the position of junior partners, or even reduced to the position of supervisors.

c. Social networks based on market relationships: These ties are configured through economic relationships in the markets, but are invariably mediated by the caste location of the two interacting parties. As discussed in several of our testimonies, caste as an ideology (in its contemporary incarnation) does not seem to function through its sociological principles/practice of purity and pollution, but works dexterously, at least in markets, to maintain a power relationship between the upper- and lower-castes. In other words, economic relationships in the market between upper-castes and lower castes are structured by the social identity of the individuals concerned, wherein the former resists the presence of the latter, or shows contempt for his/her aspirations to own capital for her/his accumulation endeavours. However, due to the ever increasing political assertion of Dalits, it is no longer possible for upper-caste owners of capital to forbid Dalits from pursuing their accumulation endeavours. As a result, Dalits are included in the market-based accumulation processes, but on unfavourable terms. The Dalits, on their part, also believe that they come not only from a dominantly 'disapproved' social location, but also from an economically weak class position. Hence, it is from this disadvantaged socio-economic position that they try and carve out their own social network in the markets. As exemplified in the various testimonies of Dalit entrepreneurs, most of them enter into unfavourable economic arrangements, even though they perceive these engagements as discriminatory. More often than not, they persist with unfavourable business relations, in their attempt to breach the dominant social network of the upper-castes, and carve out a space for themselves.

Conclusions

Our analysis shows how market outcomes are embedded in the existing social structure. Following our theoretical discussion in the second section where we argued that market outcomes in India are neither a. governed by the forces of demand and supply, nor b. structured by formal institutions. We turned to field research to show how market outcomes are shaped by existing social institutions that form India's social structure of accumulation. It would be helpful to examine the role of caste as one of the crucial components of the social structure of accumulation in India. The Dalit entrepreneurs we interviewed chose to enter the market because of its normative promise of emancipation. However, from our interviewees' accounts of their experiences, we found that caste as an ideology (a set of beliefs, norms, values, and practices) nurtures, rather than dissolves, discriminatory attitudes and behaviour by upper-castes against Dalits. We also saw that caste ideology has a social as well as an economic basis. The social basis manifests itself through the stereotyping of Dalits, who are expected to conform to dominant social constructs which mandate that they serve society manually, and render them unfit for any 'higher' economic role — that is, roles involving education, technological sophistication and continued exposure to upper-castes on the basis of either equality or acquired characteristics. The social role of the ideology of caste may not involve any immediate economic motives (for instance, bank officials who deny loans to Dalits despite their being legally entitled to them, or the refusal of upper-castes to eat food prepared in a Dalit-owned restaurant). However, it always damages the economic interests of Dalits. The explicit economic objectives of the ideology of caste can be invoked by upper-castes to ensure favourable economic returns for themselves, at the expense of Dalits (for instance, non-Dalit caste identity is used to prevent competition in markets, suppress prices, reduce the profits of Dalits, earn higher interest rates, negotiate profitable partnerships with Dalits, etc.). Thus, both the social and economic bases of caste ideology may lead to adverse economic outcomes for Dalits.

As discussed in several of the testimonies, caste ideology does not seem to function through socio-religious principles — the practice of purity and pollution. Instead it works cleverly, at least in the market, to maintain an unequal power relationship between the upper-castes and Dalits. Further, due to the ever-increasing socio-political assertion of Dalits, it is not always possible for upper-caste owners of capital to entirely prohibit Dalits from entering the market and engaging in capital accumulation. As a result, Dalits are incorporated, to some extent, in market-based accumulation processes, but on unfavourable terms. This unfavourable accommodation of Dalits is structured and maintained by social networks.

In other words, caste ideology can create solidarity between individuals belonging to the same caste, and carrying out similar economic activities. Such solidarity propels the configuration of social networks in markets, with the aim to protect and promote the economic interests of their members. Social networks are also carved out through identities of religion and region. Most of the dominant social networks in a market are coterminous with upper-castes, and may or may not overlap with religion and region of origin; they were not created explicitly to resist Dalit entrepreneurs but, as they adhere to the social and economic basis of the ideology of caste, they invariably work against the economic interests of Dalits. It also appears from the testimonies of Dalit entrepreneurs that the dominant social networks are tightly knit bodies (sometimes organised as trade bodies), which mostly work towards the economic interests of their members. Their network resources (credit, information, control over labour supply, etc.) are not available for non-members, especially Dalits. On the other hand, Dalits do appear to have weak social networks in markets.

The weak social networks of our Dalit entrepreneurs are expressed through ascriptive ties (configured through caste identity), and facilitate access to formal as well as informal credit, using local political leaders to influence the state, etc. Business ties with upper-castes (partnerships) and market relationships with dominant market players (accepting adverse inclusion as a matter of strategy) are also part of the repertoire of weak ties. The objectives of the weak networks facilitating Dalit accumulation are similar to those of the dominant social networks of the upper-castes. However, the socio-economic relationships inspired by weak networks do not support repeated exchanges. For example, while a local politician may help the Dalit entrepreneur once to access credit, there is no surety that he will help him again to resolve his problem with the municipality, as happens through the social networks of the upper-castes. In the latter case, for instance, as a matter of routine, a promissory note of credit becomes almost formalised as informal legal tender. Further, even if there is repeated exchange involving a Dalit (for instance, when a Dalit operates with an upper-caste partner, or they enter into transactions with the upper-castes), the outcomes are asymmetrically beneficial to upper-castes.

This discussion gives us convincing evidence to conclude that the operations of the modern market will not automatically dissolve caste identities, since these can restrict competition. In fact, our evidence reveals how caste can be used to meet demands to circumscribe competition. These markets seem to be efficient, though not necessarily from the perspective of Dalits, even when the capacity to enforce by formal, regulatory institutions is conspicuous by its absence.

—

Notes

1. Dalit Chamber of Commerce, http://www.dicci.org/en/dicci.html (accessed on 26 September 2011).
2. This includes technical and engineering services, financial management services, tax management services, HRD, labour management services, marketing services, business opportunity services, quality control services, training and leadership programme, etc.
3. For more information, see: Shubhangi Khapre, 'Young Dalits are More Pragmatic', *DNA*, 16 April 2006, http://www.dnaindia.com/mumbai/special_young-dalits-are-more-pragmatic_1024353 (accessed on 26 September 2011).
4. Vani K. Borooah, Amaresh Dubey and Sriya Iyer, 'The Effectiveness of Jobs Reservation: Caste, Religion and Economic Status in India',

Development and Change, 2007, 38 (3): 423–45; P. Sivanandan, 'Caste, Class and Economic Opportunity in Kerala: An Empirical Analysis', *Economic and Political Weekly*, 1979, XIV (7/8): 475–80; S. Jetley, 'Education and Occupational Mobility: A UP Village', *Economic and Political Weekly*, 26 April 1969, IV (17): 725–27.

5. See K. P. Kannan and G. Raveendran, 'India's Common People: The Regional Profile', *Economic and Political Weekly*, 2011, XLVI (38): 60–73; Amit Thorat, 'Ethnicity, Caste and Religion: Implications for Poverty Outcomes', *Economic and Political Weekly*, 2011, XLV (51): 47–53; National Commission for Enterprises in the Unorganized Sector, *The Challenge of Employment*, New Delhi: Government of India, 2006.

6. K. P. Kannan, 'Dualism, Informality and Social Inequality: An Informal Economy Perspective of the Challenge of Inclusive Development in India', *Indian Journal of Labour Economics*, 2009, 52 (1): 1–32.

7. Santosh Mehrotra, 'Well-being and Caste in Uttar Pradesh: Why UP Is Not Like Tamil Nadu', *Economic and Political Weekly*, 2006, XLI (40): 4261–71; Pallavi Chavan, 'Access to Bank Credit: Implications for Dalit Rural Households', *Economic and Political Weekly*, 2007, 42 (31): 3219–24; S. K. Thorat and Chittaranjan Senapati, 'Reservation Policy in India-Dimensions and Issues', Working Paper Series, Vol. I, No. 2, New Delhi: Indian Institute of Dalit Studies, 2006.

8. World Bank, *India's Employment Challenge: Creating Jobs, Helping Workers*, New Delhi: Oxford University Press, 2010; Himanshu, 'Employment and Wages of Dalits', mimeo., Centre De Science Humaines, http://www.csh-delhi.com/team/downloads/publiperso/Emp_wages_Dalits_himanshu.pdf (accessed on 27 September 2011).

9. Smita Narula, *Broken People: Caste Violence Against India's Untouchables*, New Delhi: Human Rights Watch, 1999; Gopal Guru, 'Understanding Violence Against Dalits in Maharashtra', *Economic and Political Weekly*, 26 February 1994, XXIX (9): 469–72; Debashis Chakraborty, D. Shyam Babu and Manashi Chakravorty, 'Atrocities on Dalits: What the District Level Data Say on Society-State Complicity', *Economic and Political Weekly*, 17–23 June 2006, XLI (24): 2478–81.

10. Barbara Harris-White and Aseem Prakash, 'Social Discrimination and Economic Citizenship', in S. Janakarajan, R. Maria Saleth and L. Venkatachalam (eds), *Indian Economy in Transition: Emerging Issues and Challenges-Essays in Honour of C.T. Kurien*, New Delhi: Sage, 2014.

11. See Gail Omvedt, 'Globalisation & Indian Tradition', http://www.ambedkar.org/News/Globalisation.htm (accessed on 28 February 2011); Chandra Bhan Prasad, 'Markets and Manu: Economic Reforms and Its Impact on Caste in India', CASI Working Paper Series, No. 08-01, Center for the Advanced Study of India, University of Pennsylvania, 2008; A. Ramaiah, 'Dalits to Accept Globalisation: Lessons from the

Past and Present', mimeo., Mumbai: Tata Institute of Social Sciences, 2004, http://ssrn.com/abstract=568582 (accessed on 28 February 2011).

12. Ashwini Deshpande, *The Grammar of Caste: Economic Discrimination in Contemporary India*, New Delhi: Oxford University Press, 2011, p. 38.

13. G. S. Becker, *The Economics of Discrimination*, Chicago: University of Chicago Press, 1971.

14. Ibid., p. 14.

15. In Becker's model, an individual can also have a positive taste of discrimination. It is not necessary that a person belong to the dominant group for her/him to articulate her/his taste for discrimination. Deshpande, *The Grammar of Caste*, pp. 41–42.

16. Deshpande, *The Grammar of Caste*, p. 38.

17. George A. Akerlof, 'The Economics of Caste and of the Rat Race and Other Woeful Tales', in George Akerlof (ed.), *Explorations in Pragmatic Economics*, Oxford: Oxford University Press, 2005, pp. 39–55.

18. Deshpande, *The Grammar of Caste*, p. 45.

19. Ibid.

20. Deepak Lal, *Hindu Equilibrium, Volume 1: Cultural Stability and Economic Stagnation: India, c.1500 BC–AD 1980*, Oxford: Clarendon Press, 1988.

21. James G. Scoville, 'Labor Market Underpinnings of a Caste Economy: Foiling the Coase Theorem', *American Journal of Economics and Sociology*, 1996, 55 (4): 385–94.

22. This is also linked to the immediate detection of persons who try to transgress their caste identity in favour of a different caste.

23. Deshpande, *The Grammar of Caste*, p. 38.

24. Biswajit Banerjee and J. B. Knight, 'Caste Discrimination in the Indian Urban Labour Market', *Journal of Development Economics*, 1985, 17 (3): 301.

25. Ashwini Deshpande, 'Recasting Economic Inequality', *Review of Social Economy*, 2000, 3: 388.

26. Douglas North defines institutions as 'humanely devised constraints that structure political, economic and social interaction. They consist of both informal constraints (sanctions, taboos, customs, traditions and codes of conduct), and formal rules (constitutions, laws, property rights)'. Please refer to Douglas C. North, 'Institutions', *The Journal of Economic Perspectives*, 1991, 5 (1): 97–102.

27. Douglas C. North, 'Institutions and Economic Theory', *The American Economist*, 1992, 1: 3. Further pointing out the lacunae in the neo-classical school, North writes: 'Institutions are unnecessary in a world of instrumental rationality; ideas and ideologies don't matter; and efficient markets — both economic and political — characterise economies'.

28. For a discussion on market (in)efficiency, see Douglas C. North, 'The New Institutional Economics and Third World Development', in John Harriss, Jane Hunter and Colin M. Lewis (eds), *The New Institutional Economics and Third World Development*, London: Routledge, 1995, pp. 19–20.

29. Joseph Stiglitz explains that a thick network of interpersonal relationships functions to resolve the allocative and distributional questions only when the markets are thin. The development of a market destroys the value of personal relationships. However, in his view, it can only acquire shape with the corresponding development of a modern capital state and associated legal institutions. The latter replaces community as the guardian of social, business and personal contracts. See Joseph Stiglitz, 'Formal and Informal Institutions', in Patha Das Gupta and Ismail Serageldin (eds), *Social Capital: A Multifaceted Perspective*, Washington: World Bank, 1999, pp. 59–68.

30. See Douglas C. North, *Institutions, Institutional Change and Economic Performance*, Cambridge: Cambridge University Press, 1990, pp. 107–31.

31. Also see, Douglas C. North, *Structure and Change in Economic History*, New York: W. W. Norton, 1981, p. 20.

32. Douglas C. North, 'Institutions', *The Journal of Economic Perspectives*, 1991, 5 (1): 111.

33. Oliver E. Williamson, 'The New Institutional Economics: Taking Stock, Looking Ahead', *Journal of Economic Literature*, 2000, 38 (3): 596.

34. Neo-classical economics and new institutional economics seem to converge on the point that the market lies in the realm of impersonal exchange, characterised by economic transactions between equal and autonomous individuals motivated by profits. All kinds of markets and diverse institutions of economic exchange — ranging from bidding, purchase and sale of goods and services in cyber space, hi-tech operations on the Mumbai Stock Exchange, utilising political connections and rent-giving for privileged information, the kinship-based wholesale gold market at Chandni Chowk in Delhi, credit exchange notes worth millions scribbled on dirty pieces of paper, wholesale grain trade and jewellery business of Delhi, UP and Rajasthan, the patronage-based retail CG road market at Ahmedabad, sand markets in Patna surviving on muscle power and political clout, the village *haat* (market) at Bakshika Talab in Lucknow where access to physical space to sell one's wares is more or less a function of 'correct' caste location, and so on — come within the universalistic framework of a singular market. Any perceptible patterns of economic exchange falling outside the framework distort the natural movements of demand and supply curves and set in motion externalities (transaction costs of various kinds) which reduce profits or raise the costs of goods and services. Hence, any such distortion will naturally wane.

35. Barbara Harriss-White, *India Working: Essays on Society and Economy*, Cambridge: Cambridge University Press, 2003, p. 197.
36. Harris-White makes a distinction between state and societal corporatism. 'In the first form, the state plays a directive role and dominates its relationship with interest groups and their relationship with each other. In the second form, associations are relatively independent from the state…. The state is not a neutral arbitrator, but actively synthesises corporatist ideals and values to serve to promote the interest of the capital' (Barbara Harriss-White, *India Working: Essays on Society and Economy*, Cambridge: Cambridge University Press, 2003, p. 190). She further explains that caste can be consistent with capitalist production relations (Harriss-White, *India Working*, pp. 190–96).
37. Karl Polanyi, *The Great Transformation: The Political and Economic Origins of Our Times*, Boston: Beacon Press, 1957.
38. Harrison C. White, 'Where Do Markets Come From?' *The American Journal of Sociology*, 1981, 87 (3): 517–47.
39. Mark Granovetter, 'The Impact of Social Structure on Economic Outcomes', *Journal of Economic Perspectives*, 2005, 19 (1): 33–50.
40. R. Burt, *Corporate Profits and Cooptation*, New York: Academic, 1983.
41. J. Podolny, 'A Status Based Model of Market Competition', *The American Journal of Sociology*, 1993, 98 (4) : 829–72.
42. Centre Pour La Recherche Économique Et Ses Applications (Center for Economic Research and its Applications).
43. R. Boyer, *The Regulation School: A Critical Introduction*, New York: Columbia University Press, 1990, pp. 25–60. For a critical summary, see Bob Jessop, 'The Social Embeddedness of The Economy and Its Implications for Economic Governance', http://Eprints.Cddc.Vt.Edu/Digitalfordism/Fordism_Materials/Jessop2.Htm (accessed on 21 August 2011).
44. As discussed, the neo-classical individual carries the baggage of caste and refuses to go against the norm out of the fear of being penalised, but he also expects such outcomes to wane in the long run. However, the authors belonging to the school of social embeddedness recognise that caste identity can coexist with the modern capitalist markets. In fact, caste can provide a basis for the formation of social networks in the realm of markets.
45. On adverse terms of inclusion in various markets, please refer to S. K. Thorat, 'Caste System and Economic Discrimination: Lessons from Theories', in S. K. Thorat, Aryama and Prashant Negi (eds), *Reservation and Private Sector: Quest for Equal Opportunity and Growth*, New Delhi: Indian Institute of Dalit Studies and Rawat Publication, 2005, pp. 73–80.
46. S. K. Thorat, 'Caste, Social Exclusion and Poverty Linkages — Concept, Measurement and Empirical Evidence', mimeo., New Delhi: Indian Institute of Dalit Studies, New Delhi, 2008.

47. Reviewed by Barbara Harriss-White in Harriss-White, *India Working*, pp. 176–78.
48. Harriss-White, *India Working*, p. 177.
49. The theory of the social structure of accumulation analyses the relationship between capital accumulation processes and the set of social institutions that affect those processes; the central idea being that capital accumulation over a long period of time is a product of the role played by supporting social institutions. For a detailed discussion of the 'Social Structure of Accumulation', see David M. Kotz, 'The Regulation Theory and Social Structure of Accumulation Approach', in David M. Kotz, Terrence McDonough and Michael Reich (eds), *The Social Structures of Accumulation: The Political Economy of Growth and Crisis*, Cambridge: Cambridge University Press, 1994, pp. 85–98; and also David M. Kotz, 'Interpreting Social Structure of Accumulation Theory', in David M. Kotz, Terrence McDonough and Michael Reich (eds), *The Social Structures of Accumulation: The Political Economy of Growth and Crisis*, Cambridge: Cambridge University Press, 1994, pp. 50–71.
50. Harriss-White, *India Working*, p. 197.
51. The school of 'social embeddedness' makes a distinction between markets as politics and politics of markets. The former implies that the state plays an important role in the formation of institutions of the market — property rights, establishment of state institutions for private trade, rules of exchange, credit facilities and other conditions under which economic agents compete, cooperate and exchange.
52. Harriss-White, *India Working*, p. 178.
53. The state-wise spread of interviews is as follows: Gujarat (8), Madhya Pradesh (15), Maharashtra (20), Rajasthan(10), Uttar Pradesh (27), and West Bengal (10).
54. This interview was conducted in Bengali by Amrita Dutta, who assisted the author in conducting the interviews in West Bengal — Hoogly and 24 Parganas. Her crucial help is duly acknowledged.
55. The Dalit entrepreneur from Agra seems to be affected by the policy regime guiding economic liberalisation. The production of leather accessories is no longer reserved as a small-scale industry [for official notification see http://www.smallindustryindia.com/publications/reserveditems/dereserve.htm (accessed on 23 May 2011)] and is presently a 'special focus' area for export (Exim Policy, 2002–2007, Ministry of Finance, Government of India). This has permitted large scale investment of both national and international capital, which in turn has ensured that small local production units (that were anyway stifled due to lack of modern technology, absence of credit and the highly unequally economic relationship between the Dalit artisanal community manufacturing leather goods and upper-castes traders/sellers) do not work for the local market

but undertake contract jobs mostly for 'unknown' big capitalists located outside their city. Earlier, leather workers would manufacture products for the local trader, either at an agreed price or under a piece wage rate agreement, where the trader would supply the raw material. In both forms of business, the earnings for the Dalit manufacturer were quite low since the traders would control prices by forming cartels. In the new scenario, the mediating agent between the outside big capitalist and local Dalit manufacturer is generally the same upper-caste local trader. Both in Agra and Kanpur (the two cities in which we interviewed leather goods manufacturers), the perception is that the current trade regime is more exploitative, since there is an additional tier of appropriation in the face of the big capitalist, while the relationship between the local trader (now the raw material supplier on behalf of big capitalist) and Dalit manufacturer continues to be one of exploitation. Due to this economic restructuring, we were told, earnings have fallen substantially along with increased dependence on the patronage of the upper-caste trader.

56. The surname Manjrekar generally refers to people belonging to the dominant Maratha community.
57. Now a renowned trader in ceramic products in Gujarat, she started as a small time coal supplier. Her business strategy was to deliver coal at the doorstep, and charge substantially less than the upper-caste suppliers, who were also not ready to deliver coal to homes. She informed us that during the 1970s, this business plan helped her upper-caste customers to forget her caste (the same people refused to buy cooking coal from her because she was a lower caste — a *bhangi*) and trade with her. The lower profit was compensated by higher sales.
58. In many cases, a portion of credit is earmarked exclusively for them but they have still failed to access it.
59. The first set of arguments is not specifically formulated for prospective borrowers belonging to the Dalit community but for understanding the reasons of credit denial to small borrowers. All Dalit entrepreneurs in our study were small borrowers, even the tiny minority who now own very big businesses. Therefore, these arguments will have important implications for understanding the credit constraints of our Dalit entrepreneurs.
60. Banks mostly fund 20–25 per cent of the projected turnover during the loan period.
61. Mukta Gajanan Joshi, 'Access to Credit by Hawkers: What Is Missing? Theory and Evidence from India', D. Phil diss., Ohio State University, 2005, pp. 17–18.
62. Interview with Sanjay Kumar, Chief General Manager, Union Bank of India, Lucknow. Mr Kumar was in charge of retail banking business.

63. 'Lending rates of commercial banks were deregulated since October 1994 subject to the condition that banks declare their Prime Lending Rates (PLRs) for a credit limit over ₹2 lakh as approved by their Boards. For credit limit up to ₹2 lakh, PLR (now Benchmark Prime Lending Rate) remains as the ceiling rate. Since April 2001, commercial banks were given freedom to lend at sub-BPLR rates (for credit limit of over ₹2 lakh) to creditworthy borrowers on the lines of a transparent and objective policy approved by their Boards'. See guidelines of Reserve Bank of India, http://rbi.org.in/rbi-sourcefiles/lendingrate/home.html (accessed on 5 November 2010).

64. The same fact has been noted by other high ranking bankers in India. For instance, see Nachiket Mor, 'Expanding Access to Financial Services — Where do we go from here?', Centre for Micro Finance Research Working Paper Series, IFMR Trust, Chennai, http://www.ifmr.ac.in/pdf/workingpapers/expandingAccess.pdf (accessed on 23 March 2008).

65. Banerjee and Duflo examine the available data on loans extended by a particular public sector bank to small borrowers and conclude that there is strong correlation between the current loan and the amount of the past loan. Thus, banks predominantly choose to extend credit to those who have a proven track record. Refer to Abhijit Banerjee and Esther Duflo, 'The Nature of Credit Constraints. Evidence from an Indian Bank', mimeo., MIT, 2001, http://www.chicagogsb.edu/research/work-shops/AppliedEcon/archive/WebArchive20012002/duflo.pdf (accessed on 9 October 2011). A similar conclusion is reached by Bahumik and Piesse; see Sumon Kumar Bhaumik and Jenifer Piesse, 'A Closer Look at Banks' Behaviour in Emerging Credit Markets? Evidence from the Indian Banking Industry', mimeo., Aditya V. Birla India Centre, London Business School, London, 2004, http://papers.ssrn.com/sol3/papers.cfm?abstract_id=606761#PaperDownload (accessed on 23 March 2010).

66. For details see http://www.crisil.com/credit-ratings-risk-assessment/crisil-ratings.htm (accessed on 14 July 2014).
Also see 'Insight: CRISL Default Study', 2004–2005, http://www.crisil.com/credit-ratings-risk-assessment/2005-crisil-rating-default-study.pdf (accessed on 20 March 2010).

67. For details, see http://www.icraratings.com/ (accessed on 14 July 2014).

68. Quoting from the report of the Reserve Bank of India (titled 'Advances to Agriculture and Weaker Sections', 2004), Ananth and Mor point out that only four out of 30 private sector banks and seven of 27 public sector banks met the target for lending to 'weaker sections'. See Bindu Ananth and Nachiket Mor, 'Financial Services Case Study: India', paper presented at OECD–World Bank Fifth Services Experts Meeting, OECD, Paris, 3–4 February, p. 5.

69. Abhijit V. Banerjee, Shawn Cole and Esther Duflo, 'Banking Reform in India', mimeo., MIT, 2004, 27–28, http://econ-www.mit.edu/files/508 (accessed on 23 June 2009); and Abhijit Banerjee and Esther Duflo, 'The Nature of Credit Constraints. Evidence from an Indian Bank', mimeo., MIT, 2001, http://www.chicagogsb.edu/research/workshops/AppliedEcon/archive/WebArchive20012002/duflo.pdf (accessed on 9 October 2011).

70. Nachiket Mor was earlier Deputy Managing Director of ICICI, India's largest private sector bank, and is currently Non-Official Director, Central Board of Reserve Bank of India. Bindu Ananth is President of Institute for Financial Management and Research Trust (IFMR).

71. The service area approach 'carves out geographical areas which are to be served by designated bank branches only. Bank branches are assigned targets based on district-level credit plans'.

72. New private sector banks are required to open a minimum of 25 per cent of their total branches in rural/semi urban areas as a condition of the licence issued to them under Section 22 of the Banking Regulations Act, 1949.

73. Ananth and Mor, 'Financial Services Case Study: India'.

74. David A. Leblang, 'Property Rights, Democracy and Economic Growth', *Political Research Quarterly*, 1996, 49 (1): 5–26.

75. Stijn Claessens and Luc Laeven, 'Financial Development, Property Rights, and Growth', *The Journal of Finance*, 2003, 58 (6): 2401–36.

76. Pranab Bardhan, 'Law and Development', in K. Dutt and J. Ros (eds), *International Handbook of Development Economics*, Vol. II, Elgar, forthcoming, pp. 1–17, http://emlab.berkeley.edu/users/webfac/bardhan/papers.htm (accessed on 27 May 2011).

77. World Development Report, *Building Institutions for Markets*, New York: Oxford University Press for World Bank, 2002; see especially Chapter 1: 'Building Institutions: Complement, Innovate, Connect, and Compete', pp. 3–27.

78. The administrative and legal structure can also create and honour property rights in a situation where they did not hitherto exist. However, here we are discussing the situation where secure property rights exist but fail to fructify in the market interest of Dalit entrepreneurs.

79. Becker, *The Economics of Discrimination*.

80. See Eleanor Zelliot, *From Untouchable to Dalit*, New Delhi: Manohar, 1992; and Rosalind O' Hanlon, *Caste, Conflict and Ideology: Mahatma Jyotirao Phule and Low Caste Protest in Nineteenth-Century Western India*, Cambridge: Cambridge University Press, 1985.

81. Mahars are classified as a Scheduled Caste community in Maharashtra. They are considered politically powerful and are reported to constitute 9 per cent of Maharashtra's population.

82. Harijan literally means 'children of God'. The term was coined by Mahatma Gandhi for the untouchables and is used all over India but has prominent usage in Gujarat, the birthplace of Gandhi. See the first chapter on discussion of 'Defence of Varna Approach'.

83. Claude Levi Strauss, 'Social Structure', in Henrietta L. Moore and Todd Sanders (eds), *Anthropology in Theory, Issues in Epistemology*, Oxford: Blackwell Publishing, 2006, p. 137.

84. Harriss-White, *India Working*, pp. 176–99.

85. Oliver Mendelsohn and Marika Vicziany, *The Untouchables: Subordination, Poverty and the State in Modern India*, Cambridge: Cambridge University Press, 2005.

86. Craig Jeffrey and Jens Lerche, 'Stating the Difference: State, Discourse and Class Reproduction in Uttar Pradesh, India, *Development and Change*, 2000, 4: 857–78.

87. Fifty-seven of our Dalit entrepreneurs were earlier wage workers in the economic activity in which they subsequently invested capital to control their own business.

88. This will be further discussed in the following section.

89. Khatik or Sonkar are classified as Scheduled Castes. There are many stories about the origin of their caste, but one that enjoys wide acceptance in central Uttar Pradesh is that they used to rear and hunt pigs.

90. Joel M. Podolny and Karen L. Page, 'Network from Organisation', *Annual Review of Sociology*, 1998, 24: 59.

91. See Harrison C. White, 'Where Do Markets Come From?', *The American Journal of Sociology*, 1981, 3: 517–47; R. Burt, *Corporate Profits and Cooptation*, New York: Academic, 1983; Mark Granovetter, 'Economic Action and Social Structure: The Problem of Embeddedness', *The American Journal of Sociology*, 1985, 91 (3): 481–510; Mark Granovetter, 'Economic Institutions as Social Construction: A Framework of Analysis', *Acta Sociologica*, 1992, 35 (1): 3–11; Podolny, 'A Status Based Model of Market Competition'; Granovetter, 'The Impact of Social Structure on Economic Outcomes'.

92. The interviewees were unanimous in their view that informal credit is most crucial in business operations. Informal credit has several forms — an advance for the goods or services to be bought from the businessperson, the time allowed to the business-person to pay for the goods purchased for onward supply, or simply accessing money from the open credit market for capital or market operational expenditures. However, a few of them also accepted that long-term credit is also contingent on the quantity of purchase; big orders can give them some space to command relatively longer credit. But many others pointed out that growth in the market and the ability to procure big orders itself hinges on one's social network.

93. The Desk to Desk Courier (DTDC) claims to be the India's largest domestic delivery network company. Its website says that it delivers letters to the remotest places in India with the help of 4,000 business partners (franchises) spread across the length and breadth of India. See http://www.dtdc.in/ (accessed on 14 July 2014).
94. Gujarati is a regional identity. However, it is again the upper-castes belonging to Patels and Kunbis that dominate this sub-sector.
95. With the informalisation of the formal sector, the lower rung jobs have been contracted out to private players. This has increased the demand for private labour contractors and supervisors who can execute contracts for the cleaning and maintenance of offices. In the context of the household, there has been a drastic increase in professional couples along with a sharp rise in crime rates of theft and murder. The latter has made households increasingly look for professional agencies from where they can hire trusted house-help.
96. Tandons are Hindu upper-caste Khatris. The term 'Khatri' is generally considered to be a Punjabi adaptation of 'Kshatriya'.
97. Three influential works exploring the role of agency in the actions of subordinate social groups are: James C. Scott, *The Moral Economy of Peasant: Rebellion and Subsistence in South East Asia*, New Haven: Yale University Press, 1976; James C. Scott, *Weapons of the Weak: Everyday Forms of Peasant Resistance*, New Haven: Yale University Press, 1985; and James C. Scott, Domination and the Arts of Resistance: Hidden Transcripts, New Haven: Yale University Press, 1990.

FOUR

Dalit Entrepreneurs and the Role of the State in the Markets

■

The Context

Opening the full range of business opportunity to all by removing the inherited and institutional barriers to entry.

Letter from Richard Nixon, President of the
United States, to Anthony Maxwell, 31 October 1972[1]

[I]n this present era of privatisation . . . Representation . . . [has to be provided] to the deprived classes, not only in Government and public institutions but in private corporations and enterprises which benefit from Government funds and facilities.

Address to the Nation by the first Dalit President of India,
K. R. Narayanan, on the eve of Republic Day, 25 January 2002[2]

मेरा बाप पटेल परिवार का हली था। वो पटेल परिवार के घर का सारा काम करता था और उसके बदले में हमारे परिवार को थोड़ा पैसा और खाना मिलता था . . . हम लोग कभी भी उजिलियत से संबंध नहीं रखते थे। हम लोगों का खाना और देखभाल पटेल करता था। वो दिन अब बदल गए, अब खेती कोई नहीं करता है सब शहर में आ गए हैं, प्रोपर्टी का धंधा जोरों पर है। मैं ठेकेदारी करता हूँ मेरा काम है लेबर और बिल्डिंग मैटीरियल सप्लाई करना और कंस्ट्रक्शन को सुपरवाइज़ करना। पैसा ज्यादातर बनिया या पटेल लगाते हैं। अब मैं पटेल और बनिया के साथ बैठकर दारू पी सकता हूँ। गुजरात में कोई जात को लेकर लड़ाई नहीं है। सब लड़ाई पैसे की है। मैं मेहनत करके बनिया और पटेल का फायदा करता हूँ, वो कभी मेरी जात नहीं पूछते हैं। पर अगर मैं अपना धंधा शुरू कर दूं तो मेरी जात पर सवाल खड़े हो जाएंगे और मेरा धंधा चौपट हो जाएगा।

My father worked for a Patel family as a hali [a bonded labourer]. He had to do all the back-breaking work and, in return, our family used to get some money and food . . . We never had any social inter-action with the *Ujiliyat* (upper-castes). Our food and welfare were assured as long as we kept our master's family happy. Those were different times. Agriculture was the primary economic activity. Now cities have changed our lives. There is a boom in real estate. I supply labour and building material, and supervise construction projects of real estate financiers and builders who are mostly Patels and Baniyas . . . Now, I also sit and drink with the Patels and Baniyas. There is no caste conflict in Gujarat. All conflict is over money . . . My hard work rakes in profits for them. They never question my caste. But if I were to try and step into their shoes and start my own business, then my caste would become an issue and they would ensure that my venture does not survive.

Sunil
A real estate contractor in Ahmedabad

Sunil's candid confession reflects the contradictory socio-economic patterns emerging in contemporary Indian society. On the one hand it shows how markets of 'modern India' can mitigate the historical social stigma associated with the lower castes. At the same time, it is a testimony to the entrenched power of caste structures, which continue to dictate the spaces and choices available to the lower castes for economic progress. While the contours of caste-based socio-economic norms delineating dominant–subordinate positions have relaxed considerably over the years, a highly unequal power relationship continues to persist between lower and upper-castes. At the macro-level this contradiction is reflected in an unprecedented economic growth rate, accompanied by increasing levels of inequality and persistent poverty. Annual growth rates hovered between 6 to 9 per cent in the last several years and 'by most accounts have surpassed expectations'.[3] On the other hand, increasing inequality over the period has created islands of prosperity and ghettos of poverty. Statistical disaggregation of the data on inequality reveals the predominance of poverty amongst social groups such as adivasis,[4] minorities[5] and Dalits.[6]

In this context, it has been argued by those who work for the cause of Dalits that the state has to play a leading role in addressing and mitigating the structural causes of their poverty and exclusion.[7] This can be better understood by taking into account three representative views: one held by an academic, another by a leading politician and the third by a conclave of activists.

Gopal Guru, an academic, argues that democracy by itself cannot be seen as a panacea for the failure of moral principles. He points to the failure of the democratic principles — 'I will rule and be ruled in turn' — which, due to the law of incumbency, effectively results in the seat of power always remaining occupied by members of upper-castes. The Dalit vision of democracy, therefore, requires democratic authority to be practiced by the state, rather than simply depending on the moral capacity of democracy.[8] Thus, Guru stresses upon the need for state institutions to step in to temper and eradicate the non-egalitarian processes of caste.

The second representative view is articulated by Kanshi Ram, the founder of the leading political party of Dalits, the Bahujan Samaj Party, in an interview given to Christophe Jaffrelot.[9] He explains that the capture of state power is essential for any transformative agenda.

> I started with the idea of social transformation and economic eman-cipation. I still want my people to advance socially and economically. But, I have realised that unless we are having [sic] political clout, we cannot advance much on those sides.

The third argument comes from the 'Bhopal Declaration', a conclave of leading intellectuals and activists working for the cause of Dalits. The conclave called for the creation of Dalit businessper-sons.[10] It declared that the Indian state should encourage private Dalit economic activity along the same lines as it did for caste Hindu capital in the decades between the 1950s and 1980s. The inspira-tion behind the creation of a Dalit entrepreneurial class which will own and invest capital in the globalising economy is drawn from the 'Black Economic Empowerment Programme' (BEEP) of South Africa,[11] and specifically from the 'Black Capitalism and Diversity' initiatives of the United States.[12]

In this scheme of things, democracy has substantive meaning only when the ongoing political assertion of Dalits is also buttressed by their economic empowerment, i.e. Dalits are encouraged by the state and assisted to sustain their economic ventures in the 'free' market.

The Bhopal declaration[13] explicitly states:

> The Government should set aside funds for ensuring capital and credit opportunities to the Dalits. Adequate investment resources are necessary to enter the market economy. The entire country's market economy, now virtually controlled by a few privileged castes, needs to be democratised. Make provisions for the development of entrepre-neurial skills, capacities for market enterprises . . . Democratisation of capital and credit and ensuring a proportionate share for the Dalits in

the market economy should be taken seriously. Diversity in the work-force will be one of the major issues that will be haunting the nation in the years to come as a result of the liberalisation of the economy, globalisation of trade and privatisation of services.

As described in the preceding paragraph, Dalits see the state as an essential institution to overcome the limits of formal democracy, to support their socio-economic empowerment, and to enable them to become owners of capital. All three viewpoints converge on the fact that the state as an institution can be restructured for norma-tive socio-political and economic objectives. Thus the restructured state, for Dalits, becomes a primary requirement for an egalitarian socio-cultural, political and economic project.

In the following section, we try to understand the Dalit perspective on the existing role of the state in influencing accumulation processes in the markets, and how Dalit entrepreneurs experience and construct this role during the course of their various economic transactions. This chapter clearly has a limited mandate: to understand the role of the state in the economic processes constituting the markets, as they affect Dalit entrepreneurs. As we will see, state mediated economic outcomes are inextricably bound with social and political structures, both at the macro and micro levels.

The Engagement of Dalit Business with the State

In his study of the state, Philip Abrams[14] suggests that a distinction be made between the two objects of analysis, the state-system and the state-idea. State-system refers to

> a palpable nexus of practice and institutional structure, centred in government, and more or less extensive, unified and dominant in any given society. And its sources, structures and variations can be examined in fairly straightforward empirical ways. There is also, a state-idea, projected, purveyed and variously believed in different societies and different times.[15]

Abrams points out that the

> state comes into being as a structuration within political practice; it starts its life as an implicit construct; it is then reified — as the

res publica, the public reification, no less — and acquires an overt symbolic identity progressively divorced from practice as an illusory account of practice.[16]

He goes on to suggest that we should avoid mistaking the latter for the former by attending to the senses in which the state does not exist, rather than those in which it does.[17] If one has to understand how the state is viewed by Dalit entrepreneurs in its ideological abstraction (state idea) and its material everyday existence (state-system), we have to take a cue from the works of Gupta, Harriss-White and Corbridge et al.,[18] and study the state anthropologically, by viewing the everyday practice of the state (the state-system). However, in doing so, one cannot exclude an analysis of the ideological construct of the state (the state-idea). In other words, the functional institutions of the state, governing everyday practice, cannot be divorced from its ideological structure. The latter not only gives birth to the former, but both of them continuously shape each other. Hence, the crucial question that emerges is: How do we understand the state from the perspective of a particular sub-set of people? This question can perhaps be addressed by disaggregating various constituent elements of the state that Dalit entrepreneurs engage with during their market operations. Dalit entrepreneurs can, then, reconstitute these experiences to develop an understanding of the state. Our attempt to represent this Dalit experience is not so much to frame a general theory of the state, but, in all modesty, to try and understand its nature from the standpoint of the Dalit entrepreneur. To do this, we make use of evidence collected during the course of field interviews of Dalit entrepreneurs.[19]

The Abstract State (State-Idea)

The state is interpreted in different ways by Dalit entrepreneurs. However, these socio-economic interpretations are interrelated in ways that are not straightforward, especially in cases where the state is perceived to be an abstract institution, whose institutions are seen to exist 'out there'. This idea of the state is notably relevant when it is seen to be wielding enormous discretionary power affecting vast socio-economic changes; or when its actions cannot be understood and explained; or when electoral weight and successful political articulation does not translate into tangible development benefits. We can elaborate on this with the help of the following discussion:

Insensitive Policies, Caste-based Social Structure and Discretionary Power

The state is perceived to be sufficiently empowered to undertake a range of actions that, seemingly, cannot be influenced — let alone controlled — by any group or individual. As a laundry owner in Lucknow articulates this:

सरकार सब कुछ कर सकती है अगर सरकार चाहे तो मेरा सब धंधा पानी बंद हो सकता है।

The state can do anything . . . If it wants, my business will cease to exist.

This particular image of the power of the state does not necessarily corroborate with Weber's famous description of the state as having 'the *monopoly of the legitimate use of physical force* within a given territory'.[20] No doubt, the state in India has the legitimacy — or can always construe a reasonable justification — to use physical force against its citizens.[21] However, the interviewee does not seem to be emphasising its enormous power to use physical force, but, rather, the state's potential capacity to inflict immense damage to his economic interests by arbitrarily imposing any number of superfluous legal notices, or by creating bureaucratic hurdles to ensure that his business ceases to exist. The statement also reflects a degree of helplessness where he, seemingly, cannot resort to any remedial measures in the event that he perceives that his right as a citizen, or as a market player, has been violated by the state. What then allows the state to violate what its citizens consider to be their rights? Kaviraj[22] writes that this chasm has emerged from two different understandings of the state-idea. The first emanates from the English-speaking bureaucratic and political elite, and the second from the vernacular local bureaucracy. The 'high' language of the Weberian state's elite officials and political executives makes little sense to local state officials whose life worlds are structured by caste, community, kin, and family location.[23] Kaviraj argues that, due to this disjunction, the state's development policies have been 'reworked beyond recognition' by the officials working lower down in the bureaucracy.[24] Kaviraj seems to indicate that such reworking has resulted in the capture of the state, with benefits accruing to the locally dominant classes and castes due to the active compliance of the local officials. Through this process, however, the rights of a majority of the citizens are being violated. We argue for the need to re-look at this important formulation, and also rework it in order to address the marginalisation and exclusion of specific social groups. Kaviraj explains the disjunction only in terms of the national and local elite. Instead, we argue that caste-based exclusion (or, for that matter, exclusion of Adivasis, women, or religious minorities) was possibly never given enough serious political consideration in the planning and policy processes, resulting in all group-specific characteristics being subsumed under the universal category of 'Indian citizen'.[25] Hence, it was not the lower level officials alone who have mirrored the iniquitous wider social structure while executing development policies. This insensitivity has also been reflected in the policies framed at the national level, by the 'secular' political and bureaucratic elite, who have 'promoted' policies geared towards universal citizenship. Such policies, couched in terms of universal citizenship, appear to be least concerned with, or most insensitive to, exclusion emanating from caste practices, accentuating low caste locations. In other words, the development schemes of the state have seen every individual from all social groups as citizens socially similar to each other, without bothering to understand the ideological and cultural basis of their exclusion. This, in turn, has prevented the state from taking specific measures that could integrate the historically deprived social groups like Dalits, into the development processes. Such insensitive policies, in combination with the attitude of the local vernacular elite who work within the caste-based social structure, have facilitated the perpetuation of socio-economic inequality. This exclusion is further aggravated by the technical and sophisticated language of the policies and programmes governing the mass of citizens, who are either illiterate or insufficiently equipped to understand the Weberian language of the government. In a different context, but one which is also true for our argument, Scott[26] suggests that the complex language of governance is perhaps the 'most effective guarantee that a social world, easily accessible to an insider, will remain opaque to an outsider'; in effect, those who cannot grasp the language are rendered mute and marginal.

With reference to the narrative from the laundry-owner in Lucknow, the interviewee belongs to the one of the lowest castes, placing him in an unequal power relationship with the state, since the state is mostly represented by officials who belong to the upper-castes. In his mind, the state and its representatives have always been the source of his marginalisation, which is further reinforced by his inability to understand and make sense of what seems like an arbitrary and complex web of policies, programmes, legal regulations, municipal laws, licensing regimes, etc. For him, like for many other Dalits, rather than the *de jure* provisions published in the official gazette, it is the word of the official, backed by the legitimate power of the state, which is the law. Thus, the policies articulated by officials cannot be questioned, even if they are perceived by the Dalit to be against existing legal norms or natural justice. The interviewee also appears to believe that if he were to make any effort to question the actions of the state, it would not go down well with the officials, and they could invoke a number of penalising laws and legal actions against him. It needs to be emphasised that the possibility of penal action instils fear in the Dalit entrepreneur and, in turn, arouses 'respect' for and confers legitimacy on the abstract state. Thus, the power of the state, seen in abstraction, is perceived through the discretionary authority of its officials.

Inability to Comprehend State Action

Another significant example of the state as an abstract entity was cited by the secretary of a leather goods co-operative located on the periphery of Ahmedabad. A group of Dalit individuals came together and registered themselves under the Co-operatives Act, and began manufacturing leather goods. The state government, through the Gujarat Industrial Development Corporation (GIDC), not only supported the co-operative financially so that it could procure fixed assets, but also purchased its finished products in bulk. However, changes in the policy discourse from the mid-1990s trimmed state allocations, and reduced budgetary support for various subsidies. The support of the state government, thus, started waning, and finally came to an end in 2003, resulting in a sharp drop in the annual turnover of the co-operative, from over ₹1 million per annum, to less than ₹0.1 million per annum. While GIDC officials informed the co-operative members that the policy decision had come directly from the state secretariat located at Gandhinagar, the state capital, the Dalit entrepreneurs were not able to identify either the department, nor an individual to whom they could assign blame for their misery. Their representation to Gandhinagar was futile since physical access to the state secretariat was denied to them.[27] Further, they could not understand the logic of such a policy measure when the state was prospering economically and their business peers in other economic sectors (who happened to be *Baniyas* or *Patels* — upper-caste traders) were benefiting from similar GIDC policies.[28] A co-operative member agitatedly posed the question:

हम लोगों को जीडीआईसी ने क्यों मना कर दिया हम लोगों की जीडीआईसी ने तब मदद की जब गुजरात गरीब था अब जब ज्यादा पैसा है तो हम लोगों का धंधा क्यों बंद कर दिया गया?

Why is the door of GIDC closed to us? They supported us when Gujarat was poorer, but when it is prospering, why are we being asked to pull down our shutters?

The collective dignity of the co-operative members was further hurt when they were served a notice by GIDC stating that their co-operative had been listed as a 'failure of the community development initiative'. This was felt to be absurd since their co-operative was consistently making profits. The action of the state defied common sense, leading to a pervading sense of helplessness, which was exacerbated by the fact that they did not know where and to whom they could complain and plead their case. We are inclined to believe that if members of the co-operative had sought formal explanation from the state, it would, in all likelihood, have been brought to light that planning/policy experts had recommended the discontinuation of certain subsidies which were adversely affecting the fiscal health of the state and theirs was one such. As a consequence, the state had been compelled to freeze funds to them in the 'larger interest' of its citizens. Given the inability of the co-operative members to understand the reasons for policy restructuring and in the absence of any logical explanation the state's measures were perceived as discriminatory and oppressive (more so because other businesses led by upper-caste entrepreneurs were still seen to be enjoying the state's patronage/benefits). It was but natural for the course of events to seed the idea in the minds of the Dalit entrepreneurs that the state was an abstract, oppressive and arbitrary wielder of power — a notion further reinforced by the fact that neither were they capable of identifying the institutions within the state where they could plead their case, nor were they able to gain physical access to the relevant state department(s).

This narrative of the abstract state idea complements Partha Chatterjee's[29] argument that the Indian state acquires a Hegelian form and chalks out plans and policies for its citizens.[30] Chatterjee argues that substantial autonomy is enjoyed by the people who hold high office in the state. This autonomy, together with a monopoly of revenue-raising power, enables the state to acquire the role of mobiliser and manager of investible resources, while also mediating and managing the recurrent socio-economic strains in the polity. This also helps the state to acquire legitimacy. Further, in Chatterjee's formulation, the state claims to know everything[31] and, hence, decides the best recipe for development for its citizens, through the institution of planning. It is assumed that the progress of the nation (universal interests) is equivalent to the progress of its citizens, irrespective of their social location (particular interests). The emphasis on 'universal interests' allows the planning exercise to take into account only objective realities without paying attention to subjective preferences. This disjunction probably emerges because the state remains elusive to many of its citizens and, thus, for lack of concrete experience, acquires an abstract form in their minds.

So why is the state abstract? Is the elusiveness of the state (the impermeable boundary between state and civil society) the main reason for its abstractedness? Or, is it so because while the state planning mechanism does make a serious attempt to address the needs of marginalised social groups, the developmental benefits promised to them are never delivered properly due to pathetic implementation?

Political Inclusion and Economic Exclusion

The question posed above needs to be grappled with because several other forceful interpretations of the Indian state do not accord with the 'centrality of the state' thesis put forward by Chatterjee. For example, Francine R. Frankel,[32] Pranab Bardhan,[33] Rudolph and Rudolph,[34] and Achin Vanaik[35] point out, from their different theoretical vantage points, the capacity of various *powerful interests* in the realm of civil society that seek to permeate the structures of state, and shape its actions in their favour. We argue that the penetration of the state by civil society is not brought about by dominant interests alone. Since the 1990s, it has been increasingly realised that political processes in India have shifted from vertical mobilisation (through patronage to factions) to fierce horizontal mobilisation[36] under the impact of what Yadav describes as the second democratic upsurge.[37] As a result of this, it is no more the case that political parties co-opt newer social groups[38] through the politics of patronage;[39] instead, historically deprived social groups, through horizontal mobilisation, force the state to articulate their concerns, either by capturing political power through their own political parties, or by wresting influence over other political parties. This historical shift in political processes is well reflected in the initiatives undertaken by the Madhya Pradesh government, which invited intellectuals and activists working for the cause of historically deprived social groups to suggest measures for their socio-economic advancement. Some of these were crucial to what came to be known as the 'Bhopal Declaration', which, among other things, strongly advocated state support for the creation of a Dalit bourgeoisie. Based on the recommendations of this document, the government of Madhya Pradesh took the decision to extend all possible support to the people from the Dalit and Adivasi communities to become entrepreneurs and traders. To meet the objective, a unique 'Rani Durgavati Scheme' for self-employment was launched under the aegis of the Department of Industry, under which the department selects beneficiaries, provides training, ensures loans, and helps them in every possible way to start their businesses.[40] The state government also pledged to compulsorily procure 30 per cent of government purchases from the entrepreneurs and sellers belonging to Scheduled Castes and Scheduled Tribes.[41] Reacting to this crucial initiative, the owner of a handloom and boutique business at Vidisha explained:

राजनीति में दलित की अब एक अहम भूमिका है। कोई भी पार्टी का बिना हमारे वोट के काम नहीं चलता है . . . वोट लेने के लिए सरकार को कुछ तो करना ही होगा। दलित के हित में निर्णय करने का मतलब है पुराने समर्थ लोगों के हित के विरूद्ध जाना, पर सरकार के पास कोई चारा नहीं हैं। हम लोगों को गुड मिलने का भरोसा तो दिलवाना ही होगा।

Dalits have become a crucial social constituency in politics. None of the political parties can afford to ignore us . . . in order to get our votes, they have to do at least something . . . Any decision in favour of Dalits means a decision against the old guards. But the government in power has no option but to give us benefits.

A doctor, who also owns a nursing home in Aurangabad further reinforces this point:

कोई भी सही में दलित के लिए काम नहीं करना चाहता है। महाराष्ट्र में राजनीतिक समीकरण की वजह से हर बजट में कोई न कोई दलित के लिए स्कीम होती है . . . कभी दलित

के कोआपरेटिव बैंक को पैसा मिलता है तो कभी शिक्षा के लिए तो कभी दलित महिलाओं के सशक्तीकरण के लिए।

None of the political parties are really interested in working for the interests of Dalits, but the electoral compulsions in Maharashtra compel the parties to make some Dalit-specific provisions in every budget . . . At times special budgetary provisions are made for allocating grants to various Dalit co-operative banks; at other times, steps are taken for the education of Dalits or special provisions are made for the empowerment of Dalit women.

Both these narratives point towards the imperatives of the political process that force political parties to respond to the fierce horizontal political mobilisation, which in turn, compels the state to take their views on board, even if such policy initiatives go against the interests of powerfully entrenched social groups. According to both interviewees, such measures are essential because of the need of the state to reproduce itself and maintain its legitimacy in the political domain. In contrast, the nature of assimilation sought in Madhya Pradesh is not in the nature of the benevolent patron state co-opting social groups from above, but, in fact, proactively responding to the demands of political assertion from below, by taking into cognizance the subjective preferences of Dalits in the policy domain. However, such Dalit-specific initiatives (as the one discussed above) do not necessarily mean that the state and its institutions become accessible to them and thus, lose their abstractness. As explained by another Dalit entrepreneur who trades in plastic products at Bhopal:

दलित के लिए नीतियां तो पचास बनती हैं, उनका फायदा हमें कभी मिलता है पर ज्यादातर नहीं मिलता है। भोपाल में नीति बनती है, अखबार में आती है, पर उसका फायदा हमें कैसे मिले, हममें से किसी को भी मालूम नहीं अगर पता भी चलता है तो जरूरी नहीं है कि हम लोगों को उसका पूरा लाभ मिलेगा।

Numerous policies are introduced for the benefit of Dalits, we are able to access some of them, but most of them remain inaccessible . . . The policies are made in Bhopal (the state capital) and are reported by the newspapers. However, the policies still remain elusive since we don't know how to capture their benefits . . . Even if we get to know of them, there is no guarantee that we will get the full benefits.

In the last three narratives documented above, the state is seen as responding to the demands of Dalits. In the last narrative, the interviewee points out that though numerous policy announcements suggest that the state is being responsive to Dalit demands, it does not necessarily follow that the benefits will flow to them. In other words, the boundaries between the state and civil society are made more porous by their political strength, but the degree of the state's abstractness still remains the same. Two related implications follow from the permeability between the state and civil society. First, as pointed out by Joel Migdal, when the state comes into contact with various groups, it clashes with and accommodates a different moral order. These engagements, which occur at numerous junctures, change the social base and aim of the state.[42] However, an increase in the number of pro-Dalit policy initiatives, resulting from aggressive political articulation by Dalits, may not necessarily translate into a pro-Dalit local administration, where the policies are actually executed. In other words, political inclusion may not necessarily mean economic inclusion. Second, according to our interviewees, changes at the top do not really make the state more accessible. Hence, it appears that the concreteness of the state is related not only to the ability of Dalit businessmen to access the state symbolically or politically, but also to their ability to stake practical claims to the benefits of development.

The Everyday State — (State-system)

It is not always the case that the state and its institutions are an abstract entity. During the course of their market operations, Dalit entrepreneurs engage with numerous departments representing the state. They perceive the state officials to be either latently biased or openly discriminatory against their interests. In the following section, we try to capture the experience of Dalit entrepreneurs in their engagements with various institutions of the state. It will be noticed that they try to simplify the state and its practices either in order to gain possible means to engage with the state, or to explain to themselves the reasons for their marginalisation. We call these practices their *theses of state simplification*.

Simplification of the State

The theses of state simplification, as we will see, comprises four discrete theses that need to be emphasised. It must be stressed that none of the following theses, with regard to the role of the state, can be interpreted on their own, but have to be read together. The theses of state simplification can be explained as follows:

Dalit entrepreneurs tend to de-link the state departments they deal with from the larger scheme of statecraft. At the same time, they also perceive state officials to be autonomous from the norms, rules and regulations of the formal state (thesis I: de-linking state departments from statecraft, and state officials from norms/rules of statecraft). This, as we will see, allows the institutions of the state to become tangible. However, this does not amount to a simple relationship between an individual and the state officials. Instead, Dalit businessmen perceive their relationships with politicians and administrators as being structured and over-determined by the values of discrimination practised by the latter. Hence, they experience the state discriminating against them vis-à-vis upper caste competitors, resulting in their unfavourable inclusion in the accumulation processes of the markets in which they transact (thesis II: unfavourable inclusion). The reasons for their unfavourable inclusion are rooted in the socio-economic and political strength of the upper-castes, which also contributes to the blurring of the boundaries between the state and civil society (thesis III: blurring of the boundaries between state and civil society: role of caste), and to their ability to carve out social networks through family, caste and marriage connections (thesis IV: role of family and its relationship to caste).

In order to better understand the simplification of the state by Dalit entrepreneurs, let us explain each of the constituent theses:

Thesis I: De-linking the state department from statecraft and state officials from norms/rules of statecraft

One of the most influential conceptions of the state in the liberal democratic order is drawn from Weber's understanding of the state's institutional design (as comprising a set of interrelated organisations which are made operational by the bureaucracy). The most important characteristics of the bureaucracy are: a. A hierarchical system of super-subordination where subordinate executives are supervised by their superiors along with a complex network of horizontal and vertical linkages between various arms of the state bureaucracy and, b. Office management governed by impersonal relationships and laws.[43]

In contrast to Weber's understanding, and the constitutional and legal architecture of the bureaucracy in India, Dalit entrepreneurs do not see the various departments as interlinked to each other through the larger schemes of statecraft. As pointed out by an interviewee in Aurangabad,

मेरा काम सिर्फ पुलिस से, सेल्स टैक्स ऑफिस से, म्युनिस्पैलिटी से, और बिजली ऑफिस से पड़ता है। सब ऑफिस अलग-अलग ढंग से काम करते हैं। और आपस में कोई लेना देना नहीं है। हरेक ऑफिस में बाप हैं, जब चाहें काम रोक दे और धंधे का नुकसान कर दे। इसलिए हर जगह अलग से व्यवहार बनाना पड़ता है। बिना व्यवहार बनाए कोई काम नहीं होता है।

I only deal with the police, sales tax office, municipality, and electricity department. These departments are not related to each other in any way and each works differently. In each office, there is an influential person, who can bring work to a halt at will and inflict huge losses to my business.[44] That's why I have to use different strategies in each office and carefully cultivate these relationships. If I don't nurture these relationships and build a rapport with each of these influential people, all my work will come to a standstill.

Similar views, de-linking the departments from the larger state apparatus, were echoed by Dalit entrepreneurs operating in Lucknow, Jaipur, Bhopal, and Pune, when describing the experiences of their interaction with the state bureaucracy. In their understanding, official rules and regulations are not executed as legally recognised bureaucratic responsibilities, but are conditional on the individual's ability (or inability) to carve out the necessary social relationships with state officials. As a result, individuals holding positions of power in the concerned state departments are seen to be de-linked (autonomous), and/or are perceived to be above the body of rules and regulation. This dual de-linking — of a given department from the larger scheme of statecraft, and of the state officials from the body of rules and regulations — transforms the state from an abstract entity into an institution which can be approached through legal as well as extra-legal means.

However, the modern state is a huge body with criss-crossing hierarchies structured by layers of officers, section heads, clerks, peons, etc. Any attempt on the part of Dalit entrepreneurs to carve out a working relationship requires that this complex hierarchy be rendered compatible with a purely functional calculus. Thus, the complex structure of the state is simplified by dissecting it into a three-layered hierarchy: a. *bada sahib* (senior officer), b. *babu*s (section officers and clerks), and c. *chaprasi* (peon). This can be seen in a statement of a Pune-based entrepreneur:

बड़े साहिब के पास कागज पहुचाने हैं तो बाबू को भी मस्का मारना होता है या तो चपरासी को पैसा खिलाना पड़ता है।

In order to ensure that an application or important paper is presented before senior officer, one must sweet talk the lower-level officials. Or else bribe the peon.[45]

This simplification of the state's hierarchy has been shaped as a result of their regular and repeated interaction with its officials. The babus can either promote their cause or equally ensure that their plea gathers dust in one of the files of the numerous departments. Similarly, the chaprasi can either facilitate their access or thwart their efforts to gain an audience with the bada sahib. Finally the bada sahib may choose to immediately address their concerns, though this crucial help is not always forthcoming.

Thus, as the last two narratives explain, engagements with state officials are not necessarily only for issues springing from official reasons. In fact, non-official social idioms are seen to be continuously discovered, used and reworked to mediate and influence official transactions. We find that Dalit entrepreneurs enter into business partnerships with the upper-castes in order to exploit their social network and gain access to the state as well as to the credit market. Similarly, Dalit entrepreneurs often make use of local political contacts and NGOs to facilitate their economic endeavours. On few occasions, Dalit entrepreneurs gain access to state offices through relatives or other sympathetic Dalit officials. For instance, a leather tannery owner in Kanpur shared with us:

मेरा बिजली का कनेक्शन कार्मिशयल यूज के लिए है। मेरा साला क्लर्क है केसू में, उसने तुरन्त लगवा दिया।

The electricity connection for commercial use was immediately installed since I received help from my brother-in-law who works as a clerk at KESU (Kanpur Electricity Supply Undertaking).

Similarly, a computer hardware seller at Aurangabad told us:

वाघमोरे[46] जो मंत्रालय में काम करता है उसको दलित लड़के जो कुछ काम चाहते हैं काफी पसंद हैं। उसने सरकार की स्कीम से जो दलित लड़कों के लिए है, मुझे तुरन्त पैसा दिला दिया। जिसकी वजह से मैंने ये दुकान बनाया।

Waghmare who works at Mantralaya [state secretariat located at Mumbai] approves of and supports Dalit youth who show initiative. He got funds released from a government scheme specifically meant for Dalit youth for me and I used that money to set up my current business.

Further, the most crucial engagements affecting economic outcomes in the markets are perceived to be negotiated not through written codes of interaction but, instead, through verbal negotiations. In fact, many of the written procedures are implemented through unwritten and verbal engagements with state officials.

For instance, a brick kiln owner in Pune, told us:

सेल्स टैक्स इन्स्पेक्टर का भतीजा मुझसे घूस का सौदा कर लेता है। घूस के हिसाब से मेरा टैक्स तय हो जाता है। मैं फिर दूसरे दिन जाकर पहले से तय टैक्स जमा कर देता हूँ।

The nephew of the sales tax inspector negotiates the bribe with me. Based on the size of the bribe agreed upon, he, on behalf of his uncle, determines the tax that I have to pay. The next day I go and deposit the tax as per our discussions the previous day.

The means of engagement with state officials, at times, can be the same for a Dalit and an upper-caste entrepreneur. However, our interviewee perceives that the outcomes from such interactions are mostly adverse to their economic interests. As we will see in the discussion ahead, the perceived biases are due to the fact that the interactions between a Dalit entrepreneur and a caste state official(s) is/are mostly mediated by the discriminatory values shaped through the ideology of caste, and not by due process, rules or procedures.

Thesis II: Unfavourable inclusion

The two examples presented in the first thesis, perhaps hold true for any number of individuals who, irrespective of their social location, undergo the experience of complex, and sometimes, ritualistic official procedures — delays, rent-seeking, inaccessibility, etc., — resulting in their exclusion from policy processes and their benefits.

However, Dalit entrepreneurs indicate that their experience of engaging with the state cannot be equated with those of individuals from other social groups, especially those belonging to the dominant social groups. They make a crucial distinction between their omission from the policy process due to the non-responsiveness, inapproachability, and the unsympathetic character of the state departments, and their marginalisation as a result of the discriminatory practices of the upper-castes who control the state bureaucracy. As testified by a leather goods manufacturer from Agra:

ऐसे भी गरीब लोगों को कोई नहीं पूछता है। हम लोगों की चप्पल घिस जाती हैं बैंक और सरकारी ऑफिस के चक्कर काटते काटते . . . उसके बाद जब पता चलता है कि हम जात के चमार हैं तो काम होना तो राम भरोसे।

As it is, no one cares for the plight of the poor. We may wear ourselves out making repeated trips to the bank and government offices to get work done. Once the officials come to know that we belong to the *Chamar*[47] caste, then there is no telling when or if at all our plea will be heard. It is all left to God Almighty's 'benign benevolence'.

This narrative makes a crucial distinction between the two types of exclusion — one due to the processes of governance, and the other, reinforced/ influenced by the values that uphold discrimination against the lower castes. It appears that exclusion due to discriminatory practices cuts across class hierarchy. Take, for instance, the following testimonial of a Dalit woman who owns a large ceramic tiles factory at Ahmedabad:

पैसा होने से हमारी जात नहीं बदल जाती है। अगर बनिया और पटेल के पास पैसा है तो उनकी सारी दुनिया इज्ज़त करती है, नेता उसका काम करता है और सरकारी अफसर उसको केबिन में बुलाकर चाय पिलाता है और उसका काम भी तुरन्त कर देता है। मेरी भी इज्ज़त है पर मुंह पे, पीठ पीछे सब लोग गाली देते हैं। कसम से, अपुन ने सब पार्टी को पैसा दिया है, सरकार में भी पैसा खिलाया है, पर आज तक किसी ने चाय के लिए नहीं पूछा। . . . पैसे से मैं सरकारी अफसर से ज्यादा मजबूत हूँ पर जात से नहीं, इसलिए पैसे की इज्जत सिर्फ मुंह पर है।

Money cannot change one's caste. The rich business people belonging to Baniya and Patel communities are respected by everybody. The political leaders help them, and when they visit government offices, they are ushered into the cabin of the officials and offered tea, while their work is also done immediately. I am also respected but only in my presence. Behind my back, I am ridiculed and abused. I swear I have

also given money to all political parties, and also to government officials, but till date, I have never been offered tea . . . I am richer than
many officials, but my caste status is lower than theirs and, hence,
I don't command respect.

This account reveals the aggrieved spirit of the woman entrepreneur who, despite acquiring wealth and prosperity, is unable to
overcome her baggage of being born as Dalit, and her consequent
undervaluation as a social being. Her political desire to claim equal
status with her upper-caste peers remains unfulfilled; moreover, she
is perturbed that upper-caste entrepreneurs are accorded privileges
by the state officials, while she can only get her work done through
informal practices such as rent-giving. In this respect, it may not be
wrong to point out that rent-giving facilitates the endeavours of both
Dalits as well as non-Dalits but, from the narrative, it appears that
member of upper-castes enjoy greater access to the state's resources
due to their social proximity to the state officials (we discuss this
issue later at greater length).

How do we make analytical sense of the exclusion specifically
experienced by Dalits, irrespective of their class location? Sen's insight
into 'passive exclusion' emanating from social processes where there
is no deliberate attempt to exclude, but which may, nevertheless,
result in exclusion due to a set of circumstances, may offer some
explanation.[48] In fact, this may help us explain the exclusion of
lower classes in general. In the case of Dalits, the narratives suggest
that the values of discrimination give shape to what Sen describes as,
'unfavourable terms of inclusion and adverse participation, rather
than what can be seen primarily as a case of exclusion as such'.[49]
Research on the development state shows that unfavourable inclusion and adverse participation is the norm in almost all types of
socio-economic projects (intellectual, cultural and developmental)
in independent India. Sarkar,[50] Nigam[51] and Pandian[52] explain that
dominant writings on various social issues — nationalism, modernity,
nation-building, etc. — consciously eclipsed the social plurality that
has always existed in the nation. In the process, the culture of lower
castes was excluded by the dominant national (read caste Hindu)
culture. Pandian opines that the commitment to the development
state, and the discipline of sociology, both chart a teleological path
of modernity that moves from lower caste practices to sanskritisation,
and on to westernisation.[53] This teleology sets caste as the 'other'
of the 'modern', while 'modern' is invariably pro-upper-caste in

orientation.[54] In the context of the governance of development programmes, empirical evidence of adverse inclusion and participation
is hard to avoid. This includes many examples of the deserving who
have been excluded and undeserving who have been included, and
of discrimination in development programmes,[55] consistently unused
budgetary allocations meant specifically for Dalits,[56] and reserved
posts in government departments remaining vacant, especially at the
higher rungs of the bureaucracy.[57] Despite more than half a century
of 'anti' and 'compensatory' discrimination policies by the central
and state governments respectively, Mendelsohn and Vicziany note
that major beneficial impacts for Dalits have come from the policies
directed to the entire population, and not from those focused specifically on 'untouchables'.[58] In other words, Dalits are deliberately
excluded from claiming rights flowing from the provisions specifically
earmarked for them. Even in cases when Dalits are economically
upwardly mobile, they are denied equal access to economic goods.
Guru[59] illustrates this point with an example from Pune where
house-builders refused to sell a flat to a Dalit client, even though the
client was ready to pay more than the market price for it. It is in this
context that the writings of Harriss-White[60] and Thorat[61] develop the
idea that discrimination leading to adverse inclusion is shaped by the
ideology of caste. In other words, a set of social arrangements with
a tangible material base that are sustained by a set of ideas, beliefs
and values. Harriss-White further argues that caste, as an ideology,
is quite dynamic, and responds to socio-economic changes without
substantially altering its essential characteristic of sustaining the
relationship of domination and subordination between the upper and
lower castes.[62] Further, the ideology of caste also socially unites the
upper-castes with respect to their relationship with Dalits.

If Dalits are unfavourably included in socio-economic processes
and the institutions or the state shapes such adverse inclusion, it
becomes crucial for us to understand how Dalit entrepreneurs make
sense of the state's actions. What are their distinct experiences which
make them believe that the state officials act mostly against their
interests?

Thesis III: Blurring the boundary between the state and civil society: The Role of Caste

Dalit entrepreneurs fully understand that the upper-castes are
not a homogeneous group, being horizontally divided by sub-caste

locations, and vertically differentiated by class positions. According to a laundry owner in Lucknow:

सरकारी दफ्तर में सबसे ज्यादा बोलबाला जात का है और पैसे का है। दफ्तर के अन्दर भी सब मुलाज़िम आपस में बनिया, ब्राह्मण, ठाकुर जात के अनुसार ही गुट बनाते हैं। अगर जात का समीकरण ठीक बैठता है तो हो सकता है कि बिना पैसे के काम हो जाए। और जब समीकरण ठीक नहीं बैठता है तो गुप्ता जी को अग्रवाल से और पाण्डेय से जानपहचान निकालने में टाइम नहीं लगता है और एक बार जानपहचान निकल आती है तो पैसा कम खिलाना पड़ता है। . . . मुझे कर्मशियल बिजली का मीटर लगवाने में पापड़ बेलने पड़ गए थे, बाबू पैसे ऐसे मांगता था जैसे पेड़ पर उगते हैं। मेरे घर में कोई पढ़ा-लिखा नहीं है जो किसी दफ्तर में काम कर सकता हो और मेरा काम भी आसान हो जाए। पैसा खिलाने के लिए भी जान पहचान बहुत जरूरी है।

The government offices predominantly operate through caste identity and rent-seeking. The social solidarity between the employees in the offices is rooted in caste identities — Baniya, Brahmin, Thakur, etc. If the caste of the citizen approaching the government office is the same as that of the official, it is quite possible that the work will get done without any bribe. Even if there is some minor misalignment of sub-castes, it is not that difficult for an upper-caste to find some social contact to approach the officials of a different sub-caste. Such social contacts invariably lead to a reduction in the size of bribe/rent. While I was trying to get an electricity connection for commercial use, the officials expected me to pay a huge bribe. They think that money grows on trees . . . My family is uneducated; hence, I don't have any contacts in any of the offices which can facilitate my work.

According to this interviewee, the relationship with government departments is invariably mediated either through corruption, or through social relationships (cultivated with the official by virtue of common caste and/or sub-caste identities). His cynical belief is that corruption is a given, perhaps an essential requirement to lubricate the bureaucratic machinery, and make it function. What seems to distress him more, is the fact that people of his caste lack social contacts to influence the government machinery and lower their transaction costs (delays and amount of rent given), whereas an upper-caste can easily find a social contact, even if the official is from a different upper sub-caste. His narrative attempts to simplify the complexities inherent in the institutions of the state that result in his adverse inclusion. But at the same time, it raises a crucial question: How do we understand this all-pervasive corruption and its relationship with caste identities in the context of the adverse inclusion of Dalits? What follows is an elaboration of the third thesis on the 'simplification of state', which hopes to provide an answer, besides offering a. a plausible explanation for the perception by Dalits of their unfavourable inclusion in the market processes due to the specific role of the state; and, b. a possible understanding of the relationship between the state and the regime of accumulation practiced by the dominant castes.

Before we proceed further, it may be helpful to briefly review the dominant understanding of corruption.

An eminent proponent of the modernisation theory, Samuel Huntington, argues that corruption is a result of the disjunction between the norms of the modern nation state, which are universal and based upon achievement, and 'traditional' values, in which differences between the ruler's families (read state officials) and the state are not recognised. Only when the distinction between the state and its representatives is widely accepted, can nepotism and corruption be defined. Further, he argues that modernisation creates new avenues of wealth and power. Those who have wealth seek political power, and those who have power seek wealth, and both may rely on corruption to meet their respective ends. Lastly, overextended and centralised bureaucracies emerge as a source of corruption.[63] Gunnar Myrdal[64] reiterates Huntington's point; he sees corruption as resulting from the institutional weakness of Asian states, and the discretionary nature of the administrative structure in post-independent countries. Drawing from the Santhanam Committee Report,[65] Myrdal points out that the industrial and commercial classes use corrupt practices not only to 'secure large, unearned profits, but also the necessary means to enable them to be in a position to pursue their vocations, or retain their positions among their own competitors'.[66] The corrupt politician and dishonest official maintain a regime of 'discretionary control' and regulation, due to their vested interest of rent-seeking.[67] Bardhan describes rent-seeking as 'the use of public office for private gains', which has its roots in a. the 'monopoly power of bureaucrats', and, b. the lack of democratic institutions promoting accountability and transparency at different levels of governance. Bardhan further argues that rent-seeking, in the long run, has an adverse impact on investment and growth and, therefore, the process of economic growth will ultimately generate enough interest in the reduction of corruption.[68] The natural culmination of these arguments was, perhaps, reflected in the Structural Adjustment Programmes (inspired by the World Bank) in late-developing countries. The use of public office for private gain was described as rent-seeking which primarily resulted from an over-extended state, and the complex matrix of laws and licensing regimes. This ushered in the discourse of thinning down the state, and calls for transparency and accountability in its operations and good governance.

Notwithstanding the fact that these writings are divided by important ideological differences, all these accounts emphasise the centrality of the state. They make a distinction between the state as an institution, and the officials representing the state. Further analysis reveals that the state and its officials are seen to enjoy a certain kind of autonomy with regard to the 'constraints' imposed on them in the form of norms, rules, and procedures of the state, which allows them, in turn, to favour one party over the other for an *economic incentive*. It is, then, this acquired autonomy by state officials that facilitates the articulation of dominant economic interests within the state. Further, the natural outcome of this particular diagnosis of rent-seeking will be a demand for a restructuring (maybe thinning down) of the state, in order to temper, or altogether stop, rent-seeking. In this sense, the state, too, is seen to command some sort of autonomy from its own employees who manage its apparatus, allowing it to enact measures to put an end to the practice of rent-seeking.

We argue that the dominant discourse on corruption is internally contradictory; the state is corrupt and has to cleanse itself. Further, evidence from across India indicates that the liberalisation of the hitherto 'rigid' centralised bureaucracy has resulted in newer forms of regulatory control and corruption.[69] Our reasoning is that the research discussed above explains the phenomenon of corruption as a self-reproducing institution to be overcome by the formal restructuring of the state; however, it falls short of clarifying the reasons why corruption sustains and thrives.

Another set of scholars who attempt to explain the causes of corruption see it either as a cultural practice configuring relationships with the state, or as a manifestation of specific socio-political processes.

In his ethnographic analysis of corruption and the local state, Gupta argues that corruption 'draws attention to powerful cultural practices by which the state is symbolically represented to its employees, and to the citizens of the nations'.[70] He further explains:

The discourse of corruption is central to our understanding of the relationship between the state and social groups precisely because it plays this dual role of enabling the people to construct the state symbolically, and to define themselves as citizens. For it is through such representation, and through the public practices of various government agencies, that the state comes to be marked and delineated from other organisations and institutions in social life.[71]

Thus, corruption appears to be the central idiom through which the citizens' relationship with the state is structured. Gupta gives central importance to illegal monetary transactions propelling the violation of norms and standards of conduct which blurs the boundaries between *state and society* (emphasis added). This invocation of cultural practices in order to understand corruption also confers autonomy on the state and its officials similar to that discussed by the political economists previously. Accordingly, the capacity of social processes to influence outcomes in the political and administrative domain is crucially ignored.

Mushtaq Khan[72] addresses this gap. He stresses on the peculiarity of the social and political structures that create and sustain the blurred boundaries between state and society and, thereby, consistently allow private interests to be reflected in state action. Such a blurring of boundaries should not be seen merely in the light of the autonomous institution of rent-seeking and rent-giving, but as a product of wider socio-economic and political processes. Perhaps this is what Mushtaq Khan has in mind when he flags the role of patron-client politics (under democracy) in capturing economic resources, which, in turn, blurs the gap between state and society. Khan argues that pyramidal patron–client networks emerge as the most rational form of organisation for faction leaders, who use the network to buttress their own position in the political power structure:

> What political factions seek is not the construction of a coalition that can mobilise votes to allow a transparent renegotiation of taxes and subsidies, but a coalition that can mobilise organisational power at the lowest cost to the faction leader, to achieve distribution of assets and incomes using a combination of legal, quasi-legal, or even illegal methods.[73]

Due to this specific feature of socio-political accumulation, Khan thinks that the 'newer' ideas of transparency and accountability are unlikely to benefit a broad range of groups, since these do very little to undermine the dominance of patron-client networks and the informal networks mediating the exercise of power.

We agree with Khan that rent-seeking, and rent-giving, both reflect the socio-political process of accumulation and, that the 'democrat-isation' of this process cannot but exclude social groups from the range of economic/development benefits. However, the field material discussed in detail below does not permit us to term the relationship between the dominant castes and the state as one of patron and client. In fact, the evidence cited in the passages below will show that the practice of rent-giving and accepting cannot be neatly slotted into any of the theories discussed above — it is not merely an economic transaction for private gain, nor is it a disjunct between modern universal values and traditional norms, and it can certainly not be ascribed to an institutional incapacity of a centralised bureaucracy. The violation of rules and norms, and the flouting of legal imperatives take place when the interests of the dominant castes (for instance, Brahmins, Baniyas) and the state feed each other, thus, further facilitating the segmentation of markets along caste lines, while entailing the unfavourable inclusion of Dalits.

We turn to our field evidence:

The fact that corruption is embedded in socio-political processes was clearly articulated by the secretary of the leather co-operative in Ahmedabad:

नेता से जान पहचान से काफी काम आसान हो जाता है। पटेल और बनिया गुजरात की सरकार चलाते हैं। सभी सरकारी आर्डर उनके धंधे का फायदा करते हैं।

Being personally acquainted with the political leadership facilitates business . . . The Gujarat government is run by Patels and Baniyas; all government circulars invariably further their business interests in the market.

This narrative reveals how leading players in economy and society, who are also members of the dominant castes, can penetrate the state and mould its policies to further their own interests. Here, two points need to be emphasised: first, the pattern described by the interviewee from Ahmedabad is not merely that of the market needing the state as a secular regulator, but describes the economic strength of certain castes who use the state to fulfil their economic objective of accumulation in the markets; second, the narrative elucidates the symbiotic relationship between the state and markets as being controlled by the dominant castes, wherein the power of the former translates into the strength of the latter, and vice-versa.

This description resonates with Harriss-White's delineation of caste as a powerful institution mediating between the state and markets and, in turn, blurring the dividing line between them. She explains:

> Market exchange and competition are impossible without collective actions, which are grounded in caste and caste-like groups . . . In elaboration of the 'dual culture' of positive discrimination in market-based economic and social advancement, the caste association has developed another dual role. They both woo the state for concessions and repel the state's own attempt to regulate.[74]

This, however, begs another question: If caste provides a basis for collective action, why are Dalits as a social group not able to articulate their economic interests collectively, and challenge their unfavourable inclusion?

Here, a statement from the secretary of the leather co-operative in Ahmedabad is worth noting:

> दलित का सरकार में कोई साथी नहीं है, न हम लोगों की संख्या धंधे में ज्यादा है। जितने लोग हैं, छोटा मोटा धंधा करते हैं। हम लोग बड़ा पैसा कभी भी किसी पार्टी को नहीं दे सकते हैं। बनिया पटेल के पास बड़ा धंधा है और पैसा है। उनकी सरकार है, उन्हीं के आदमी इलेक्शन जीतते हैं और मिनिस्टर बनते हैं, मिनिस्टर बनने के बाद उन्हीं का काम करते हैं। इस गठबंधन को तोड़ना हम लोगों के लिए समंदर को मीठा करने के बराबर है।

> Dalit entrepreneurs don't have any major contacts in the government. And not many of us are businesspersons, the ones who are, have small businesses and hence, hence, we cannot make big political donations . . . It is the Patels and Baniyas[75] who have big businesses and lots of money. They are the ones who make big political donations; their people contest elections and become ministers in the government. Once in office, they work for their own community. Breaking this nexus, for us, is like attempting to sweeten sea water.

Dalit entrepreneurs are not able to successfully articulate their economic interests within the government because of their miniscule and insignificant economic power.[76] The speaker understands that the interests of dominant players in the markets are primarily articulated through caste solidarity, and that it is this caste solidarity that facilitates the symbiotic alliance between economic power and political power, where each becomes the source of the other's strength. Thus, if the market needs the state, the reverse is also true — the state, too, needs the market. The Dalit perceives that this interdependence is self-reproducing, and detrimental to the interest of any socially weak player in the market. Dalit entrepreneurs believe they do not have the numerical or economic strength necessary to create, cultivate and sustain friendly relations with the elected representatives of the state. Had this been otherwise, it would have been easier for them to shape policies that would favour their economic interests. It was repeatedly explained to us that the macro reality (discussed above) of a symbiotic relationship between the dominant castes and state is also reproduced at the micro level. For instance, a leather shoe manufacturer in Agra reveals:

जिसे भी वोट की राजनीति करनी है वो पैसे से दबंग जात का काम तुरन्त करता है।

If one has the ambition to enter and survive in electoral politics, one has to work for the members of economically dominant castes.

Here, our interviewee is referring to the local corporator (the elected representative in the local municipality), who was perceived as a 'genuine' person, i.e. one who would like to help everyone in his constituency. However, the municipal corporator could not ignore the demands of rich, upper-caste traders because of his ambition to contest the state legislative assembly elections. At the next rung of the political ladder, the corporator would require a substantial amount of funds which could only be provided by rich traders; our entrepreneur interviewee perceived that it was the anticipation of future financial requirements that propelled the corporator to help rich, upper-caste traders to flout various municipal laws, and facilitate their access to various local officials. Thus, the imperatives of electoral politics ensure that the interests of the dominant castes are not ignored.

But it is not only the need for political funds that impels local politicians to work in favour of the dominant castes. As pointed out by an automobile workshop owner:

इस इलाके में ठाकुर[77] का बोलबाला है . . . कुर्मी,[78] चमार,[79] और धोबी[80] संख्या में ज्यादा हैं पर सरकारी ऑफिस, पुलिस में ठाकुर की ही चलती है। मेरी पुरानी दुकान ठाकुर साहिब के पिछवाड़े थी। उनके आदमियों ने तोड़ दी। जब मैंने रोकना चाहा तो हाथापाई हुई, पुलिस

ने पारषद के कहने पर मुझे अन्दर कर दिया। हम लोगों की वजह से ही पारषद जीता है
पर काम ठाकुर का ही करता है। अब यहां दुकान खोली है, पुराने ग्राहक खतम हो गए,
धीमें धीमें नये ग्राहक आ रहे हैं, 8 साल की मेहनत बेकार हो गई।

Thakurs are the most powerful community in this area . . . They
have considerable clout in local government, politics, and police,
even though a majority of the population belongs to the Kurmi,
Chamar and Dhobi castes . . . My old workshop was located just
behind Thakur Sahib's backyard. It was demolished by Thakur's men,
I tried to stop them and a scuffle ensued . . . I was arrested and the
local corporator facilitated my arrest. He won the election because
of us but he invariably helps Thakurs. I have opened the shop at this
new location now. I have lost all my old customers and am trying to
establish relationships with new ones gradually. Eight years of effort
in building a customer-base have gone to waste.

Here, we see the social power of the upper-castes in influencing
political representatives, as well as police officials, to act in their
favour and against the economic interests of the Dalit entrepreneur.
The numerical weight of the lower castes in the electoral arena does
not necessarily translate into protection of their economic interests.

Political funding and social dominance, however, are not the only
means to develop proximity with the institutions of the state. There
are other social institutions, for instance, family and marriage, which
facilitate access or proximity to state power; to analyse these social
structures and practices, we shift our attention from macro-level
political and social structures, to micro processes that primarily
emanate within the domain of the family and have a critical impact
on macro structures, for example, the nature of the state and its relationship with the market. The micro processes that we will discuss
are based on our interviewees' perceptions of the role of family and
caste in using the resources of the state which, in turn, facilitates the
reproduction of inequality and the unfavourable inclusion of Dalits.

Thesis IV: Blurring of the boundary between state and civil society: Role of Family and its Relationship with Caste

André Béteille has argued consistently that caste has undergone a
fundamental change under the impact of modernity, and has ceased
to play an active role in the reproduction of inequality, at least at
the middle and upper levels of the social hierarchy.[81] He believes that

family is the crucial 'institution through whose agency inequality is reproduced in the strategic domain of the society'.[82] Our field evidence does not seem to favour family over caste in the reproduction of inequality, but sees these institutions as two sides of the same coin.

Our Dalit interviewees perceive that their upper-caste business competitors are invariably in a superior social position because they have a better relationship with state officials. For instance, it is perceived that social relationships between businessmen and the state are predominantly the product of kinship/family relations — चाचा, ताउ, मौसी, मामा[83] [Uncles and Aunts], or developed through caste-inspired camaraderie:

> देशस्थ ब्राह्मण या भोसले अपनी कास्ट के लोगों का काम जल्दी से कर देते हैं पर दलित का काम हमेशा रोक देगा।

A Deshastha Brahmin[84] or a Bhonsle[85] official will immediately help people of his caste but will always stall the work of Dalits.[86]

Dalit businessmen see family, or extended family (i.e. relationships within the same sub-caste), as significantly influencing social relationships between market players and the state. We are told that family relationships provide access to state resources, as does caste identity. Both family and caste, however, are closely intertwined, so any social linkages with state officials that are based on family relationships are invariably, therefore, also caste linkages.[87] They facilitate the appropriation of illegal benefits from the state (listed below) and, hence, should be seen as a form of capital referred to by Bourdieu as cultural and social capital.[88] In our context, Dalits perceive that the families of upper-caste entrepreneurs command a stock of cultural capital (by way of knowledge and skills), and social capital (in the form of social networks — acquired mostly from the past, but also developed and sustained by present cultural and material capital). For Dalits, this combination of cultural, social and material capital (in most cases, access to material capital comes from family ties in upper-caste families), gives upper-castes not only unequal access to the means of production, marketable talent, and contacts, but also relatively disproportionate access to state power. In fact, family connections based on caste are seen to facilitate influence to the extent that the local municipality will go soft on illegal encroachments,[89] on trading in certain goods without 'official permissions' (read licences),[90] on manipulating sales tax payments with the help of 'willing' tax officials,[91] on physical threats to competitors with the help of the local police,[92] on evading or manipulating electricity tariffs,[93] etc.

The examples cited above are essentially attempts to lower the transaction costs. However, outcomes in the markets can also be critically influenced by the power of the state through, what Harriss-White calls, 'non competition'.[94] For instance, the social alliance with state officials is not only a source of strength, but also a deterrent, if it is perceived that market competitors have access to officials in the state through their family connections. An ironsmith in Vidisha explains:

> दो साल पहले दिवाली पर मैंने अपनी दुकान के सामने पटाखे की दुकान लगाई। बगल वाले अग्रवाल[95] ने भी पटाखे की दुकान लगाई। उसकी बिक्री जब कम हो रही थी तब उसके आदमी ने मुझसे आकर बोला कि मैं सारे पटाखे उसे खरीद के दाम पर बेच दूं वरना वो पुलिस में शिकायत कर देगा। मैंने उसकी बात मान ली क्योंकि उसका बहनोई सब इंस्पेक्टर है। मेरे पास पटाखे बेचने का लाइसेंस नहीं था, ना ही उसके पास था, पर उसका बहनोई उसका लाइसेंस था।

> Two years ago during Diwali, I tried to sell fireworks. The neighbouring shop owned by Agarwal was also selling crackers. My sale was better. An employee in his shop came and told me to sell all my crackers to him at my procurement price. He threatened me that his boss would lodge a complaint with the police. I was selling crackers without a licence; so was he. But, his licence was his brother-in-law, who is a police sub-inspector.

This testimony shows how a weaker market player (who, incidentally, also belongs to a lower caste), is unable to operate informally on the theoretical principles of the 'free' market, against his more powerful upper-caste market competitor. In other words, the state institutions introduce non-competition in the market by ensuring that even if lower castes have the ability to enter the market (informally), and perform better than their upper-caste competitor (also transacting informally), they still face the possibility of suffering serious losses in the market because of the partisan attitude of the state.

Béteille's formulation, discussed earlier, that caste has witnessed fundamental changes, that family, and not caste, is the primary institution reproducing inequality, calls for some critical refinement.[96] We agree with Béteille that the family provides the basis for cultural and social capital, giving an edge to some individual(s) over others who lack in such capital. However, the social capital (and social networks) which is configured by family relations and yet operates beyond the immediate family is more often than not rooted in caste, allowing disproportionate access to resources irrespective of whether these are controlled by the state or in the hands of non-state actors. Upper-castes' social affinity, and not family, therefore, forms the crucial basis for the blurred lines between the state and civil society, and results in the unfavourable inclusion of Dalits. While we also agree that caste has significantly changed, both sociologically and economically, under the impact of modernity, and has become somewhat secularised, nonetheless, as argued by Basile and Harriss-White, the form of the transformation and secularisation of caste is 'corporatist'[97] — 'economic regulation that limits class conflict *inter alia* by involving both capital and labour in the market'.[98] The corporatist project, and changes in caste imply, as Jaiswal has also argued that only those aspects of caste have changed that are in conflict with the capitalist mode of production and, hence, are disappearing with the impact of industrialisation.[99] However, the institution of endogamy, the primary feature that sustains the caste system, still seems to be more or less intact, and quite in harmony with capitalist modernity, besides serving as a crucial connection between family and caste. For instance, our evidence indicates that the social capital (social network) of upper-caste entrepreneurs acquires a more robust shape through marriage alliances within the same sub-caste. At least 13 of our interviewees (three in Lucknow, two each in Aurangabad, Pune and Ahmedabad, and one each in, Vidisha, Kanpur, Agra, and Jaipur) told us that their upper-caste business competitors were fortunate to have either their son, or daughter, or some close relatives, married to either a government official, or to the son or daughter of a government official. A chemist based in Aurangabad describes the benefits of such social alliances:

पेठ[100] और मैंने साथ धंधा शुरू किया था। पेठे का दमाद सिविल हास्पिटल में सर्जन है। इसलिए उसको वहां दवाई सप्लाई करने का कान्ट्रैक्ट मिल गया। पेठे ने कान्ट्रैक्ट से काफी पैसा कमाया। मुनाफे से उसने ट्रान्सपोर्ट का धंधा शुरू कर लिया।

Pethe and I started our medical shop together. Pethe's son-in-law is a surgeon at the Civil Hospital. This helped him secure a contract to supply medicines to the Civil Hospital . . . and earn handsomely. Now he has invested his surplus to start a transport business.

In this context, marriage not only delimits social relationships between castes, and within sub-castes, but also has a crucial and powerful impact on managing and influencing official decisions, thus affecting market outcomes.

The institution of endogamy operates to ensure that such social resources are not available to Dalits. As observed by a laundry owner in Lucknow:

हम लोगों की लड़की लड़को की शादी आपस में ही होती है। सभी लोग की औकात बराबर होती है, हम सब लोग की किस्मत में बड़े लोग की सेवा करना लिखा है। कोई फरक नहीं पड़ता चाहें हम छोटा मोटा धंधा करें, बनिया की दुकान में काम करें या फिर मजदूरी। कौन सरकारी अफसर धोबी की लड़की से शादी करेगा शादी का सम्बंध बराबर लोगों से होता है।

Our girls and boys marry within the community. All of us have a similar social status; all of us are destined to earn our livelihood by serving the rich and powerful. It does not matter whether we do petty business, or get employed in shops owned by upper-castes, or work as labourers; the end result is the same. Which government official will marry a *Dhobi*'s daughter? Marriage alliances are always between people of equal social status.

Our interviewee informed us that Dalits, like any other caste, mostly marry within their community. However, unlike the upper-castes, their reasons for doing so are not based on social or religious beliefs, but on the stricture of forming alliances with those who are socially equal. The narrator articulates his cynicism at the rigidity of the caste mandate — in his social experience and perception, most state officials are from upper-castes, thus making it extremely difficult to form social relationships through marriage alliances. The perception of the Dalit entrepreneur that state officials, especially at middle and the higher echelons, belong to upper-castes is validated by the latest available figures.[101] The last four narratives seem to indicate that family and caste are inextricably interlinked and reinforce the social relationships limiting the role of Dalits in the state.

Summing up: A Comment on the Experiences of Dalit Entrepreneurs and the Character of the State

As we have explained earlier, Dalit entrepreneurs face unfavourable inclusion in the market due to biases with respect to the role of the state. In their everyday engagement with the state, they experience two different avatars of the state: the state-idea and the state-system. The former is understood in terms of the centralisation and coordination of what they experience as domination by the state — the state-idea is an abstract but oppressive force. The state-system, on the other hand, is experienced as a symbiotic relationship between the state and the dominant castes, resulting in a feeble state that is open to local control and appropriation by these dominant castes. At the same time, contrarily, the state is powerful enough to ignore the interests of Dalits who, while being electorally significant, are politically and economically weak. However, both notions of the state have to be seen as reinforcing and shaping each other, leading to the blurring of boundaries, rather than as distinct and mutually exclusive categories. We will now explain how that 'blurring' works.

The perception of the state as an abstract institution is because of its seemingly omnipotent status, whereby its powers are often exercised in a discretionary manner. This 'abstraction' is intensified when the state's policy initiatives are made known to Dalits through political publicity and media reports, but are subsequently found to be not implemented on the ground. The 'abstraction' is further reinforced when the state's 'disciplinary' actions, although affecting the Dalits drastically, are not explained to them, nor are they able to gain access to the state to question or seek clarifications. In other words, the state appears to be an abstract entity whose actions are unaccountable or intangible, and its institutions are inaccessible. This leads to disappointment and anger, especially since they seem to be shaped by the institutionalised interests of the dominant castes. However, this does not translate into collective unrest. Indeed, while it has resulted in fierce political assertion in the past, such assertion does not necessarily translate itself into obliterating the perceived discriminatory characteristics of the state. Given this scenario, why is the state, then, still seen as legitimate and powerful?

Abrams explains that the state-idea is an ideological project:

> It is first and foremost an exercise in legitimation — and what is it being legitimised is, we may assume, something which if seen directly and as itself would be illegitimate, an unacceptable domination. Why else does all the legitimation work? The state in sum is a bid to elicit support for or tolerance of the insupportable and intolerable by presenting them as something legitimate, disinterested domination.[102]

As an ideological project, the Indian state invokes constitutional measures to guarantee political citizenship. It also tempers the universal notion of citizenship, and makes special provisions for various kinds of affirmative action in favour of socially and economically backward classes. Further, under the provisos of political democracy, the state penetrates society with an array of legislative provisions, policies and programmes, both economic and non-economic, formulated and executed for Dalits (avowedly for overcoming their historical deprivation), as well as non-Dalits. In the face of its vast reach, the state has become an integral part of the life-world of Dalits and non-Dalits. Moreover, its support is seen as critical for the former because of their historical deprivation, and the state's immense role creates a perception that it is the only institution that can possibly mitigate the marginalisation of Dalits in the markets. Most of the testimonials that we have documented condemn the state's avowed efforts to tackle structural violence against Dalits.

However, the state as an idea appears to be quite legitimate, and extremely powerful in the socio-economic imagery of Dalit entrepreneurs, even if its practical actions are perceived to be shaped by the institutionalised interests of the dominant castes. The construct of the state in the imaginations of Dalit entrepreneurs is, therefore, contradictory: the state is the problem, but the state is also the solution. Accordingly, a normative construct of the state is repeatedly invoked in order to explain the gap between the expected role of the state and its actual behaviour — the latter having resulted in the violation of economic rights of Dalits in the market. The normative construct is a beacon on which to focus aspirations — the state is expected to take on their cause and mitigate the structural constraints they face. There are important implications that flow from this normative construct of the state-idea. In exploring them, our discussion will move more towards explaining the state-system as experienced by the Dalit entrepreneurs.

The normative construct of the state emphasises the role of political democracy, wherein political mobilisation and assertion is a vehicle for capturing or influencing state power. State power, in turn, becomes an instrument to meet the dual demands of a. socio-political empowerment (through democratic relationships in civil society), and b. economic empowerment (through equitable entitlement in the market).[103] However, political democracy is neither a necessary, nor a sufficient condition for claiming equitable entitlements under the existing market conditions. Political democracy mostly operates through formal institutions, whereas market outcomes are mostly dictated by informal practices. Formal institutions operate under secular norms most appreciated in electoral arrangements,[104] whereas informal practices tend to be cemented through institutions such as caste, religion, gender, ethnicity, age, region, locality, family relations, etc. These influence state action and shape market outcomes. Yet, as detailed earlier with the help of our 'four theses of state simplification', Dalits constantly struggle against social obstacles for configuring or accessing such networks. However, the legitimacy of the state is still upheld because, as Nayyar points out, those excluded by the market are still sought to be included by political democracy.[105] Therefore, under the conditions of political democracy, the institutions of the state-system, through their complex functioning, act as incentives for Dalit political expectation, and are able to conceal the caste character of the state with the help of real progress towards political inclusion.

The caste character of the state is reflected in the fact that the power of the state (embodied in its legal provisions) is primarily perceived as the power of the dominant upper-castes, both in and for itself, and also over the lower castes. The extensive testimonies of Dalit entrepreneurs demonstrate that, contrary to popular conceptions of the state in liberal theory (which suggest that the state is a neutral arbitrator among conflicting interests), and in Marxist theory (where the state is either an executive arm of the bourgeoisie or may become relatively autonomous only when there is a balance of forces between dominant classes), the Indian state is a casteist entity! The Dalit experience of the character of the state stresses two crucial points:

a. The state is a key institution with respect to outcomes in the economy (even the informal economy) that result in the unfavourable inclusion of Dalit entrepreneurs. In such contexts, caste and family become critical institutions that make porous the boundaries between state, market and civil society.

b. Dominant upper-castes and the state (represented by political parties, leaders, and state officials) cannot be seen as independent of each other, and have their respective interests served by each other. However, the relationships between upper-castes and Dalits on the one hand, and the linkages between upper-castes/Dalits with the state on the other, are not static; it is the specificity of socio-political and economic conditions that may place one in a better bargaining position than the other.

Hence, adhering to Harriss-White,[106] caste can be seen as a social structure of accumulation[107] (SSA) in the market. The SSA develops through what she calls 'Politics of Markets', which includes the following:

a. Ushering in non-competition with the help of social networks, through which market exchange is construed;
b. defending economic interests with the active help of the state;
c. manipulating party politics (funding all political parties rather than getting identified with one);
d. enforcing market contracts through social rules rather than state sanctions.

In the context of our analysis, points a. and d. would imply the *withdrawal* of the state in support of the dominant castes; point b. would require the presence of an active state *supporting* the interests of dominant castes; and point c. refers to the means used by the dominant castes to *access* the state. The field evidence analysed in this chapter confirms these conclusions.

Thus, it is the politics of caste that enables upper-castes to articulate their economic interests within the institutions of the state, while also ensuring that Dalit entrepreneurs are not included on equitable terms in the transactions which constitute the process of accumulation. It is in this context that Dalit entrepreneurs invoke the normative construct of the state-idea. Thus, the normative role of the state is not an ethical concept, but an urgent invocation, necessary to explain Dalit disadvantage, and invoked to protect their economic interests. As detailed in Thesis I of Simplification of the State, the use of extra-legal means to access the state by Dalit entrepreneurs does not put them on par with their upper-caste peers. The critical requirement for Dalits, therefore, is that economic transactions based on custom be replaced with those based on secular rules and norms, and that these transactions be enforced by a state-system that is impartial to caste.

Notes

1. Richard Nixon, letter to Anthony Maxwell, 31 October 1972, folder: Ex Fg 21-17, Office of Minority Business Enterprises [2 of 2], box 7, FG 21- Department of Commerce, Central Files, Nixon Presidential Materials, quoted in Dean Kotlowski, 'Black Power-Nixon Style: The Nixon Administration and Minority Business Enterprise', *The Business History Review*, 1998, 72 (3): 445.

2. Quoted in Government of Madhya Pradesh, *The Bhopal Declaration*, 2002, 1, http://www.ambedkar.org/ (accessed on 30 June 2008).

3. Government of India, 2009–10, *Economic Survey*, New Delhi: Ministry of Finance, 2010.

4. See Dev Nathan, Sandip Sarkar, Hareshwar Dayal, and Sunil Mishra, 'Development and Deprivation of Scheduled Tribes', *Economic and Political Weekly*, 2006, XLVI (46): 4824–27.

5. Government of India, 2006, *Social, Economic and Educational Status of Indian Muslim*, New Delhi: Ministry of Minority Affairs, 2006.

6. Since this book is on Dalits, it may be pertinent to point out that in the year 2011–12, nearly 30 per cent Dalits were below the poverty line. More than 32 per cent of rural Dalits are poor while 22 per cent of Dalits residing in urban areas are poor.

7. On economic exclusion, see S. K. Thorat, 'Caste System and Economic Discrimination: Lessons from Theories', in S. K. Thorat, Aryama and Prashant Negi (eds), *Reservation and Private Sector: Quest for Equal Opportunity and Growth*, New Delhi: Indian Institute of Dalit Studies and Rawat Publication, 2006, pp. 73–80; on the exclusion of Dalits from delivery of government's developmental programmes, see Oliver Mendelsohn and Marika Vicziany, *The Untouchables: Subordination, Poverty and the State in Modern India*, Cambridge: Cambridge University Press, 2005; Joel Lee and Sukhadeo Thorat, 'Dalits and the Right to Food: Discrimination and Exclusion in Food Related Government Programs', mimeo., New Delhi: Indian Institute of Dalit Studies, 2007; on exclusion from government jobs, see Craig Jeffrey, Roger Jeffery and Patricia Jeffery, 'Degrees without Freedom: The Impact of Formal Education on Dalit Young Men in North India', *Development and Change*, 2004, 35 (5): 963–86; Anand Teltumbde, 'Pursuing Equality in the Land of Hierarchy: Positive Discrimination Policies in India', mimeo., New Delhi: Institute for Human Development, 2007; on exclusion from the financial sector, see Smita Gupta, 'State Finances and Dalits', mimeo., New Delhi: Institute for Human Development, 2007.

8. Gopal Guru, 'Dalit Vision of India: From Bahishkrit to Inclusive Bharat', *Futures*, 2004, 36: 760.

9. Christophe Jaffrelot, *India's Silent Revolution: The Rise of Low Caste in North India*, London: Hurst and Company, 2003, p. 393.
10. Government of Madhya Pradesh, *The Bhopal Declaration*, 2002. Also see Aditya Nigam, 'In Search of a Bourgeoisie: Dalit Politics Enters a New Phase', *Economic and Political Weekly*, 30 March–5 April 2002, XXXVII (13): 1190–93.
11. In South Africa, one of the crucial pillars of the African National Congress's guiding principles of the National Democratic Revolution was to facilitate a strong nationalist and productive black capitalist class. See O. C. Iheduru, 'Social Concentration, Labour Unions and the Creation of a Black Bourgeoisie in South Africa', *Commonwealth & Comparative Politics*, 2002, 40 (2): 47–85. Commentators hailed it as a revolutionary response to the process of globalisation. BEEP, propelled and encouraged by the state, enabled the black majority labour unions to form union-owned investment companies for wealth accumulation and, in turn, to transform workers into both labour and capital, employees and employers. Roger Southall, 'The ANC & Black Capitalism in South Africa', *Review of African Political Economy*, 2004, 31 (100): 313–28.
12. In the United States, Richard Nixon laid the seeds for Black Capitalism by initially inviting blacks, later extending the appeal to Hispanics and Indians, to acquire a stake in the free market economy. The Nixon administration laid the foundations for two crucial institutions: the Office of Minority Business Enterprise (which later came to be known as the Minority Development Business Agency), and the Minority Enterprise Small Businesses Corporations (funded by Small Business Administration and private sponsors). The former supervised the expansion of federal procurement from firms owned by African Americans and Hispanic Americans. The mandate of the latter was to loan money to minority entrepreneurs (Dean Kotlowski, 'Black Power-Nixon Style: The Nixon Administration and Minority Business Enterprise', *The Business History Review*, 1998, 72 (3): 445). These two initiatives charted out the Supplier Diversity Programme. In 2002, around 15,000 minority business enterprises supplied goods and services to around 3,500 public and privately owned firms (Mayank Shah and Ram Monder, 'Supplier Diversity and Minority Business Enterprise Development: A Case Study of Three US Multinationals', *Supply Chain Management: An International Journal*, 2006, 11 (1): 75–81).
It was also pointed out that the US ruling regime was politically compelled to take such measures because of the growing socio-political assertion of the Black community. See Robert E. Weems Jr. and Lewis Randolph, 'The Ideological Origins of Richard M. Nixon's "Black Capitalism" Initiative', http://web.ebscohost.com/ehost/pdf?vid=2&hid=107&sid=073e804f-932e-4523-80fc-1292ad813570%40sessionmgr102 (accessed on 2 June 2008).

13. Government of Madhya Pradesh, *The Bhopal Declaration*, 2002, p. 25.
14. Philip Abrams, 'Notes on the Difficulty of Studying the State (1977)', *Journal of Historical Sociology*, 1988, 1 (1): 58–89.
15. Ibid., p. 82.
16. Abrams, 'Notes on the Difficulty of Studying the State'.
17. Ibid.
18. Akhil Gupta, 'Blurred Boundaries: The Discourse of Corruption, the Culture of Politics, and the Imagined State', *American Ethnologist*, 1995, 22 (2): 375–402; Barbara Harriss-White, *India Working: Essays on Society and Economy*, Cambridge: Cambridge University Press, 2003, p. 75; Stuart Corbridge, Glyn Williams, Manoj Srivastava, and Rene Veron, *Seeing the State: Governance and Governmentality in India*, Cambridge: Cambridge University Press, 2005.
19. See Introduction — Chapter One — for a description of the methods used in the field research.
20. Emphasis added; Max Weber, 'Politics as Vocation', in H. H. Gerth and C. Wright Mills (eds), *From Max Weber: Essays in Sociology*, New York: Oxford University Press, 1946, p. 78.
21. For instance, the Supreme Court, in the case of Sardar Sarovar Project, directed all concerned state governments to ensure that those who were displaced because their lands and homes would be submerged by the dam, be rehabilitated through the principle of 'land for land'. However, this principle has been extensively violated, and any protest against it crushed by the police and paramilitary forces. See Sanjay Sangvai, 'No Full Stops for the Narmada: Life after the Verdict', *Economic and Political Weekly*, 8–14 December 2001, XXXVI (49): 4524–26. These protests are seen in the mainstream as going against the interest of the nation and, hence, the violence of the state is considered legitimate. Similarly, in Odisha, despite vehement protests by Dongaria Kondha Adivasis, the Odisha government has allowed mining by corporate groups and, in the process, trampled on the livelihood of locals. See Geetanjoy Sahu, 'Mining in the Niyamgiri Hills and Tribal Rights', *Economic and Political Weekly*, 12–18 April 2008, XLIII (15): 19–21. A review of land acquisition for establishing Special Economic Zones in various states will reveal a similar story.
22. Sudipta Kaviraj, 'On State, Society and Discourse in India', in Stuart Corbridge (ed.), *Development: Critical Concepts in Social Science*, London and New York: Routledge, 2000, pp. 426–43.
23. Somewhat similar arguments but from a different theoretical location were made by a few other authors. Myron Weiner (Myron Weiner, *Political Change in South Asia*, Calcutta: Firma K. L. Mukhopadhyay, 1963, pp. 115–51) pointed out the existence of two political cultures,

one that is situated in districts and localities, both urban and rural, and the other that is found in the national capital, whose members occupy important administrative and political positions. He called the former an 'elite political culture' and the latter a 'mass political culture'. The elite culture sought to develop and modernise India — its economy, its political institutions, and some aspects of social customs. The mass political culture largely manifested 'traditional' elements. Morris Jones, (W. H. Morris Jones, *The Government and Politics of India*, London: Hutchinson University Library, 1964, pp. 44–92) also characterises Indian polity and society through three idioms — 'Modern', 'Traditional' and 'Saintly' — and all of them fundamentally differ from each other. T. N. Madan (T. N. Madan, 'Whither Indian Secularism?', *Modern Asian Studies*, 1993, 27 (3): 667–97) presents a comparable argument. While explaining the crisis of Indian secularism, he argues that the state project of constitutional secularism is alien to the social beliefs and practices of common people.

24. Kaviraj, 'On State, Society and Discourse in India', p. 442.
25. Niraja Gopal Jayal, 'Five Caveats to Citizenship', mimeo., Jawaharlal Nehru University, New Delhi, 1999.
26. James C. Scott, *Seeing Like a State: How Certain Schemes to Improve the Human Conditions Have Failed*, New Haven: Yale University Press, 1998, p. 60.
27. Technically, all citizens can physically access the state and its officials. However, the Dalit entrepreneurs were perturbed because they were unable to identify or meet the decision makers and thereby enquire the reasons for such an adverse decision, and find out whether it could be at all be changed or reversed.
28. Gujarat has seen a series of policies promoting manufacturing and industrial growth, which includes subsidies, single window clearance, industrial parks, special economic zones, loan subsidies, etc.
29. Partha Chatterjee, 'Development Planning in India', in Partha Chatterjee (ed.), *State and Politics in India*, New Delhi: Oxford University Press, 1997, pp. 271–97.
30. Chatterjee points out that Hegel's penetrating logic shows that the universal rationality of the state is concretely expressed at two institutional levels — the bureaucracy as the universal class and monarchy (sovereign will of the state, in case of India) as the immediate existent will of the state. In India, 'it was in the universal function of development of national society as a whole that the post-colonial state would find its distinctive content'. The bureaucracy as the universal class was expected to work for the universal goals of the nation. The institutions of planning provided rational determination and pursuit of these universal goals [Chatterjee, 'Development Planning in India', pp. 278–79].

31. Chatterjee describes the process of planning in the Hegelian incarnation of state as the domain of rational determination and the pursuit of these universal goals of development. Development implies a linear path, directed towards a goal, or a series of goals separated by stages. It entails the fixing of priorities between long run and short run goals and making conscious choices between alternative paths (Chatterjee, *State and Politics in India*, p. 277).

32. In her historical account, Frankel observes that domestic policy outcome was the result of complex interactions among different levels of state (national state and federal units): the relationship between different federal units, political regimes and party, politics within the ruling party, state leaders who controlled rural politics through politics of patronage, and co-option through strategic use of government programmes and subsidies. Further, she argues about the role of international actors in influencing policy outcomes. See Francine R. Frankel, *India's Political Economy, 1947–1977: The Gradual Revolution*, Princeton: Princeton University Press, 1978.

33. Pranab Bardhan argues that the state is captured by a coalition of the dominant propertied class. Since none of the partners of the dominant coalition is more powerful than the other, it provides an opportunity for the state to acquire relative autonomy from them. See Pranab Bardhan, *The Political Economy of Development in India*, Oxford: Clarendon, 1988.

34. Rudolph and Rudolph characterise the Indian state as a 'self determining third actor' but still a dichotomous weak/strong state. The state is strong because it mediates between different powerful propertied classes, thereby giving it considerable autonomy, though such autonomy is specific to space and time. At the same time, the state is weak because of the constraints imposed on its autonomy by demand groups (organised labour, bullock capitalists, rich farmers, and high ranking bureaucrats). See Lloyd I. Rudolph and Susanne Hoeber Rudolph, *The Modernity of Indian Tradition*, Chicago: The University of Chicago Press, 1967.

35. Achin Vanaik sees the state as an organisation having a distinct will and interests, and policy outcomes can be understood by interpreting the relationship between state as an organisation and the dominant classes. See Achin Vanaik, *The Painful Transition: Bourgeois Democracy in India*, London: Verso, 1990.

36. These terms were first used by Rudolph and Rudolph to describe the mobilisation of lower castes by their own leaders in South India (horizontal mobilisation) while contrasting it with vertical mobilisation where the political mobilisation was top-down, i.e., lower castes depended on upper-castes in clientelistic relationships. See Lloyd I. Rudolph and Susanne Hoeber Rudolph, *The Modernity of Indian Tradition*, Chicago:

The University of Chicago Press, 1967. However, the nature of political mobilisation seems to be similar in the north and south.

37. Yogendra Yadav argues that the present wave of democratisation, where the lower castes are asserting their presence in the political domain, is the second democratic upsurge in India. The first began in the 1960s when the Congress party started losing its dominance. See Yogendra Yadav, 'Understanding the Second Democratic Upsurge: Trends of Bahujan Participation in Electoral Politics in the 1990s', in Francine R. Frankel, Zoya Hasan, Rajeev Bhargava, and Balveer Arora (eds), *Transforming India: Social and Political Dynamics of Democracy*, Delhi: Oxford University Press, 2000, pp. 120–45. Ashutosh Varshney ('Is India Becoming More Democratic?' *The Journal of Asian Studies*, 2001, 59 (1):12) believes that it is the fourth democratic upsurge. The first two have been attributed to the rise of mass politics under Gandhi in the 1920s, and the third one with the universalisation of adult franchise after Independence.

38. The primary shift that we indicate is the decisive movement from a dominant one-party system to a 'competitive multi-party system' — the existence of two parties at the state level, the diversity of which collates to give the appearance of multi-party system at the national level. See Yogendra Yadav, 'Understanding the Second Democratic Upsurge: Trends of Bahujan Participation in Electoral Politics in the 1990s', in Francine R. Frankel, Zoya Hasan, Rajeev Bhargava, and Balveer Arora (eds), *Transforming India: Social and Political Dynamics of Democracy*, Delhi: Oxford University Press, 2000, pp. 132–35. Under the former, it can generally be said that the state and party collapse into one entity, and a patron–client relationship is evolved through the politics of patronage between the dominant party and various social groups; while, under the multi-party system, lower castes as social groups, and other regional groups are represented by their own political parties or their leaders.

39. A caveat is in order. The politics of patronage may still hold true as far as the political integration of Adivasis and minorities is concerned.

40. Government of Madhya Pradesh, Scheduled Caste and Scheduled Tribe Welfare Department.

41. Ibid.

42. Joel S. Migdal, 'The State in Society: An Approach to Struggles for Domination', in Joel S. Migdal, Atul Kohli and Vivienne Shue (eds), *State Power and Social Forces: Domination and Transformation in the Third World*, Cambridge: Cambridge University Press, 1994, p. 12.

43. Max Weber, 'Politics as Vocation', in H. H. Gerth and C. Wright Mills (eds), *From Max Weber: Essays in Sociology*, New York: Oxford University Press, 1946, pp. 78–82.

44. The interviewee uses the term 'baap' to refer to the key influential officer with whom he needs to interact in a particular department.

45. The distinction between them is that the former usually travels in a white ambassador (senior government servants travel in a white car called 'Ambassador', manufactured by Hindustan Motors) or a jeep, works in a private office cabin in the government building with highly restricted access to outsiders; whereas clerks and peons can be approached directly, and it is easier to request or plead with them to negotiate the case or amount of bribe with them.

46. Waghmare generally belong to the Mahar caste — a Dalit sub-caste.

47. The Chamar caste is one of the Dalit castes. People belonging to this caste were traditionally employed in leather works, and were responsible for leather tanning — the process whereby raw hides of animals are converted into leather. As per the values of the caste-based social order, the profession is considered to be highly polluting in nature.

48. Amartya Sen, 'Social Exclusion: Concept, Application, and Scrutiny', *Social Development*, 2000: 14–18, http://www.flacso.org/biblioteca/ sen_social_exclusion.pdf (accessed on 2 June 2008) makes a distinction between 'active' and 'passive' exclusion. The former explains state-promoted exclusion though deliberate policy measures. 'When, however, the deprivation comes about through social processes in which there is no deliberate attempt to exclude, the exclusion can be seen as a passive kind' [Sen, 'Social Exclusion: Concept, Application, and Scrutiny', p. 15, http://www.flacso.org/biblioteca/sen_social_exclusion.pdf (accessed on 2 June 2008)].

49. Sen, 'Social Exclusion: Concept, Application, and Scrutiny'.

50. Sarkar argues that in dominant historiography, the analysis of political action is grounded in categories of imperialism, nationalism and colonialism, which amounts to the failure of historiography to take note of social plurality (Sumit Sarkar, *Writing Social History*, New Delhi: Oxford University Press, 1998, pp. 358–90). In Sarkar's words: 'such an assumption involves an uncritical acceptance of the holistic ideological claims of "Indian" nationalism and "Hindu" and Muslim communalism — claims that have sought to homogenise a multitude of differences of regions, class, caste and gender' (p. 358).

51. Nigam (Aditya Nigam, 'Secularism, Modernity, Nation', *Economic and Political Weekly*, 25 November–1 December 2000, XXXV (48): 4256–68) reviews the work of various authors and Dalit thinkers who have critiqued the dominant understanding of Secularism, Modernity and Nation. He also points out that the present critique of caste by Dalits is not based on untouchability and ritual practice associated with the caste in the private sphere, but needs to be understood as a sustained struggle against the modern incarnation of caste. He further argues that

modern upper-caste privileges are not articulated in the old language of caste; the new discourse speaks through the idioms of efficiency, merit and even hygiene.

52. M. S. S. Pandian, 'One Step Outside Modernity: Caste, Identity Politics and Public Sphere', mimeo., South-South Exchange Programme for Research on the History of Development (SEPHIS), and the Council for the Development of Social Science Research in Africa (CODESRIA), Amsterdam/Dakar, 2001.

53. Pandian is pointing towards the writings of M. N. Srinivas. See M. N. Srinivas, *Social Change in Modern India*, New Delhi: Orient Longman, 1972.

54. Pandian also indicates that 'it would be a mistake to [argue that] lower castes [reject] modernity. It is at once a critique of the modern for its failure as well as an invitation to it to deliver its promises'. In other words, the lower castes' relation to modernity can best be described as 'antagonistic indebtedness'. See Pandian, 'One Step Outside Modernity : Caste, Identity Politics and Public Sphere', mimeo., South-South Exchange Programme for Research on the History of Development (SEPHIS), and the Council for the Development of Social Science Research in Africa (CODESRIA), Amsterdam/Dakar, 2001, p. 19; Geetha and Rajdurai (V. Geetha and S. V. Rajdurai, *Towards a Non Brahmin Millennium: From Iyothee Thass to Periyar*, Calcutta: Samya, 1998, p. 56) will agree with Pandian that Dalits are indebted to the British colonial rule-inspired discourse of modernity because they note that modernity provided them the language of rights, and the secularisation of public space, both essential products of western education, and the modern processes unleashed by the British rule.

55. For instance, see Joel Lee and Sukhadeo Thorat, 'Dalits and the Right to Food: Discrimination and Exclusion in Food Related Government Programs', mimeo., Indian Institute of Dalit Studies, New Delhi, 2007.

56. See Smita Gupta, 'State Finances and Dalits', mimeo., Institute for Human Development, New Delhi, 2007.

57. See Anand Teltumbde, 'Pursuing Equality in the Land of Hierarchy: Positive Discrimination Policies in India', mimeo., Institute for Human Development, New Delhi, 2007.

58. Oliver Mendelsohn and Marika Vicziany, *The Untouchables: Subordination, Poverty and the State in Modern India*, Cambridge: Cambridge University Press, 2005, p. 119.

59. Guru, 'Dalit Vision of India: From Bahishkrit to Inclusive Bharat', *Futures*, 2004, 36: 759.

60. Barbara Harriss-White, *India Working: Essays on Society and Economy*, Cambridge: Cambridge University Press, 2003, p. 197.

61. S. K. Thorat, 'Caste System and Economic Discrimination: Lessons from Theories', in S. K. Thorat, Aryama and Prashant Negi (eds), *Reservation and Private Sector: Quest for Equal Opportunity and Growth*, New Delhi: Indian Institute of Dalit Studies and Rawat Publication, 2006, p. 77.

62. Harriss-White, *India Working*, p. 197.

63. Samuel P. Huntington, *Political Order in Changing Societies*, New Haven Conn: Yale University Press, 1968, pp. 59–62.

64. Gunnar Myrdal, *Asian Drama: An Inquiry into Poverty of Nations, Volume II*, New York: Twentieth Century, 1968, pp. 937–60.

65. This committee established by the Government of India, Ministry of Home Affairs in 1964, prepared a report on corruption, titled *Report of the Committee on Prevention of Corruption*, often called the Santhanam Committee Report after chairperson of the committee. See Myrdal, *Asian Drama*, p. 937, footnote 1.

66. Government of India, *Report of the Committee on Prevention of Corruption (Santhanam Committee Report)*, pp. 11–12; Myrdal, *Asian Drama*, p. 937.

67. Myrdal, *Asian Drama: An Inquiry into Poverty of Nations, Volume II*, p. 951.

68. Pranab Bardhan, 'Corruption and Development: A Review of Issues', *Journal of Economic Literature*, 1997, 35 (3): 1320–46.

69. The coming of economic liberalisation and new forms of regulatory control has not reduced corruption. For an analysis of corruption in newly liberalised sectors of economy, see Desmond Fernandes and Leo Saldanha, 'Deep Politics, Liberalisation and Corruption: The Mangalore Power Company Controversy', 2000, http://elj.warwick.ac.uk/global/issue/2000-1/fernandes.html (accessed on 7 June 2008); P. Purkayastha, 'Telecom Policy: Another Scam? Rigging Tender for Foreign Entry', *Frontline*, 16 June 1995: 34–37. The recent scams in the telecom sector, natural gas extraction, etc., are considered to be the biggest in terms of the quantum of illegal gratification and embezzlement involved. Moreover, measures (indeed numerous such measures have been taken inspired by structural adjustment policies) for tackling corruption do not affect more than 20 per cent of the economic activities. Harriss-White (*India Working*, pp. 3–16) points out that economic activities constituting almost 80 per cent of the economy in India are not regulated by formal institutions of the state. She also reviews the study of Roy (Rathin Roy, 'State Failure: Political-Fiscal Implications of the Black Economy', in Barbara Harriss-White and Gordon White (eds), *Liberalisation and New Corruption, IDS Bulletin*, Sussex: Institute of Development Studies, 1996, pp. 22–31) that points out that corruption

(cash as medium for rent-giving) accounts for merely 5 per cent of the total tax evasion in India. Drawing from Roy, Harriss-White argues that it is the tax evasion which is more problematic, and that it has its roots in the social structure.

70. Akhil Gupta, 'Blurred Boundaries: The Discourse of Corruption, the Culture of Politics, and the Imagined State', *American Ethnologist*, 1995, 22 (2): 385.

71. Ibid., p. 389.

72. Mushtaq H. Khan, 'Markets, States and Democracy: Patron-Client Networks and the Case for Democracy in Developing countries', *Democratization*, 2005, 12 (5): 704–24.

73. Ibid., p. 719.

74. Harriss-White, *India Working*, p. 197.

75. Pranab Bardhan, 'Law and Development', in A. K. Dutt and J. Ros, eds, *International Handbook of Development Economics*, Cheltenham: Elgar, 2008, pp. 381–93.

76. Due to the lack of available information, we are unable to comment on the social and political unity of Dalit entrepreneurs and Dalit labourers to combat upper-caste domination. However, the case study of Arni (a district in Tamil Nadu) by Basile and Barbara Harriss-White points out that differential class positions prevent the Dalit entrepreneur from allying with a Dalit labour. They give the example of Dalit urban sanitary workers in Arni who are organised, and have muscle power as well as the numbers, but represent interests contradictory to those of Dalit businessmen. See Elisabetta Basile and Barbara Harriss-White, 'Corporative Capitalism: Civil Society and the Politics of Accumulation in Small Town India', QEH Working Paper Series – QEH WPS 38, Oxford: Queen Elizabeth House, 2000, pp. 15–21.

77. Thakur is a Kshatriya sub-caste.

78. Kurmis are, generally, a Kshatriya sub-caste (that has acquired some status in states like Gujarat, Andhra Pradesh, through the process of sanskritisation). The government classifies them as Other Backward Classes.

79. Chamars are a Dalit sub-caste.

80. Dhobis are a Dalit sub-caste.

81. André Béteille, 'The Reproduction of Inequality: Occupation, Caste and Family', *Contributions to Indian Sociology*, 1991, 3: 3–28.

82. Ibid., p. 26.

83. As told to us by a general merchant in Lucknow.

84. Deshastha Brahmins are a Hindu Brahmin sub-caste, mostly residing in Maharashtra.

85. Bhonsles belong to the clan of Marathas, a dominant Marathi-speaking caste of warriors, commoners and peasants.

86. As narrated by a sanitary goods shop owner at Pune.
87. A caveat is in order. When we claim that caste still is factor in structuring socio-economic relationships, we try to indicate caste as a social block with a clear demarcation between upper-castes and lower castes. Upper-castes as a social group constitution of myriad jatis have more affinity with each other inspite of their internal differences.
88. Pierre Bourdieu, 'The Forms of Capital', Richard Nice transl., Goettingen: Otto Schartz & Co., 1983, pp. 183–98. We use the concept of social capital in the manner deployed by Bourdieu, who was interested in understanding how social classes reproduce themselves and explained how it was command over durable relationships which facilitates access to (economic) resources. In this sense, social capital is not an attribute of society as a whole but an instrument of power which in turn differs between classes.
89. As told to us by a general merchant in Lucknow.
90. As narrated by an ironsmith in Vidisha.
91. As mentioned by a leather goods manufacturer in Agra.
92. As a leather goods manufacturer in Kanpur informed us.
93. As described by a teacher who runs coaching classes.
94. Harriss-White, *India Working*, p. 50.
95. Agarwal is a surname used by Vaishyas/Baniyas.
96. Another caveat is in order. Béteille's formulation is not based in the context of market operations, but only among the service class Indian belonging to the middle and upper classes. However, his conclusion has an important influence on subsequent scholarly discussion on caste, family and inequality.
97. Elisabetta Basile and Barbara Harriss-White, 'Corporative Capitalism: Civil Society and the Politics of Accumulation in Small Town India', QEH Working Paper Series – QEH WPS 38, Oxford: Queen Elizabeth House, 2000, pp. 39–47; Harriss-White, *India Working*, p. 197.
98. As a corporatist project, caste plays three crucial roles: it provides the ideological backcloth, supplies the institutional structure on which corporatist institutions evolve, and helps to create the overlap between economy and society. See Basile and Harriss-White, 'Corporative Capitalism'.
99. Suvira Jaiswal, 'Caste: Ideology and Context', *Social Scientist*, 1997, 25 (288): 10.
100. Pethe is a surname found among Chitpawan/Konkanastha Brahmins in Maharashtra.

101.

	Representation of Dalits in Services of all the Central Ministries/Departments as on 1 January 1999			Representation of Dalits in Services of all the Central Ministries/Departments as on 1 January 2003			Representation of Dalits in Services of all the Central Ministries/Departments as on 1 January 2005		
Group	Total Employees	SCs	Group	Total Employees	SCs	Group	Total Employees	SCs
A	93,520	10,558 (11.29)	A	85,938	10,256 (11.93)	A	80,589	9,551 (11.9)
B	104,963	13,306 (12.68)	B	181,905	26,040 (14.32)	B	139,958	19,194 (13.7)
C	239,642,694	378,115 (15.78)	C	2,121,697	345,718 (16.29)	C	2,036,103	333,708 (16.4)
D (Excluding sweepers)	949,353	189,761 (19.99)	D (Excluding Sweepers)	879,805	158,206 (17.98)	D (Excluding sweepers)	767,224	140,469 (18.3)
Sweepers	96,435	63,233 (65.57)	Sweepers	126,131	73,881 (58.57)	Sweepers	61,174	48,067 (59.2)
Total excluding sweepers	3,544,262	591,740 (16.7)	Total excluding sweepers	3,269,345	540,220 (16.52)	Total excluding sweepers	3,023,874	502,922 (16.63)
Total including sweepers	3,640,697	654,973 (17.99)	Total including sweepers	3,395,476	614,101 (18.09)	Total including sweepers	3,105,048	550,989 (17.74)

As is clear from this table, the bulk of the Dalit population is concentrated in the lower rungs, especially in the category of sweepers (a caste profession).

Source: National Commission for Scheduled Castes and Scheduled Tribes, Sixth Report, 1999–2000, p. 182; National Commission for Scheduled Caste, First Annual Report 2004–05, p. 183; National Commission for Scheduled Caste, Second Annual Report 2005–06, p. 179.

Note: Figures in parenthesis denote percentage.

102. Abrams, 'Notes on the Difficulty of Studying the State', p. 76.
103. The issue of the economic empowerment of Dalits through markets has been most influentially argued by the Bhopal Declaration.
104. This is not to deny that political democracy in India does not use informal networks to mobilise votes but still, the basic principle of political democracy is one person one vote.
105. Deepak Nayyar, 'Economic Development and Political Democracy: Interaction of Economics and Politics in Independent India', *Economic and Political Weekly*, 1998, XXXIV (49): 3121–22.
106. Harriss-White, *India Working*, pp. 50–53.
107. Besides caste, Harriss-White includes gender, religion and age as crucial social factors in regulating market outcomes.

FIVE

Market-based Profit Accumulation and Civil Society

◘

The previous chapters give us enough evidence to conclude that economic transactions in market settings are, more often than not, embedded in social relationships structured around caste locations. This is particularly true when it comes to market relationships between upper-castes and Dalits. This brings us to the important question of the relationships between caste and market-based accumulation processes, that is, caste and markets. To this end, this chapter critically examines the role (supportive or otherwise) that formal and informal civil society institutions play in the endeavours of Dalit entrepreneurs to earn profits in the markets. The chapter argues that the role of formal and informal institutions can be best captured through the study of the character of caste-inspired social networks in the accumulation process in the markets. While doing so, the chapter engages with the dominant theories of civil society and puts forward a case for viewing civil society as the site of accumulation rather than only as a site for democratisation.[1]

Towards Understanding Accumulation in Markets: The Primacy of Social Networks

The discussion in Chapter Three has shown us that dominant economic theories are almost blind to the role of social identities in influencing market outcomes. Chapters Three and Four also deal with the role of formal and informal institutions in shaping the accumulative endeavours of Dalit entrepreneurs. More importantly, the third chapter contested the faith of dominant theoretical frameworks that social identities will gradually dissolve in the face of market competition.[2] It was the 'school of social embeddedness' that enabled us to make theoretical sense of the business histories of Dalit entrepreneurs studied in this book. In other words, it provided us a framework to understand how social networks find their basis in caste identities and influence market outcomes. The narratives of the Dalit business persons also informed us that the institution of caste re-adapts itself and promotes market competition instead of restricting it. They also flag the crucial role of ideology in sustaining the function of social identities in the context of market-based competition. Similarly, the narratives in Chapter Four help us to argue that social identities are invariably articulated by and in turn influence the formal institutions constituting the state, leading to informalisation of the state's apparatus. Chapters Three and Four apprise us of institutionalised patterns, both in the realm of markets as well as the state, which have a structural propensity to operate under the influence of caste and in turn lead to unfavourable inclusion of Dalit entrepreneurs when they enter the markets as owners of capital. Instead of just documenting the shortcomings of the neo-classical approach and numerous analytical understandings of the state, this chapter elaborates on the institutionalised patterns which contribute to profit accumulation for upper-caste business persons as well as to the adverse inclusion of Dalit entrepreneurs.

Social Networks in the Markets

The study of social networks in the markets entails the examination of how markets operate as social structures. In recent times, social networks have been deployed as important conceptual apparatuses to understand socio-economic interaction of individuals in a typical market setting. Nan Lin has used the concept of *social resources* — temporary and borrowed resources accessible through one's direct (immediate family) and indirect ties (friends' friend) — to explain differential returns in the labour market.[3] Granovetter uses the concept of *embeddedness* to stress the role of personal relations and structures (or networks) of such relations in generating information and trust, and discouraging malfeasance in any economic transaction.[4] In other words, Granovetter argues that economic relationships between individuals do not exist in an abstract idealised market but are embedded in actual social networks. He also invokes the concept of *strength of weak ties* to describe a market situation that enables individuals to reach people who are not accessible via strong ties,[5] a concept further developed by Ronald Burt.[6] Burt, while looking for the reasons behind competitive advantage, points to the possibility of *structural holes* within non-redundant relationships that aid the flow of information and in turn allow benefits to some market players over others. Burt highlights the crucial advantage that may be enjoyed by individuals who can tie into multiple networks that are largely separated from one another. The availability of channels of information and other resources that allow flow from one network to the other are to be understood as structural holes in the network.

These sociological concepts are analytically insightful and provide a robust conceptual apparatus to document and analyse the social instruments deployed to compete in the markets. However, being an empirical exercise, the stress is on the role of information acquired though relationships based on trust.

In the Indian context, social networks acquire their roots in the dominant religious discourse, shared meanings, cultural practices, and local beliefs, which form the basis of collective action. Besides providing such information, social networks facilitate economic endeavours in the markets through numerous actions, both economic and non-economic in nature. These include supplying ideological justification for the exclusion of certain market players from legitimate economic endeavours, providing access to state resources, regulating the entry and exit of labour and informal credit, facilitating business by providing access to the required physical space, deploying the collective strength of social networks to reward its members, and punish market competitors by means that may include violent intimidation.

The social network when seen through this prism may seem similar to the social structure as conceptualised in the literature thus far.[7] Are social structure and social network one and the same then? We argue that when the social structure is viewed through the lens of social network we understand the existing social relations, at a given point of time, which connect certain individuals together. The social network approach is then fundamentally a relation-centred approach. It provides us with the flexibility to examine short term social ties forged in a market situation which are derived from a long standing social structure. For instance, caste as an institution has long endured as a social structure. Despite undergoing considerable sociological and economic change, it is still quite influential in determining how individuals connect with one another.[8] In our context, caste is a long-standing social structure which translates into a 'particular' social phenomenon when it connects different individuals and facilitates the formation of social networks. Therefore, studying social structures is not the same as studying social networks, though the latter draws from the former. A particular social relationship between two or more persons in the market (social networks) exists only as part of a wide network of social relations, involving many other persons (social structure). This social network is the object of our investigation.

The four components of social networks which aid in profit accumulation are listed below.

The Normative Component

Normative roots of social networks consist of norms and informally binding regulations that are mutually recognised and enforceable sanctions against violators. These norms and rules could either facilitate or hinder economic transactions in the market. In existing economic theory it is argued that the robustness of social networks is based on the level of trust which members of the network enjoy with each other. Trust acquires the shape of informal institutions and forms the basis for enforcing mutually acceptable norms and sanctions. The basis of trust between members of a social network is perceived uncertainty. In the face of uncertainty, the members are willing to take calculated risks and trust others. Trust is not altruistic in nature; it is promoted by self-interest. Members believe that they will be better off in the long run (even if they face short term loss) if they abide by the established and accepted norms of the social network(s).[9] In other words, trust acquires an economic function when market players follow the expected norms and help each other by sharing information about mutually beneficial economic transactions.

Moving away from the economic perspective discussed above, we can situate the basis of social networks in the norms governing the social structure. For instance, the normative principles of caste bequeath norms which reproduce social relations and institutions in a hierarchal order. In other words, the ideology of caste normatively mandates the *maintenance of hierarchy* in relationships between different social groups. Hierarchy becomes the basis of difference between 'us'/the self and 'them'/the other. For the difference to be maintained and hierarchy to be socially legitimised, *status quo* in relationships between different social groups has to be retained through a normative framework of socio-cultural, political and economic relationships, practices and statutes. For instance, the normative framework privileges and naturalises the rights of the upper-caste(s) over those of lower caste(s), and the latter is expected to serve the labour and other economic interests of the upper-castes.[10] This normative understanding of caste becomes the basis of social networks where the upper-castes, though divided by vertical and horizontal class location as well as different sub-caste locations, form a loose social network to mutually help and safeguard each other's economic interests vis-à-vis Dalit entrepreneurs. This is not to say that upper-caste entrepreneurs are not part of other social networks based on their sub-caste or sub-sector of trade and business. In the Indian context, there is often an overlap between the two.

The Structural Component

The second component of the social networks affecting Dalit entrepreneurs is structural. The structural component generally acquires its roots in the normative constructs of social relations. Accordingly, norms can be functionally defined as behavioural expectations that are at least partially fulfilled by the majority of the economic agents in the markets. Norms influence and shape structures. In other words, structures represent constraints on the options that individuals and collectives are likely to exercise (shared rules), and also identify categories of social actors and their appropriate and socially accepted activities or relationships. However, these structural constraints are open to modification and alterations over time through individual choices and actions.

In a market relationship, a Dalit entrepreneur is connected to upper-caste entrepreneurs in a one-to-one relationship (Figure 5.1). This primarily means that social ties in the markets are structurally conditioned in a manner that Dalit entrepreneurs either do not have any social networks to bank upon or the networks are extremely weak. On the other hand, upper-caste entrepreneurs are not only connected to each other (social networks), they are also able to do business with Dalit entrepreneurs on terms mostly set by them (Figure 5.1). This argument is somewhat similar to certain tenets of the theory of structuration as put forth by Giddens.[11] In the theory of structuration, it is argued that cultural/social constraints do not completely determine human actions. Instead, structures set bounds

Figure 5.1 Dalit Entrepreneurs in Market Networks

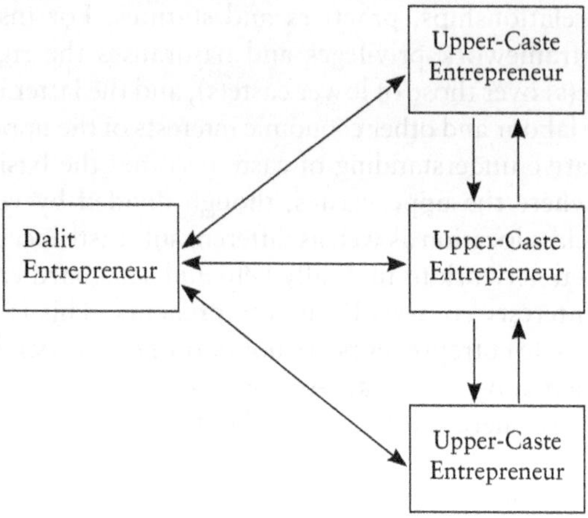

Source: Author.

on the individual/group rationality by constraining their actions, thereby increasing the possibility of a certain kind of behaviour. However, both perfect rationality as well as bounded rationality is rare. They are reworked and modified by individuals as per the existing socio-economic, political situation. Therefore, we find that Dalits are now able to enter the market to trade in goods and services, something that would not have been appreciated or allowed by the upper-castes earlier. However, they are unable to participate in social networks facilitating and regulating market transactions, which continue to be controlled by the upper-castes. These structural conditions leave Dalit entrepreneurs with no choice but to operate in the market on terms set by the upper-caste entrepreneurs (also refer to discussion in Chapter Three).

The Resource Component

Resources are the means through which economic agents in the market endeavour to achieve their economic goals.

A key question here is why do businesses controlled by upper-caste entrepreneurs differ from those controlled by Dalits in terms of market penetration and profitability? We look at this question through an analysis of the resources which contribute to profitability and accumulation in business. Here resources comprise wherewithal (both tangible and intangible) that market actors can bank upon as they pursue their goals in the markets. These resources may display individual characteristics as well as network characteristics. Through an analysis of resources, it is possible to understand the structural resources (un)available to market players though their network ties.

In examining the reasons for profitability, a stream of international literature depicts business enterprises as autonomous entities gaining competitive advantage either through external business organisations[12] or through internal resources and capabilities.[13] This formulation signifying the role of atomistic actors competing for profit against each other in the market does not seem to capture the reality of markets which are invariably segmented by social identities. Another stream of international literature fills this gap and points out that businesses are also embedded in social, professional and exchange relationships with other economic agents in the market.[14] In the context of Dalit entrepreneurs in India, several studies (including the detailed fieldwork captured in this book) recognise the social embeddedness of market relationships, while they explore the reasons for the lower profitability of Dalit-owned economic enterprises in comparison to similarly situated upper-caste economic enterprises.[15] The reason for such an unfavourable outcome for Dalits usually lies in their inability to access network resources. Network resources imply the ability to use one's own resources as well as the resources of his or her contacts.

Outcomes in the markets are contingent on resources available in the markets as well the ability to use the power of the state in a typical market situation. Caste provides a basis to undermine the formal basis of markets by facilitating informal collusions and supporting the creation of social networks. In other words, embedded relationships, both horizontal and vertical, with suppliers, customers, and competitors on the one hand and state officials on the other, help the upper-caste entrepreneurs to lower their transaction costs. Arguing differently, despite huge differences within them, the upper-castes are more likely to be in a position to use their kith and kin relationships, marriage alliances, camaraderie developed in common social spaces (for instance, temples, clubs, social collectives like neighbourhood associations, morning walk groups, etc.) as informal resources in the markets.

Upper-caste identity, ideological compatibility and the conse-quent acceptance of basic social norms governing inter-social group relationships enable upper-caste entrepreneurs to carve out social relationships with other similarly situated individuals, both in the realm of markets as well as the state. Access to state officials facili-tates procurement of licenses for business endeavours, lowers the evaluation of tax (especially sales tax), deploys the power of state to threaten competitors, makes possible priority/preferential treat-ment for leasing physical space to do business, allows violations of municipal laws without any fear of penalty, etc. Social networks also foster close relationships with the local units of political parties and their leaders in order to access the state's resources and influence state officials through political contacts. It is a two-way relationship where political parties seek electoral favours in return for helping social networks with state-controlled resources.

In the realm of markets, caste-inspired networks enable members to source short term loans and procure labour from their business peers in order to fulfil their business commitments. Besides this, social networks also create conditions for blocking the entry of new market entrants at best, or at least including them unfavourably (Figure 5.2). This brings us to the last characteristic of social net-works, that is, its dynamism. The dynamic component of the market will also explain the unequal relationship between upper-caste and Dalit entrepreneurs.

The Dynamic Component

An analysis of the dynamic component of the social network helps us to interpret changing social relationships in the markets from the standpoint of Dalits. The very fact that they can enter the market and trade in goods and services is a robust indicator of changing social relationships. However, Dalits perceive that the change is not deep or wide enough to create an equal economic and social relationship between Dalits and upper-castes.

The dynamic component of social networks also tells us that in market-based competition, the strength of social networks is invoked by the upper-castes while competing with both other upper-caste business rivals as well as Dalits. Social alliances are configured and re-configured to meet the demands of the market. However, upper-caste social networks created to compete in the market against simi-larly situated caste peers (upper-castes) do not derive their strength

Figure 5.2 Social Networks, Resources and Market Outcomes

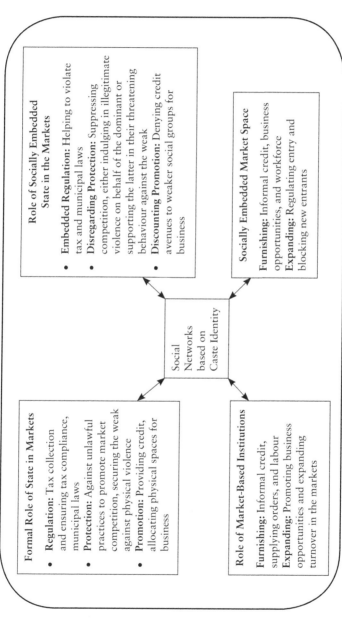

Role of Socially Embedded State in the Markets

- **Embedded Regulation:** Helping to violate tax and municipal laws
- **Disregarding Protection:** Suppressing competition, either indulging in illegitimate violence on behalf of the dominant or supporting the latter in their threatening behaviour against the weak
- **Discounting Promotion:** Denying credit avenues to weaker social groups for business

Socially Embedded Market Space

Furnishing: Informal credit, business opportunities, and workforce
Expanding: Regulating entry and blocking new entrants

Social Networks based on Caste Identity

Formal Role of State in Markets

- **Regulation:** Tax collection and ensuring tax compliance, municipal laws
- **Protection:** Against unlawful practices to promote market competition, securing the weak against physical violence
- **Promotion:** Providing credit, allocating physical spaces for business

Role of Market-Based Institutions

Furnishing: Informal credit, supplying orders, and labour
Expanding: Promoting business opportunities and expanding turnover in the markets

Source: Author.

from the ideology of caste. They are forged in the wake of market competition and are dissolved after the objective has been realised. On the other hand, when the logic of social networks is invoked against Dalits, it is relatively long-lasting in its effects.

The dynamism inherent in markets allows Dalits to gain an entry but the terms of business interaction are mostly unfavourable for them. They are generally not in a position to access informal credit or other resources held by the upper-caste–controlled social networks. While the state and its institutions are seen to step in proactively to safeguard the economic interests of the upper-castes, the same institutions are perceived to be inactive or absent when Dalits require state intervention to protect their business interests. The state is often seen to be aggressively jeopardizing the economic interest of the Dalits, especially when the upper-castes are (in)direct beneficiaries of its action. Access to the state and its resources is gained not only through family and caste relationships, but also by paying rent to state officials. In such a situation, the social network of the upper-castes helps them bargain for lower rents, which is not possible for Dalits, thereby raising the transaction costs of the latter. Moreover, even if Dalits are able to get access to the social network controlling state and market-based resources through some social or political links, they are not able to summon these resources every time they require such help. On the other hand, the upper-castes can bank on these resources repeatedly. This weak social position of Dalit entrepreneurs forces them to accept the adverse terms of business relationships defined and executed by the upper-castes.

Summarising the Role of Caste-Inspired Social Networks

Social networks attempt to maintain the social hierarchy between upper-castes and Dalits in the face of continuous protest and assertion by the Dalits. In their political role, social networks help their members to lobby for their interests within the apparatus of the state. Social networks are also vehicles for political mobilisation. Local political leaders vie for their support during electoral contests. This two-way relationship, where politicians need social networks and the latter require the favour of political leaders to access state resources, creates specific conditions where the power of the state becomes the resource of social networks and vice-versa. In their economic avatar, social networks help their members to create and sustain informal institutions of credit, regulate labour and guard the chain of supply and demand in the interests of their members. We can safely draw a few conclusions from the above description of the role of caste-inspired social networks that invariably help accumulation and profit generation in the markets.

First, caste provides an institutional avenue to social networks to create conditions for overlap between society, economy and politics. On the one hand, it connects families to the wider society, and on the other to the state and the market. While mediating between different domains, it ensures that interests and views articulated in any one particular domain (eg. family/society) are reflected and expressed in other domains (eg. state and markets). In effect, the boundaries between state, market and civil society are blurred and consequently, a new conceptual space is created where these three elements (state, market and society) interact and produce an institutionalised structure for the exclusion of and discrimination against Dalits in the market. This can be termed as the *exclusionary role* of caste in the realm of the market.

Second, while creating the conditions for overlap, caste-inspired social networks are able to bring about convergence between the hierarchical notion of social structure and economic interests favouring the members of upper-caste-controlled social networks. The ideology of the caste system ordaining a lower social status to Dalits is sought to be invoked and cemented by the upper-castes when they face tough market competition from Dalit business peers. Dalits are forced to carry out economic transactions in the markets on unequal terms structured by upper-caste market peers. If they refuse to abide by these, the sociological understanding of their caste location is invoked to either push them outside the market or to force them to trade with upper-castes on terms which are far more beneficial to the latter. In this sense, caste is perceptibly structured to *augment the economic interests* of the upper-castes.

Third, a caste-inspired social network allows its members (upper-castes) access to the state apparatus — both administrative and coercive — which in turn provides them the social strength to threaten or indulge in actual violence against non-members (Dalits) without any fear of penalty from the state, especially in cases where the Dalits question dominant caste-inspired socio-economic norms. Caste, thus, becomes a basis of coercion, hierarchy, conformity, manipulation, unaccountability, and corruption. This feature can be characterised as the *coercive and manipulative* avatar of caste.

Finally, caste becomes the basis for translating individual interests into collective consciousness. This can be seen as a dialectical interaction where the collective worldview of caste influences the individual, who in turn reinforces the collective belief through social practices and actions. This is the *collectivisation* spirit of caste.

Thus, the ideology of caste practised by upper-castes impinges on the interests of Dalit entrepreneurs in the markets through four manifest attributes — its exclusionary characteristic, the feature of augmenting the economic interests of the dominant caste, the power to coerce and manipulate and lastly, the basis it provides for collective action as discussed earlier.

In this context, we need to discuss how caste identity can play such a crucial role, especially when we are informed of the 'partial dissolution of a rigid, segmental and hierarchical social structure . . . with increasing social mobility, both horizontal and vertical'.[16] It has also been pointed out that 'the allegiance of the individual to his village, his sub-caste and his lineage has, to some extent, loosened. Along with this, the individual is being progressively drawn into networks of interpersonal relations which cut right across the boundaries of village, sub-caste and lineage'.[17]

In spite of social loosening, the upper-caste identity is still a force to reckon with, given that this social group still commands the majority of resources — economic, cultural and social — available to society as whole.[18] The upper-caste identity is still perceived to be consolidated in its disapproval of Dalits. With the increasing political assertion of Dalits and subsequent successful inroads they have made in electoral democracy,

> the attitude of upper-caste is seen to be quite contemptuous since they are perceived to be undeserving and still getting access to the dwindling state's benefits (jobs due to reservation).... It is normal to quote some stray incidents to put across the point that Dalits are unworthy of senior government jobs because they tend to be corrupt, arrogant and badly behaved.[19]

Second, the cultural capital historically acquired by the dominant caste along with family and kith and kin helps them to forge relationships with upper-caste members who may belong to a different sub-caste.[20] These social relationships are further strengthened through social spaces like temples, caste associations, upper-caste religious and social gatherings, festivals, clubs, etc., which provide avenues for social interaction and the consequent strengthening of social relationships. Third, the relationship with other upper-caste members is often cemented through marriage and conjugal ties either within the same sub-caste or with a member of a different sub-caste located on the right side of the purity and pollution ladder.[21] These institutions, though informal in nature, are powerful and instrumental in connecting people who belong to upper-castes. Together with these reasons, the social contempt against Dalits further helps to create robust 'closed' social networks exclusively representing the upper-castes.[22]

We have explained that social networks carved out on the basis of caste perform a variety of social, political and economic roles which contribute to profit accumulation in the markets. How do we understand the role of social networks inspired by caste location? Caste becomes the basis for a peculiar context-specific social solidarity, an essential feature for social networks to survive and perform their expected functions.

Therefore, the primary question we need to address is: can caste be considered a specific form of the Indian civil society, a thesis accepted by several authors?[23] We propose that it is indeed, and elaborate our argument by situating it in the existing debate on civil society.

Caste as Civil Society

Civil society is a concept with a long intellectual history. In the Indian context, it has been interpreted variously. We pick up the dominant strand of the civil society debate in India and argue against it to point out that civil society should be seen primarily as a site of accumulation, a thesis which is also supported by the four attributes of caste discussed earlier in the chapter, as well as by the traditional theorists on civil society. However, this understanding does not sit well with the otherwise rich debate in India on civil society.

Scholars pursuing the liberal democratic tradition argue that civil society cannot be detached from the state and has to be seen as part of the democratic constitutional state.[24] Mahajan draws from the theoretical framework provided by Hegel and suggests that a modern constitutional universal state (embodied in universal law) becomes the basis for assuring non-discrimination while promoting social equality.[25] In substance, she argues that in order to sustain, civil society requires a set of rational impersonal rules which only the state can guarantee. Béteille, another noted scholar within the liberal democratic school, conceptualises civil society as mediating institutions (universities, schools, libraries, banks, hospitals, newspapers, publishing houses, etc.) free from the state as well as from any traditional loyalties.[26] It is very clear that these characteristics of civil society do not complement the experience of Dalit entrepreneurs. Scholars point out that these authors discuss civil society and its associated concepts only as normative ideals of the liberal ideology and do not situate them in the actual social context on ground. This is a serious limitation as it prevents any understanding about the prevalent state of affairs,[27] about how the state can foster a uniform relationship with civil society and its citizens, irrespective of all other identities.[28]

The second argument on civil society has been put forth by the (neo) Marxists and left-of-centre liberal scholars.[29] They understand civil society as the realm outside and against the state, a domain of new social movements, civil liberties movements and various other protest formations. These movements and protest collectives are seen as the basis of substantive democracy,[30] or a foundation of creative society calling for a decentralised, participatory and accountable state,[31] or acting as a counter hegemonic force against the state trampling the rights of its citizens.[32] Kothari, a non–Marxist, progressive liberal scholar, also argues that civil society is an arena outside the state which has the potential to empower people and push the agenda of humane governance.[33] We argue that Dalits would agree with the substance of these Indian Marxist arguments that view civil society as the site of struggle, protest and assertion. For instance, Omvedt as well as Guru draw our attention to the fact that all the anti-caste movements starting from the 19th century, although placed outside the state, sought to establish, enlarge and make increasingly effective the public sphere, and carve out a basis of democratic citizenship.[34] In spite of this broad similarity with the Marxist understanding of civil society, there are certain crucial departures. The Marxist notion, while situating civil society outside the state, tends to homogenise it, thereby ignoring the social diversity as well as horizontal and vertical social differences within civil society. Therefore, the particulars are subsumed under the universal. In other words, this perspective fails to recognise that the individuals who constitute civil society are divided along the axes of caste, gender, religion, and other social identities. This is the precisely the reason why Dalits would not agree even with an intellectually nuanced conception of a political society — a site where political negotiations and transactions are pursued by subaltern groups excluded by the state and modernist civil society.[35]

In the context of our study, the dominant form of civil society experienced by Dalits is not emancipatory but exclusionary, coercive and supportive of the economic interests of the upper-castes. Caste becomes a dominant form of civil society because of its ability to translate individual interests into the interest of a collective. It helps its members to develop their own norms and regulations for interacting with Dalits on the one hand and the state and markets on the other. They are informal in nature but nonetheless institutionalised. Thus, it is in civil society that the seeds of exclusion and marginalisation are sown and nurtured. In the experience of Dalits, the institutions of state and market are reflections of the exclusionary trends present in the realm of civil society.

Therefore, conceptualising civil society as aligned with the state (liberal democratic conception) or against the state (Marxist conception) does not sit well with the experience of Dalit entrepreneurs. In effect, caste is able to throw up a unique socio-political and economic condition where the boundaries between the state, market and civil society are blurred. It can be seen as functioning neither along with the state nor against it.

In order to understand the role of civil society in shaping accumulative instincts, we need to fall back on the authors who do not see civil society as the primary vehicle of democratisation or as only facilitating the unfolding of the rule of law, impersonal institutions and universal state. We need to recognise that some of the traditional theorists coming from diverse ideological standpoints also view civil society as a site of accumulation. This point which is extremely crucial to our study has not received emphasis in the Indian debate on civil society (put forth both by Marxist as well as liberals), though they draw their theoretical framework from these very traditional theorists.

Accordingly, we will draw from three traditional theorists to emphasise that civil society is a site which supports accumulation in the markets. However, while doing so, we also point towards a few crucial points which Dalits would agree with and some others which they would oppose.

In the first conception of civil society, we put forth the views of Locke, Adam Smith and Hegel. These writers come from different ideological vantage points but seem to agree on two important counts: a. they view civil society as a site of accumulation; b. they consider the state a regulator and protector of rights whether in an active/positive role (of guaranteeing social economic entitlements) or a negative one of protecting liberties under *laissez faire* conditions. For Locke, the status of the citizen, which essentially means his/her right to life, liberty and property, can only be acquired and legally guaranteed in civil society.[36] The defence of the right to property and justification of the consequent inequality set the tone for liberal bourgeois civil society. Although Locke does not talk about 'some special mechanism — for example, the market or division of labour — which could engender and sustain civil society',[37] the logical conclusion of a Lockean perspective would be that markets and commercial classes should obey the rule of law and the administrative state. Following Locke, Hegel provides a more nuanced and penetrating understanding — the civil society in the modern world 'intervene[s] between the family and the state'.[38] True to the bourgeois democratic spirit, civil society is constituted by individuals who belong to different classes that are neither divinely ordained (for instance, the Indian caste system left the division of classes to the accident of birth) nor politically constructed (for instance, the allotment of classes to individuals left to the ruling class).[39] However, civil society for Hegel is contradictory in nature. The contradiction is manifested in the increasing accumulation through the economic expansion of civil society, while at the same time the mass of people lack the purchasing power to enjoy the fruits of the civil society (market) which in turn results in 'distress and dependence of the class tied to work of that sort'.[40] This analysis of civil society leads Hegel to call for an intervention of a universal state.

If Locke implicitly and Hegel explicitly want the state to step in to temper the inequality and oppression experienced due to the expansion of civil society, Adam Smith is completely against state intervention of any kind. Smith distinguishes between the civilised society of economic activity and the political society in the sphere of state. The former is constituted by self-regulating independent networks of economic relations among individuals and groups competing in the market.[41] A civilised society produces the best results under *laissez faire* conditions. In Smith's view, it is civilised because the essence of market exchange is not based on deception or domination but persuasion.

There are some important lessons to be learnt from these three conceptions of civil society. First, all of them converge on the viewpoint that civil society is indeed a site of accumulation. It is in the realm of civil society that the accumulative endeavours of individuals are actualised. Further, inequality also acquires its roots in civil society. However, it would be crucial to note that these inequalities are based on class distinction and not ordained by any religious belief. For Dalit entrepreneurs, class-based inequality is a universal reality, but their marginalisation is more specific and is shaped by caste and not class location. Dalit entrepreneurs will want a universal state abolishing caste-based inequality and also moderating inequalities based on class location. The Hegelian form of the state has much to contribute towards the actualisation of the Dalits' normative vision, but the existing state is seen to be quite biased in favour of upper-castes and thereby contributes to the unfavourable inclusion of Dalits in the markets. Further, for Dalits, the Smithian state would be a social disaster in a normative sense since it will not leave any space to envision an institution that can assure rectificatory justice. Last, but not the least, Hegel's and Smith's conceptions of civil society only partially explain the experience of Dalit entrepreneurs in markets. The respective theories are however powerful enough to explain the blurring of the boundaries between civil society and markets which in turn results in class-based inequality. But at the same time, their theoretical articulation, contrary to the experience of Dalits, sees the state as separate and independent of forces operating in the realm of civil society and markets.

The second conception of civil society represented by the Marxist school addresses this theoretical lacuna of seeing civil society as separate from the state. The Marxist theoretician, whether subscribing to the instrumental or deterministic approach, sees the state as upholding the class interest of the dominant classes.[42] Civil society in a capitalist state emerges with the destruction of the institutions which gave expression to feudal relationships, while also providing the freedom to own property.[43] Civil society is seen as the site of crass materialism where the right to private property is cemented and private accumulation is carried on, and political institutions (state) are merely a cover to sustain and promote particular interests.[44] However, this particular interest has been seen to be promoted more by force rather than consent. Gramsci introduced a fundamental innovation in Marxist thought by arguing that civil society does not belong to the sub-structure/material base, but to the superstructure.[45] While agreeing with Marx that civil society is the sphere of accumulation, Gramsci insightfully adds that it is also a domain where the consent of the subalterns to be ruled and dominated is negotiated, obtained and sustained by the dominant classes. Civil society thus comprises not only all economic relationships but also political and cultural relationships. There is an inter-penetration of civil society into the state and vice versa, which in turn becomes the source of hegemony (consent backed by force) of the ruling block.[46]

Dalit entrepreneurs, while experiencing unfavourable inclusion in the markets, will appreciate the Marxist school in that it recognises that civil society, state and markets are collapsed in the interest of the dominant class. However, they would still be uncomfortable on certain counts. First, their experience indicates that class by itself is not a homogenous category; it is divided by various social identities. Technically, the Dalit entrepreneurs and the upper-caste business peers belong to same class but different caste. This crucial difference enables the upper-caste entrepreneurs to extract disproportionate, more often than not illegitimate and illegal, favours from the state and its officials.[47] Second, the electoral institutions of a democratic state may allow Dalits to become a part of the state. However, this does not mean that their political empowerment can easily and surely translate into economic empowerment. The state and its institutions are still seen to be dominated by upper-castes that only offer lip service to their real economic cause. Third, they do not believe that political agencies will spearhead and articulate their socio-economic interests. In other words, Dalits do not extend unquestioned consent to the views of the state and those articulated by the dominant caste through socio-political and religious institutions controlled by them in the realm of civil society. In other words, the Dalit entrepreneurs are not under the spell of the 'hegemony of the ruling block' in the Gramscian sense. Civil society for them is also a realm of continuous political struggle and protest against the domination of the upper-castes. Their successful attempts to enter the markets as owners of capital as well as the succinct articulation of their experience of unfavourable inclusion is by itself a testimony that they are contemptuously aware of the numerous interconnected socio-economic and political patterns ensuring they remain socially inferior.

Thus, caste in its avatar of a dominant form of civil society successfully lobbies and represents the economic interest of its members, both in the market and the state. It is in this background that Basile and Harriss-White undertake an exploration crucially missed in the debate on civil society in India.[48] They set themselves the task of understanding 'within the set of institutions underpinning capitalist accumulation, what is the role played by civil social organisation'.[49] Social structure of accumulation implies that capitalism cannot be reduced to the market, and the market to the economic domain, and therefore seeks to examine the complex of social institutions in which accumulation is embedded.[50] Harriss-White in her later work shows that the economy, especially at the local level, is regulated by social institutions of caste, religion, gender, and age.[51] For Basile and Harriss-White, caste groups are dynamic institutions and indeed a specific form of civil society, because they often take an organised form and articulate the interest — economic as well as political — of their members.[52]

In the context of our study, caste as an institution performs the crucial role of civil society (helping the accumulative endeavours) by unfolding the politics of markets — use of formal and informal institutions by individuals and groups towards achieving their goals in a typical market setting.[53] Generally, such actions are pursued or undertaken by an individual or a group on account of perceived differences between social groups ('us' and 'them'). Perceived difference is a sociological category with the avowed aim to retain hierarchical social relationships between different social groups. In the case of caste system-inspired relationships, it is legitimised by religious doctrines. In a market relationship, sociological beliefs are invoked and deployed by upper-castes to discriminate against Dalits (earning them less economic returns when other tangible attributes are similar) and thus create market entry and operational bottlenecks. Dalits perceive that the invocation of sociological beliefs to sustain discrimination in a modern democratic setting is an instrument to stifle the possibility of increased and intense market competition. Therefore, the use of all available formal and informal institutions to retain the difference between 'us' and 'them', in a political environment where the macro institutions of democracy and economic regulations have ensured the entry of Dalits in the markets as the owners of capital, is termed as unfavourable inclusion. In other words, Dalit capital is included in the markets dominated by the upper-castes but on unfavourable and unequal terms.

Thus, caste helps to develop a 'set of concrete interpersonal relationships linking the individual to other individuals who are members of diverse systems of enduring groups and categories'.[54] These individuals can be market-based entrepreneurs, state officials, religious leaders, local musclemen, or members and officials of various caste-based associations. In other words, caste when understood as civil society helps us to appreciate the instrumentality by which relationships based on 'trust' and socio-cultural compatibility are forged, religious and caste values respecting social hierarchy between social groups are invoked and practised, sanctions on individuals disregarding the norms of caste-based hierarchy are imposed and, in extreme circumstances, violence is used in an attempt to preserve social dominance. The individuals upholding these values are also members of the state and markets. It is not unusual for these beliefs and values to be reflected in the actions of state officials while they discharge their duties, or in the business dealings of market entrepreneurs.

Therefore, a group of people who have a broadly similar socio-cultural, economic and political worldviews and also command various types of resources are drawn to help each other in a typical market situation. This includes regulation of credit and labour supply in the market, procurement of market contracts, setting prices, regulating the entry of new market players, etc. This in turn contributes to the accumulative endeavours of the entrepreneurs belonging to upper-castes, who strategically use their access to state officials and informal regulatory institutions present in the markets to ensure that Dalit entrepreneurs have no choice but to continue doing business with them under adverse terms of exchange. Any disrespect by the Dalit entrepreneurs towards the upper-caste-established code of conduct governing market operations may result in systematic and permanent exclusion or even physical violence against them.

While caste as a form of civil society explicitly helps in the process of accumulation, it unfolds an institutional process that results in a unique possibility of blurring the line separating the state, markets and civil society. Civil society as a site of accumulation is not a new conceptualisation. As discussed above, the traditional theory of civil society, authors as diverse as Locke, Adam Smith, Marx, and Gramsci have earlier pointed out to a similar possibility.

However, before concluding, we would like to reiterate a few specific characteristics of caste as civil society.

Caste as a form of civil society in its accumulative avatar, while blurring the boundaries between state, market and civil society, creates a sort of autonomous space where profit endeavours are materialised and Dalits are unfavourably incorporated in this process. This space, which is the source of discrimination and unfavourable inclusion of Dalits, is actualised at the intersection of state, market and civil society. This intersecting space develops its own rules and norms of socio-economic relationship between upper-castes and Dalits.

Second, this intersecting space is the zone of engagement between the sustained attempts of the upper-castes to discriminate against Dalits who are the owners of capital in the markets and persistent efforts by the latter to strategise, assert and undertake trade in goods and services. As a result of this complex interaction, Dalits are included in the markets but on unfavourable terms.

Finally, this zone is also used by Dalits to employ the same strategy as the upper-castes to seek favours from the state and carve out a network in the realm of markets. However, unlike the upper-castes, their networks are quite weak and cannot be called in for support as and when required. In other words, the caste inspired social networks enable the upper-caste entrepreneurs to unfailingly access formal and informal institutions which facilitate their accumulation endeavours. While Dalits would also like to use similar institutions, they are not always successful in doing so.

It is in this sense that civil society is not only the site of accumulation but also a site of struggle. The claim that it favours the upper-castes in their accumulation endeavours to the disadvantage of Dalits in the markets is also a claim that the Dalit has achieved their current position through sustained struggle and determination to leave behind their history of oppression. Argued differently, it is their successful attempt to leave behind their caste-ordained professions and enter the market as economic agents. However, civil society in the form of caste creates bottlenecks for them and they sincerely hope that their continuous struggle will help them to be included in the market on equal terms.

Notes

1. In line with 'traditional theorists' such as Locke, Smith, Hegel, Marx, and Gramsci.
2. As per these frameworks, social identities restrict market competition and impede institutional change.
3. See Nan Lin, 'Social Resource and Instrumental Action', in Peter Marsden and Nan Lin (eds), *Social Structure and Network Analysis*, Beverly Hills: Sage, 1982, pp. 131–45; Nan Lin, 'Social Resources and Occupational Status Attainment', in R. L. Breiger (ed.), *Social Mobility and Social Structure*, New York: Cambridge University Press, 1990, pp. 247–71.
4. Mark Granovetter, 'Economic Action and Social Structure: The Problem of Embeddedness', *American Journal of Sociology*, November 1985, 91 (3): 481–510.
5. Mark Granovetter, 'The Strength of Weak Ties', *American Journal of Sociology*, May 1973, 78 (6): 1360–80.
6. Ronald Burt, *Structural Holes: The Social Structure of Competition*, Cambridge, MA: Harvard University Press, 1992.
7. See Radcliffe-Brown, 'On Social Structure', *The Journal of the Royal Anthropological Institute of Great Britain and Ireland*, 1940, 70 (1): 1–12.
8. See M. N. Srinivas and André Béteille, 'Networks in Indian Social Structure', *Man*, November–December 1964, 64 (212): 165–68.
9. See G. Akerlof, 'The Market for Lemons: Quality, Uncertainty and the Market Mechanism', *The Quarterly Journal of Economics*, 1970, 84 (3): 488–500; G. Akerlof, 'Labour Contracts and Partial Gift Exchange', *The Quarterly Journal of Economics*, 1982, 97 (4): 543–69; Oliver Williamson, *The Economic Institutions of Capitalism*, New York: Free Press, 1985.
10. The caste system as theorised by Ambedkar [B. R. Ambedkar, 'Caste in India: The Mechanism, Genesis and Development', *Annihilation of Caste*, Jalandhar: Bheema Patrika Publication, 1916, [reprinted 1936], http://www.stopfundinghate.org/resources/AmbedkarAnnihilationofCastes. pdf (accessed on 29 February 2011)] is an economic as well as social organisation of roles and responsibilities in the society. In its pure form, it not only fixes the economic rights (occupation) and social position of each caste by birth, but also delineates socio-economic penalties if an individual transcends occupational boundaries. The occupations are classified as 'pure' and 'polluted', where the former become the domain of upper-caste(s) and the latter a preserve of the lower caste(s). Thus, each individual caste is linked with the other in such a hierarchical manner that privileges of high caste, both in the economic and social domain, become the reason for the subordinate position of the lower

castes. Further, these debilitating features for the lower castes acquire sanction and legitimacy through Hindu religious texts. Also see, C. J. Fuller (ed.), *Caste Today*, New Delhi: Oxford University Press, 1996; M. N. Srinivas, *Caste: Its Twentieth Century Avatar*, New Delhi: Viking, 1996.

11. Anthony Giddens, *New Rules of Sociological Methods*, London: Hutchinson, 1976; Anthony Giddens, *Central Problems in Social Theory*, Berkeley, CA: University of California Press, 1979.

12. For instance, M. E. Porter, *Competitive Strategy*, New York: Free Press, 1980.

13. J. Barney, 'Firm Resources and Sustained Competitive Advantage', *Journal of Management*, 1991, 17 (1): 99–120.

14. For representative arguments see Nan Lin, 'Social Resource and Instrumental Action', in Peter Marsden and Nan Lin (eds), *Social Structure and Network Analysis*, Beverly Hills: Sage, 1982, pp. 131–45; Nan Lin, 'Social Resources and Occupational Status Attainment', in R. L. Breiger (ed.), *Social Mobility and Social Structure*, New York: Cambridge University Press, 1990, pp. 247–71; Granovetter, 'Economic Action and Social Structure: The Problem of Embeddedness'; Granovetter, 'The Strength of Weak Ties'; Ronald Burt, *Structural Holes: The Social Structure of Competition*, Cambridge, MA: Harvard University Press, 1992.

15. Lakshmi Iyer, Tarun Khanna and Ashutosh Varshney, 'Caste and Entrepreneurship in India', Harvard Business School Working Paper, 18 October 2011, http://www.hbs.edu/research/pdf/12-028.pdf (accessed on 11 January 2012). Jodhka has studied the efforts of Dalits to do business in north-west India; see Surinder S. Jodhka, 'Dalits in Business: Self-Employed Scheduled Castes in North-West India', *Economic and Political Weekly*, 2010, XLV (11): 488–500. Sudha Pai has also studied the efforts of Dalits to take advantage of a Madhya Pradesh government scheme to help Dalits to start their own business through guaranteed state procurement and credit facility; see Sudha Pai, *Developmental State and the Dalit Question in Madhya Pradesh: Congress Response*, New Delhi: Routledge, 2012.

16. M. N. Srinivas and André Béteille, 'Networks in Indian Social Structure', *Man*, November–December 1964, 64: 165.

17. Srinivas and Béteille, 'Networks in Indian Social Structure', p. 164.

18. See Sonalde Desai and Amresh Dubey, 'Caste in 21st Century India: Competing Narratives', *Economic and Political Weekly*, 2011, 46: 40–49.

19. As told to us by a doctor, also a proprietor of a nursing home at Aurangabad. Several perceptions and examples of a similar nature are documented by Deshpande and Newman; see Ashwini Deshpande and Katherine Newman, 'Where the Path Leads: The Role of Caste in

Post-University Employment Expectations', *Economic and Political Weekly*, 13–19 October 2007, XLII (41) : 4133–40.

20. One of the important means to acquire cultural capital is the cultivation of education and skills. Based on the Indian Human Development Survey (IHDS), a nationwide survey of 41,554 households, Desai and Dubey conclude that 'Access to productive resources, particularly education and skills remain closely associated with caste. Children from lower castes continue to be educationally disadvantaged compared to children from the upper-caste . . . Caste associations for wealthy castes organise private schools and colleges as well as charitable trusts through which members obtain scholarships and loans for higher education. While these schools are ostensibly open to all, members of the caste that established the school often receive priority. Scholarships are given based on recommendations from members of the caste based governing body'. See Sonalde Desai and Amresh Dubey, 'Caste in 21st Century India: Competing Narratives', *Economic and Political Weekly*, 2011, XLVI (11): 46–48.

21. The IHDS documents that 'caste and kin remain at the centre of Indian civic life, with nearly 95 per cent of the female respondents reporting getting married within their own caste'. See Desai and Dubey, 'Caste in 21st Century India', p. 47.

22. Also see Saurabh Arora and Bulat Sanditov, 'Caste as Community? Networks of Social Affinity in a South Indian Village', UNU Wider working paper, http://www.merit.unu.edu/publications/wppdf/2009/wp2009-037.pdf (accessed on 21 November 2011).

23. Nicholas Dirks, 'Castes of Mind', *Representation*, 1992, 37: 56–78; Satish Saberwal, 'Democracy and Civil Society in India: Integral or Accidental', *Sociological Bulletin*, September 2001, 50 (2) : 193–205; T. K. Oommen, 'Civil Society: Religion, Caste and Language in India', *Sociological Bulletin*, September 2001, 50 (2): 219–35; Aseem Prakash, 'Re-imagination of the State and Gujarat's Electoral Verdict', *Economic and Political Weekly*, April 2003, XXXVIII (16): 1601–10.

24. Gurpreet Mahajan, 'Civil Society and its Avatars: What about Freedom and Democracy', *Economic and Political Weekly*, 15 May 1997, XXXIV(20): 1188–96; Dipankar Gupta, 'Civil Society in the Indian Context: Letting the State off the Hook', *Contemporary Sociology*, May 1999, 26 (3): 305–7.

25. Mahajan, 'Civil Society and its Avatars: What about Freedom and Democracy', p. 1196.

26. André Béteille, 'Civil Society and Its Institutions', in C. M. Elliot (ed.), *Civil Society and Democracy*, Delhi: Oxford University Press, 1995, pp. 191–210; André Béteille, 'Universities as Public Institutions', *Economic and Political Weekly*, 30 July–5 August 2005, XL (31): 3377–81.

27. Sanjay Kumar, 'Civil Society in Society', *Economic and Political Weekly*, 29 July–4 August 2005, XXXV (31) : 2276–79.

28. G. Vijay and G. Ajay, 'Civil Society, State and Social Movements', *Economic and Political Weekly*, 18–24 March 2000, XXXV (12): 1035–36.

29. A caveat is in order before we discuss the conceptualisation of civil society outside the domain of the state. Marx has regarded civil society as a sphere of crass materialism, and where the hegemony of the ruling class is conceived, practiced and sustained; see Karl Marx, *On the Jewish Question*, http://www.marxists.org/archive/marx/works/1844/ jewish-question (accessed on 21 July 2010). However, the discussion emanating from Marxist/ Neo-Marxist scholars sees civil society as a domain outside the state, resisting domination and marginalisation. Hence the question arises, why is their writing considered part of the Marxist intellectual tradition? Gouldner's reading of Marx informs us about two 'analytical' Marxisms: Critical Marxism and Scientific Marxism. According to him, 'Critical Marxism leans towards a perspective in which human decisions can make an important difference, towards a voluntarism in which human courage and determination count, while Scientific Marxism stresses the lawful regularities that inhere in things and set limits on human will, counter posing determinism to voluntarism. Critical Marxism pursues a policy of active interventionism, organising instruments such as Party "vanguard" or military forces that facilitate intervention; Scientific Marxism leans towards an evolutionism in which the requisite of change have their own rates of maturation and, believing history to be on "their side", until things come their way' (Alvin Gouldner, *The Two Marxisms: Contradictions and Anomalies in the Development of Theory*, London: Macmillan Press, 1980, pp. 59–60). However, he cautions us by arguing that both Marxisms are 'analytical distinctions, or ideal type rather than concrete historical groups and persons' (Gouldner, *The Two Marxisms*, p. 61). When the civil society argument is invoked by Marxists/Neo-Marxists, they are talking about a network of associations of people and social relations bound together for the achievement of a certain political project(s).

30. G. Vijay and G. Ajay, 'Civil Society, State and Social Movements', *Economic and Political Weekly*, 18–24 March 2000, XXXV (12): 1035–36.

31. Manoranjan Mohanty, 'Social Movement in Creative Society: Of Autonomy and Interconnections', in Manoranjan Mohanty, P. N. Mukherjee and Olle Tornquist (eds), *People's Rights: Social Movement and State in the Third World*, New Delhi: Sage, 1998, pp. 63–78.

32. Neera Chandhoke, *State and Civil Society. Explorations in Political Theory*, New Delhi: Sage, 1995; Neera Chandhoke, 'The Assertion

of Civil Society Against the State', in Manoranjan Mohanty, P. N. Mukherjee and Olle Tornquist (eds), *People's Rights: Social Movement and State in the Third World*, New Delhi: Sage, 1998, pp. 23–41; Neera Chandhoke, *The Conceits of Civil Society*, New Delhi: Oxford University Press, 2003.

33. Rajni Kothari, *State Against Democracy: In Search of Humane Governance*, New Delhi: Ajanta, 1988.

34. Gail Omvedt, 'Peasants, Dalits and Women: Democracy and India's New Social Movements', *Journal of Contemporary Asia*, January 1994, 24 (1): 35–48; Gopal Guru, 'Social Justice', in Niraja Jayal and Pratap Bhanu Mehta (eds), *The Oxford Companion to Politics in India*, New Delhi: Oxford University Press, 2010, pp. 363–64.

35. Political society for Chatterjee is different from civil society. Civil society — associational life based on equality, autonomy, freedom of entry and exit and duties of members and other such principles — is still 'restricted to fairly small sections of citizens' [Partha Chatterjee, 'On Civil and Political Society in Post-Colonial Democracy', in Sudipta Kaviraj and Sunil Khilnani (eds), *Civil Society: History and Possibilities*, Cambridge: Cambridge University Press, 2001, p. 172]. According to Chatterjee, the primary difference between civil society and political society is as follows: Civil society as per classical theory (Hegel and Marx), is constituted by the homogenous family — the nuclear family of 'modern bourgeois patriarchy'. Each individual in the family is classified as a citizen having certain rights against the state with corresponding duties. Political society, on the other hand, is constituted by population, 'differentiated but classifiable and enumerable' [Partha Chatterjee, 'On Civil and Political Society in Post-Colonial Democracy', in Sudipta Kaviraj and Sunil Khilnani (eds), *Civil Society: History and Possibilities*, Cambridge: Cambridge University Press, 2001, p. 173]. The subaltern groups, in order to pursue their basic needs and subsistence livelihood requirements negotiate with the civil society as well as state — the domains of which are controlled by the dominant classes — through ad-hoc contextual strategies and strategic manoeuvres. While doing so, they neither claim hegemonic leadership in civil society, nor do they try and capture state power (Kuan-Hsing Chen, 'Civil society and Min-Jian: On Political Society and Popular Democracy', *Cultural Studies*, 2003, 17 (6): 880). Accordingly, Chatterjee argues that the 'politics of democratization must therefore be carried out not in the classical transactions between state and civil society but in the much less well-defined legally ambiguous, contextually and strategically demarcated terrain of political society' (Partha Chatterjee, 'Community in the East', *Economic and Political Weekly*, 1998, XXXIII (6): 280).

36. John Locke, 'An Essay Concerning the True Original, Extent and End of Civil Government', in Earnest Barker (ed.), *Social Contract: Locke Hume Rousseau*, with an Introduction by Earnest Barker, London: Oxford University Press, 1960, pp. 3–143.

37. Sunil Khilnani, 'The Development of Civil Society', in Sudipta Kaviraj and Sunil Khilnani (eds), *Civil Society: History and Possibility*, Cambridge: Cambridge University Press, 2001, p. 19.

38. G. W. F. Hegel, *Hegel's Philosophy of Right*, Oxford: Clarendon Press, 1967, 182: 266.

39. Ibid., 206: 133.

40. Hegel, *Hegel's Philosophy of Right*, 242:149/242–149.

41. Adam Smith, *Wealth of Nations*, North Carolina: Hayes Barton Press, 2005.

42. The debate is found in the writings of Ralph Miliband and N. Poulantsaz as they discuss their views on the autonomy of the state. Miliband is associated with the instrumentalist view. He analyses the social origins and current interest of the economic and political elites and then goes on to analyse the fundamental features of actually existing states in the capitalist society and the constraints on their autonomy. See Ralph Miliband, *The State in a Capitalist Society*, London: Weidenfeld and Nicoloson, 1969. Poulantsaz is associated with the deterministic view of the state. He criticises Miliband for analysing the state in terms of officials manning the state apparatus, arguing instead, that the state has to be seen in relation to its structurally determined role in capitalist society. In other words, classes should not be seen as simple economic forces situated outside and independent of the state, capable of manipulating it in their interest. See N. Poulantsaz, *Political Power and Social Classes*, London: New Left Books, 1973; and N. Poulantsaz, *State, Power, Socialism*, London: Verso, 1978; also see Amy Beth Bridges, 'Nicos Poulantsaz and the Marxist Theory of the State', *Politics & Society*, 1974, 4 (2): 161–90.

43. Karl Marx, *A Critique of the German Ideology*, Moscow: Progress Publishers, 1968, http://www.marxists.org/archive/marx/works/download/Marx_The_German_Ideology.pdf (accessed on 28 July 2010).

44. Karl Marx, *On The Jewish Question*, Paris: *Deutsch-Französische Jahrbücher*, 1844, http://www.marxists.org/archive/marx/works/1844/jewish-question (accessed on 28 July 2010).

45. Norberto Bobbio, *Which Socialism? Marxism, Socialism and Democracy*, Cambridge: Polity, 1987, p. 148. Further, in order to understand the relationship between base and superstructure in Gramscian thought, we can read Femia. While undertaking an exhaustive review of Gramsci's writings, Femia points out four possible models: a. consciousness (superstructure) determines base, b. consciousness (superstructure) and base

interact on equal basis, c. base determines the form of consciousness (superstructure), d. base determines what form of consciousness is possible. Gramsci fits into the last category. See Joseph Femia, 'Hegemony and Consciousness in the Thought of Antonio Gramsci', *Political Studies*, 1975, 23 (1): 29–48. Others have stressed that the Marxist concept of 'superstructure' can no longer be construed as a pale reflection of a socio-economic organisation; see Thomas Bates, 'Gramsci and the Theory of Hegemony', *Journal of the History of Ideas*, 1975, 36 (2): 353.

46. Antonio Gramsci, *Selections From the Prison Notebooks*, London: Lawrence and Wishart, 1971, pp. 244, 366–73.

47. In the Indian context, Partha Chatterjee argues that civil society is the domain of equality and rights, where citizenship status has been acquired and respected. Political society is the domain where political negotiations and transactions are pursued by subaltern groups excluded by the state and modernist civil society. This powerful articulation, while being sensitive to the struggle of the subalterns, somehow fails to acknowledge that the subalterns are not a homogenous group but divided by various social identities. See Partha Chatterjee, 'On Civil and Political Society in Post-Colonial Democracy', in Sudipta Kaviraj and Sunil Khilnani (eds), *Civil Society: History and Possibilities*, Cambridge: Cambridge University Press, 2001, pp. 165–73.

48. Elisabetta Basile and Barbara Harriss-White, 'Corporative Capitalism: Civil Society and the Politics of Accumulation in Small Town India', QEH Working Paper Series - QEHWP S38, Oxford: Queen Elizabeth House, 2000.

49. Basile and Harriss-White, 'Corporative Capitalism', p. 3.

50. Ibid.

51. Barbara Harriss-White, *India Working: Essays on Society and Economy*, Cambridge: Cambridge University Press, 2003.

52. While caste has undergone major transformation (sociological norms of 'purity' and 'pollution' have considerably weakened) under the impact of modernisation, 'caste still persists as a fundamental principle of social organisation even if under different guise' (Basile and Harriss-White, 'Corporative Capitalism', p. 6). Caste is still the basis for political mobilisation and articulating political interests [Lucia Michelutti, 'We (Yadavs) are a Caste of Politicians: Caste and Modern Politics in a North Indian Town', *Contributions to Indian Sociology*, 2004, 38 (3): 43–71; Sudha Pai, *Dalit Assertion and the Unfinished Democratic Revolution: The Bahujan Samaj Party in Uttar Pradesh*, New Delhi: Sage, 2002; Ian Duncan, 'Dalits and Politics in Rural North India: The Bahujan Samaj Party in Uttar Pradesh', *Journal of Peasant Studies*, 1999, 27 (1): 35–60] as well as for structuring and influencing economic endeavours either as

owners of capital [E. Wayne Nafziger and Terrell Dek, 'Entrepreneurial Human Capital and the Long-Run Survival of Firms in India', *World Development*, 1996, 24 (4): 689–96; Pariyaram Chaco, *Caste, Business and Entrepreneurship in South India*, New Delhi: Kanishka Publishing House, 1991] or as contributors of labour for surplus generation (Jonathan Parry, 'Lords of Labour: Working and Shirking in Bhilai', *Contributions to Indian Sociology*, 1999, 33 (1–2): 108–40).

53. Also refer to Chapter Four.
54. Srinivas and Béteille, 'Networks in Indian Social Structure', p. 166.

Six

Intersectionality, Discrimination and Unfavourable Inclusion

◼

मेरा नाम मुन्ना है। मेरी उम्र 33 साल है। मैं हरदोई का रहने वाला हूँ। मेरा बाप मेहतर था। करीब दस साल पहले दमें से उसकी मौत हो गई, मेरी माँ भी मेहतरानी थी। बचपन में मैंने भी बाप के साथ काम किया था। उस समय आजकल की तरह इंगलिश संडास नहीं होते थे। सारी गंदगी लोहे की गाड़ी में भरके ले जाना होता था। अब अंग्रेजी सिस्टम है। 19 साल की उमर तक मैंने भी पंजे से गंदगी साफ की है। फिर धीरे धीरे लोगों ने मेहतर रखना छोड़ दिया। मुझे शुरू से मेहतर का काम अच्छा नहीं लगता था लेकिन और कोई चारा नहीं था। म्युनिस्पैलिटी में रोज के भत्ते की नौकरी मिली। सड़क की सफाई करता था। जो पैसा मिलता था उसमे से ठेकेदार को हिस्सा देना पड़ता था। फिर मैंने सोचा कि अपना काम किया जाए। मैंने अपने चाचा और साले से 2000 रूपये का उधार लिया। रूपया उधार लेकर ठेले पर अंडा बेचना शुरू किया। टेला शराब के ठेके के सामने लगाता था। थोड़े दिन बाद ठेके के मालिक के भतीजे ने ठेके के अन्दर ही अंडे और मिक्सचर का काउन्टर खोल लिया। उस दिन से उन लोगों ने मेरे ठेले का नाम मेहतर का ठेला रख दिया और अपने काउन्टर के सामने एक तख्ती पर लिख दिया कि मुन्ना मेहतर का अंडा खाओ और नर्क में जाओ। मेरा अंडा खाओ और शिव रस के गुन गाओ। मेरी बहुत बेइज्जती हो गई। मेरी आमदनी भी घट गई। उसके बाद मेरा नाम ही मुन्ना मेहतर पड़ गया। गली के बच्चे मुझे मुन्ना मेहतर के नाम से जानने लगे। मुझसे अपनी बेइज्जती सही नहीं गई। मैंने काम बन्द कर दिया और कई महीने घर पर बैठा रहा। उसके बाद मैं अपने जीजा के पास लखनऊ आ गया। कुछ महीनों तक मैंने मजदूरी की, उसके बाद मैंने सिक्योरिटी गार्ड का काम किया। मैंने कुछ पैसा जमा किया, कुछ पैसा जीजा, भाई और चाचा से लिया, और फिर मैंने ये फलों का धंधा बैठाया। मैंने तीन साल तक होलसेल बाजार से फल खरीदा और ठेले गाड़ी पर घर घर जाकर बेचा, उसके बाद ये नगर महापालिका की दुकान मिल गई। बाबू ने 5000 घूस लिया। मेरे जीजा तो महापालिका में क्लर्क है। उसने मेरी काफी मदद की। दुकान तो छोटी है पर काम चल जाता है। मेरा काम धीरे धीरे बढ़ने लगा। कई होटल में फल सप्लाई करता हूँ।

मैं टेम्पो खरीदना चाहता था। पर मेरी जात की वजह से मुझे बैंक ने उधार नहीं दिया। बाबू ने मुझसे बोला था कि मैं तुम्हें पैसे दिलवा दूंगा। मैं बहुत खुश होकर उसके घर एक आम की पेटी ले गया, उसकी घरवाली ने मेरी जात पूछी, मैंने बता दिया, सोचा शहर में जात से क्या लेना देना और बाबू लोग तो पढ़े लिखे हैं। मेमसाहेब ने आम वापस कर दिए। और फिर मैं कई बार दौड़ा पर मुझे पैसा नहीं दिया। मैंने बनिया से पैसा उधार लिया, एक लाख के बदले मुझे हर महीने 5000 अगले तीन साल तक देने हैं। और हर हफ्ते दो किलो फल फ्री में देता हूँ। और जो बाकी फल बेचते हैं और होलसेलर मेरे मुह पर कुछ नहीं

कहते पर आपस में मजाक करते हैं कि जमादार भी साहब बन गया है। जब देवी जागरण होता है तो मुझसे न चंदा लेते हैं और न मुझे बुलाते हैं। होटल के मैनेजर से भी बोला पर मैनेजर ने सुना नहीं क्योंकि मैं टेम्पो से एकदम टाइम पे फल पहुंचा देता हूँ और मण्डी से कम पैसा लेता हूँ।

My name is Munna. I am 33 years old. I belong to Hardoi. My father used to clean dry latrines. He suffered from tuberculosis and died around 10 years ago. My mother also used to clean latrines. In my childhood, I too helped my parents in their work. During those days, there were no English toilets. We would haul the filth away in an iron-cart. Gradually, the traditional latrines were replaced by sewer-connected toilets. The demand for toilet cleaners also went down. I never liked cleaning latrines but there was no other option. After this, I started working as a daily wage sweeper in the local municipality. I had to give a portion of my wages to the labour contractor. I decided to start my own business. I borrowed ₹ 2000 from my uncle and my brother-in-law and started selling boiled eggs and omelette on a cart in front of a country liquor shop. After some time, the nephew of the owner of the liquor shop started selling eggs and savoury snacks from within the liquor shop. He started referring to my stall as a 'toilet cleaner's cart'. They placed a placard in front of their egg counter which said 'Eat eggs from the Toilet Cleaner's Cart and burn in hell! Eat eggs from our counter and enjoy Lord Shiva's Nectar' [In Hindu mythology, Lord Shiva is said to have a soft corner for cannabis and associated products, hence any sort of intoxicant is loosely associated with his name]. I felt really insulted and humiliated. My income also went down. 'Munna — the toilet cleaner' became my nickname — the local kids would hail me by it and tease me. I could not stand the humiliation. I closed the business and for the next few months, I just sat home without any work. After that, I came to Lucknow and started staying with my brother-in-law. First, I worked as daily wage labourer. Thereafter, I worked as security guard. I also saved some money which I pooled with some funds I borrowed from my brother-in-law and uncle and started retailing fruits. I carted fruits from door to door for three years. Then, I got this shop from the Lucknow municipality. I had to bribe the clerk with ₹5000. The shop is small but somehow I am able to manage. Gradually, my business has started expanding. I supply fruits to several hotels.

I wanted to buy a tempo for transportation. However, due to my caste, I never got a loan from the bank. The bank official assured me that he would get me the loan. I was very happy. I took a carton full of mangoes as a gift to his house. His wife enquired after my caste. I told her my caste because I didn't think that it would bother an urban educated family. But she returned my mangoes. I did not get the loan either, despite my repeated visits to the bank. Finally, I took a loan of ₹1 lakh from the local merchant (baniya). I have to repay him through a monthly instalment of ₹5000 for the next three years. Apart from this, every week, I have to give him 2 kg of fruits for free.

Though the other wholesale fruit dealers are not rude to me directly, I am aware that they ridicule me behind my back, saying that even a toilet cleaner has become a gentleman . . . They neither invite me for community religious events nor seek my contribution. They also tried to influence the hotel manager against me using my caste. However, the manager ignored it since I always supply fruits on time and at rates which are slightly below the market rates.

[Munna, fruit wholesaler, Lucknow]

This testimony lucidly highlights the paradoxes in the life of a Dalit who has moved out of his historically ordained and religiously sanctioned occupation to a modern profession. Munna is an owner of capital who has invested money in the wholesale business of fruits. This trajectory of economic upward mobility is marked by repeated humiliation and marginalisation because of his ascriptive identity. His caste location ensured that his initial livelihood options were limited to clearing human faeces. Due to a conjunction of circumstances, he was able to move out of this inhuman occupation but his caste identity and his association with an 'impure' occupation refuses to leave him. His attempt at selling small food items came to a dead end. It was followed by a foray into wholesale fruit business which is presently reasonably successful. Munna's testimony highlights a few interrelated aspects of Indian caste society. First, the caste structure seems to have acquired a certain flexibility, which enables Dalits to move out of their traditional occupations and enter modern professions without adopting the cultural practices of the upper-castes. Second, after a fair bit of struggle, Munna was able to start his wholesale business of fruits and supplies produce to a reasonably high-end restaurant in the city. This is the changing aspect of caste society. However, there are also the unchanging aspects of caste society, which are quite alarming and disturbing.

As we can see from Munna's testimony, caste identity can confer an unfair advantage or disadvantage (depending on one's caste location) vis a vis one's competitors in the market. Invoking Munna's caste identity was sufficient to drive him out of his business of selling eggs. However, even more disturbing is the fact that the logic of social 'impurity' of the food items he sold was also accepted by the customers of 'modern India', which enabled his upper-caste business peers to drive him out of the market in the first place. Although even his later competitors in the wholesale fruit market sought to use his caste identity against him, this time it did not work, mainly because his efficiency and competitive prices were appreciated by clients. Therefore caste in its contemporary avatar is often deployed to manage competition in the market in a manner which is mostly detrimental to the economic interests of Dalits.

In the realm of the state, we see that Munna perceives that he was denied a loan not because he was ineligible but due to his caste location. In the absence of institutional credit, he had to borrow money from the informal credit market at a fairly high interest rate.

However, it is in the realm of civil society that the ascriptive baggage is most pronounced — he is considered an 'untouchable' and hence not invited to religious gatherings, besides having to bear the humiliation of being labelled a 'toilet cleaner'. The patterns of discrimination, hence, seem to be rooted in civil society and then manifest themselves in the institutions of the state and markets in various forms.

Accordingly, the main argument of this chapter is that discrimination against Dalits and their unfavourable inclusion in the markets is carved out and sustained at the intersection of state, market and civil society, a fact which has also been highlighted throughout this book. In other words, discrimination and unfavourable inclusion in the market cannot be seen as being effected through a single institution. They are practiced and sustained through a combination of several institutions that operate simultaneously.

How do we make analytical sense of these multiple institutions that (re)produce and sustain such discrimination? It is our claim that the conceptual approach of intersectionality can facilitate an understanding of this complex phenomenon.

Intersectionality

The concept of intersectionality can be employed to examine the lived experiences of Dalit entrepreneurs at multiple points of intersection that have thus far been neglected in academic analysis. In other words, we need an approach to reflect multiple subordinate locations as opposed to a single (non)institutionalised cause of subordination.

It is not possible, for instance, to understand the denial of access to government resources to a Dalit women entrepreneur (which she is legally entitled to) through the usual lens of social theory that constructs binary opposites — corrupt male officials versus helpless women clients, or patronising upper-caste government official versus lower caste dependent/feeble client — because the former only focuses on unaccountable power structures of the state while the latter puts forth the dichotomy between the upper- and lower-castes. The analytical nodes of binary opposites may fail to capture the Dalit woman's experience of exclusion/marginalisation at multiple nodes — state, caste and patriarchy. Let us take the instance of a Dalit male entrepreneur who is denied access to credit by a government bank, faces the threat of violence from an upper-caste business competitor, and is being forced to under-price his business product to economically overcome the stigma of caste in the market. He faces discrimination and consequent deprivation at the intersection of caste and class on the one hand, and state and civil society on the other. In yet another case, a Dalit entrepreneur was able to access bank credit and procures the requisite license from the state government with a relative's help, but the informal network of upper-caste business peers that controlled the supply chain and business orders ensured that he earned less than the normal profit. We claim that the possibility of multiple and conflicting experiences of subordination, control and power requires a wider terrain of analyses, a conceptual and analytical challenge which can be addressed through the approach of intersectionality.

The conceptual approach of intersectionality has been borrowed from feminist studies, where it is used to examine how various social, cultural and biological categories like race, gender, class, ethnicity, and religion interact and create multiple and often simultaneous conditions of discrimination and social inequality. In other words, feminist discourse, while challenging dominant theorisation that sees race, class and gender as separate issues argues that it is the combined impact of these issues that affect individual social positions.[1] This is termed as the race–gender–class matrix or the interlocking system of oppression and marginalisation. For instance, the seminal works of Kimberle Crenshaw have made us aware of the colour blindness of law in taking into account discrimination against black women, which was intersectional in nature.[2] Similarly Browne and Misra show how race and gender intersect in the labour market and thereby create structural conditions of discrimination and marginalisation.[3] Likewise, the concept of intersectionality has been used to understand the social determinants of women's health.[4] Thus, intersectionality as a conceptual framework to analyse the lives of women in general, and women of colour in particular, highlights the multiple and overlapping socio-economic and political spaces that create subordination and marginalisation. It is also argued that it is necessary to recognise and generate a list of such intersectional spaces where marginalisation and discrimination acquire roots and sustain themselves. This also works as an intellectual critique of the 'single axis' framework and allows us to examine the multiple variables that simultaneously contribute to the marginalisation of 'weaker' social groups.

Borrowing this approach from feminist discourse, the present work puts forth the following claim: discrimination and unfavourable inclusion of Dalit entrepreneurs takes place at the intersection of the state, market and civil society. Intersectionality challenges the currently dominant conceptualisation of somewhat rigid analytical boundaries between these institutions. It seeks to blur boundaries as the consequent overlapping space is instrumental in the (re)production of discrimination/unfavourable inclusion.

Here, it would be appropriate to delineate our interpretation of intersectionality in the context of our study of Dalit entrepreneurs, while borrowing extensively from feminist theories.

Feminist discourse analyses gender inequality by pointing towards the multiple and simultaneously operating conditions responsible for creating and sustaining larger structural social inequality and discrimination. In doing so, it focuses on the interaction of various social, cultural and biological categories like race, gender, class, ethnicity, and religion. In crux, the scholars writing on intersectionality argue that these forms of social stratification need to be studied in relation to each other, conceptualising them, for example as a 'matrix of domination'[5] or 'complex inequality'[6] or intersectional[7] or 'integrative'[8] or as a 'race–class–gender' approach.[9] These analyses highlight the implications of such intersections on practical politics, since 'women of colour are situated within at least two subordinated groups that frequently pursue conflicting political agendas'.[10] Thus, intersectionality in feminist literature is concerned with the interaction between aspects of social differences and identity (race, gender, ethnicity, class, etc.), that generate systematic oppressions (racisms, sexism, etc.) at macro and micro levels in complex, interrelated ways.

Accordingly, the emphasis in feminist literature is on the multiple axes of the subordination experienced by women. In other words, a woman of colour will experience subordination differently from a white woman. Thus the distinct experiences of women that shape their access to status and power becomes central to the analysis.

Taking these important insights as building blocks, we use the experiences of Dalit entrepreneurs to understand the reasons behind the genesis and perpetuation of the discrimination and unfavourable inclusion that they are subjected to. However, unlike feminist theory which analyses (informal) social institutions (ethnicity, religion, race, etc.), we focus on formal institutions (state and the market) where the informal institutions (for instance, the ideology of caste) are articulated.

Accordingly, our analysis of intersectionality is shaped by two central tenets. First, the values associated with the ideology of caste as present in civil society are reflected in institutions that constitute the state and market. This mirroring of values results in the blurring of boundaries between state, market and civil society. Second, the intersection and interaction between state, market and society creates a unique domain that transcends the original character of each, and has its own sets of norms, rules and behavioural patterns, different from and contradictory to the assumed rationalities of state planning and markets.

Why Intersectionality is Crucial

Intersectionality serves certain theoretical and practical ends. We present four specific arguments to support our claim that this approach conceptually enriches our understanding of discrimination against Dalits and their unfavourable inclusion in the market. The arguments are as follows:

The Interconnectedness Argument

The importance of analytically contesting the binaries of state–markets, state–civil society and market–civil society has already been discussed. More important to note is the interconnectedness of various institutions that interact with and shape each other, and often act simultaneously in sustaining discrimination, socio-economic maldistribution, cultural misrecognition and consequent marginalisation of Dalits.

Social Exclusion versus Discrimination Argument

The focus on intersectional spaces causing and sustaining discrimination allows us to differentiate between exclusion and consequent marginalisation due to class location, and discrimination and the consequent socio-economic maldistribution and cultural misrecognition due to caste location. In other words, exclusion and consequent marginalisation can be caused due to unequal access to social primary goods[11] or inequality of distribution of impersonal resources (e.g. financial resources) and the absence of a mechanism for compensating people with far less personal resources[12] or little access to basic capabilities.[13] These frameworks, while explaining the varieties of exclusion, are not adequately equipped to explain the socio-economic maldistribution and cultural misrecognition of Dalits sustained by the historical practice of the caste ideology, which draws its legitimacy from Hindu religion. The absence of an effective theoretical framework translates into a methodological failure to identify the spaces where discrimination acquires its roots and is also sustained.

We propose that the approach of intersectionality is useful in addressing this theoretical shortcoming; it reveals how the power of neither social group (upper-caste or Dalit) is constituted at a given moment but is determined and constrained by the history of relationships between social groups. This determines the formation of social networks (see Chapter Five) which are then played out in formal institutions, and thereby enable caste identity to play out in the intersecting space between state, markets and civil society. Thus, this approach is able to identify the socio-political and economic arrangements that contribute towards the discrimination against Dalits through an array of formal and informal institutions.

Hence, the claim of intersectionality is to provide a framework that is intellectually alert and sensitive to what historically marginalised social groups, such as Dalits, would want to know. The emphasis is on exploring, analysing and prioritising the study of 'the powerful, their institutions, their policies, and practices instead of focussing only on those whom the powerful govern'.[14] The study of spaces where the state, markets and civil society interact allows us to trace the conceptual practices of power and how they shape everyday social relations. 'Understanding how our lives are governed not primarily by individuals but more powerfully by institutions, conceptual schemes, and their "texts" which are seemingly far removed from our everyday lives, is crucial for designing effective projects of social transformation.'[15] Towards this end, it is essential to understand how social power is operationalised and sustained as well as the agency available to Dalits in engaging with and contesting the social power of dominant social groups.

The Agency and Social Power Argument

The framework of social power derived from caste draws its sustenance necessarily through group identity. Social power as experienced at the intersecting spaces can be described as having two interrelated dimensions. First is the relationship between structure[16] and agency.[17] The dominant upper-caste would like to see this relationship between structure (caste system) and agency (ability of upper-castes to prevail over Dalits and thereby marginalising their protest and struggles) in the case of Dalits, in the manner of Lukes' conception of power, that is, the unquestioned reproduction of the upper-caste worldview where Dalits are relegated to serve their social and material interests.[18] However, in practice, the power dynamics between upper-castes and Dalits are far more complex. Dalits, while recognising subordination, continuously question it, protest against it, assert their political agency, and in the process, interrogate and question the structure–agency dualism. The upper-caste-inspired caste structure is a product of human agency but, at the same time, it also produces conditions for opposition. Thus, power is never held by the upper-caste in the form of total power. Instead, Dalits continuously strive towards altering the balance of power, albeit with limited success.[19] The result is their unwavering commitment to overcome their subordination, in the form of repeated assertions, (re)negotiations and subversion of the upper-caste stranglehold.

If there is any truth in our claim that Dalits are aware of their oppression, subordination and discrimination by upper-castes, how do we then explain the fact that they are allowed to enter the market, albeit not on equal terms?

The intersecting space is a social field where the practice of discrimination is accepted by the discriminated, not in a conscious or willing manner. Instead, it is due to what Rafanell and Gorringe describe as 'clearly motivated by identifiable calculative practices'.[20] 'Power can continue to be exercised not because it overrides calculative agency *but precisely because of it*[21] (emphasis original). In other words, Dalit entrepreneurs have either come out of their caste-ordained professions or resisted the tremendous pressure of their former employers to perform manual labour for their benefit, and chosen to enter the market as owners of capital. In this situation, they do realise that their capacity to resist or entirely oppose the illegitimate demands of their business peers is limited. Hence, their choice is to engage with them through an intelligent assessment of constraints in the specific context. Accordingly, they try to organise their personal goals and ambitions strategically in a changed context, where they have to continuously overcome the upper-caste-inspired threat of social exclusion.

Even from the vantage point of the upper-castes, social power is not permanent. It needs to be continuously reinvented and new ways and means are discovered to maintain status quo. This is where the role of social networks explained earlier becomes crucial. The social network in this manifestation is the collective power of upper-castes to blur the boundaries between state, markets and civil society. The intersecting space is in fact an innovation motivated by the collective social power of the upper-castes (so as to extract undue and unlawful benefits from the local state), which is created and sustained through a variety of social relationships. The continuous social assertion of the Dalits has not only resulted in re-negotiation of power within different social groups amongst upper-castes (for instance, an unspoken social contract to articulate their collective voices against Dalits instead of articulating the socio-economic differences within), but have also led to their re-engagement with Dalits where by their access to the market can no longer be restricted. Informal institutions, therefore, need to be erected to ensure that they are unfavourably included.

An analysis of power must thus appreciate that the upper-castes will not voluntarily abdicate their social power over Dalits. Therefore the need for formal rectificatory institutions that can compensate for historical wrongs. The rectificatory institutions where they exist are still controlled by upper-castes who may not be ideologically friendly to this idea and hence the execution of the compensatory policies will be marred by repeated failures. It is then natural and necessary that Dalits recognise these intersectional spaces in order to constantly assert themselves and claim what is legitimately due to them.

The Epistemic Superiority Argument

Intersectionality provides an epistemic basis for understanding the changing political economy and political sociology of caste. Drawing upon feminist intersectionality theorists, we also argue that the concept makes us appreciate that historically 'marginalised subjects have an epistemic advantage, a particular perspective which the scholar should consider, if not adapt, when crafting a normative vision of a just society'.[22] This becomes especially important in the present context as the caste system, while sharing several similarities with the past, is also assuming new forms and is being reconstructed and adapted to suit the current scenario. The power relationship effected through the ideology of caste is no longer restricted to the apparent sociological 'superiority' of some social groups and 'inferiority' of others. The order of caste relationships, as pointed out in previous chapters, has become more subtle and elusive as forms of discrimination acquire new forms, while still seeking to maintain an unequal power relationship between Dalits and upper-castes. Therefore, the emphasis is on understanding and articulating the perspective of the historically marginalised and recognising that experiences of marginalisation cannot be ascribed individually to state, market or civil society, but are rather simultaneous and interlinked.

Having outlined the four crucial socio-political attributes of this 'intersecting space' that creates conditions for the unfavourable inclusion of Dalit entrepreneurs, we now discuss how it differs from the existing theories of state, market and civil society.

Situating Intersectionality in the Existing Theory of State, Markets and Civil Society

As we have already described, the claim of the intersectionality approach is to explain the attempts of business persons/entrepreneurs from upper-castes to engage with Dalit entrepreneurs on unequal terms in the course of market transactions. In this endeavour, upper-caste entrepreneurs benefit from formal as well as informal institutions in the realm of state, market and civil society. Our claim is as follows:

a. The formal and informal institutions situated in the realms of the state, market and civil society interact and give birth to intersecting spaces where the ideology of discrimination is nurtured and sustained. In practice, the ideology of discrimination translates into the unfavourable inclusion of Dalits in market operations.

b. Although these intersecting spaces continue to remain part of the state, market and civil society, they tend to develop their own norms and rules which are different from the expected rationality of the state and markets on the one hand, and mirror the unequal relationships present in the realm of civil society on the other.

Both a. and b. essentially imply that this entire process takes place under the influence of the ideology of caste.

This understanding of intersectionality has some serious points of difference with the existing theories of state, markets and civil society. These are discussed ahead.

Claim I: Theoretical Stress on Social Identity

The claim of intersectionality is that it gives due emphasis to caste identity in shaping outcomes in the markets as well as influencing the state's actions which are crucial to market outcomes. Almost all dominant theories of state, markets and civil society are oblivious to this claim.

As far as the theory of state is concerned, we first juxtapose the claim of intersectionality against the society-centred theory of state. Under the theoretical framework of Marxism, the most prominent aspect of the theories of state is the issue of the state's autonomy. Autonomy is important because the institutions of the state are looked upon to create enabling conditions for equitable participation in the market as well as to ensure that the regulatory arms of the state are neutral. The Marxist school of thought views the state 'as a system of political domination with specific effects on class struggle'.[23] The thesis of relative autonomy implies that the state may not be directly controlled by the capitalist class and enjoys a degree of autonomy from any such control. Thus the state (or state officials) can pursue policies that may be in opposition to the immediate interest of the dominant class(es). However, it is also stressed that the state is never so autonomous as to undermine the long term interests of the dominant class(es).[24] Two conclusions can be drawn from the relative autonomy thesis: First, whether the state is seen in an instrumentalist or deterministic fashion,[25] state power is seen to be deployed in the long term interests of the dominant classes. Second, the state is not seen to be serving universal interest. Marxists would believe that the 'capitalist state intervene(s) *against capital as well as the working class* — especially when individual capitalists or fractions of capital threaten the interests of capital in general'[26] (emphasis mine). Note that state intervention is only for social groups defined through the (lack of) control of the means of production and not for any social groups defined through ascriptive identities. Thus, Marxism articulates one version of a society-centred approach to study the state which fails to take into account the role of ascriptive identities in shaping the ideology and practice of the state and associated institutions.

Differing significantly from this is an alternative society-centred approach to studying the state, the pluralist–structural functional approach, the broad points of which are as follows. This approach refuses to use the concept of state and instead uses the term 'government'. State is seen as too formalistic and legal, whereas government is perceived as reflecting the arena where economic interest groups and social movements contest/ally with each other to shape public policy. The government itself is not taken very seriously and can never be an independent (or autonomous) actor, since it is only an arena where 'societal inputs' (demands) lead to 'governmental outputs' (allocation).[27] First, the primary difference between the Marxist and pluralist–structural functional approaches is that the former points out to the domination of the state/government by one section of society whereas the latter argues that state policies are influenced by many interest groups and not one (the ruling class). The state's autonomy is invariably infringed upon in the pluralist tradition whereas for Marxists, the state is relatively autonomous, on certain occasions, to pursue the specific agenda of capital that is, protecting the long term interests of the capitalist class. Second, Marxist theories of state in general and state autonomy in particular are blind to the possibility that any social group (defined through ascriptive identities) can infringe upon the autonomy of the state. The pluralist–structural functional approach is opposed to the idea that any particular social group can ever dominate the state. This means that the concentration of power in one or a few social groups cannot be a permanent aspect of a social structure. Here, power is tied up with one or more issues, which may lead different social groups to make strategic alliances for a momentary or semi-permanent duration.[28]

These formulations by scholars of Marxist and pluralist persuasions do not sit comfortably with the business histories of Dalit entrepreneurs. At the micro level, the state is seen to be easily accessed through the caste and family network. In the view of Dalit entrepreneurs, the state is neither an instrument of class rule nor structurally embedded in class relations, providing cohesiveness and stability to class-based domination. Structurally as well as functionally, the state's actions reflect a bias towards (dominant) upper-castes and, more often than not, articulate their socio-economic interests. The pluralist–structural functional approach is also at odds with the Dalit view because it fails to recognise that the values, beliefs and ideas shaping the social structure are derived from the ideology of caste. Caste domination itself is not temporary but a sustained and long-lasting social pattern. The power of upper-castes over Dalits is not contingent on the prevailing socio-political and economic circumstances, but is more permanent in nature, deriving its legitimacy from religion and religious scriptures.

In contrast to society-centred approaches, statist theories argue that the state is a force in and by itself and does not promote the interests of a class or social group.[29] State officials and managers are able to exercise autonomy in their own right and accordingly pursue their own distinctive interests.[30] In the context of state autonomy, the statists argue against the theoretical primacy of class or capital. Instead, they point to the 'unified sense of ideological purpose (throwing up the) possibility and desirability of state intervention to ensure political order and promote economic development'.[31] Arguing further, Peter Evans has proposed the concept of embedded autonomy[32] — close ties between bureaucrats and businesses, whereby the former retains the ability to formulate and act on preferences autonomously — as the key to the developmental state's effectiveness.[33] Thus, statists stress on the ideological commitments and a sense of purpose on the part of state functionaries to not only carve out an autonomous action plan but also to execute it in the universal interest of the nation.

However, Dalit entrepreneurs refuse to agree with even the statist approach. They point to the embeddedness of state officials in the social structure, which includes factors like caste, kith and kin, and family-inspired networks, all of which enable the upper-castes to access the resources of the state rather than a macro ideological

objective catering to universal interests.[34] The same has been documented and analysed in detail in Chapter Four of this book.

The role of identity in the context of theories of markets has been
analysed by several scholars who can perhaps be safely clubbed under
the disciplinary boundaries of economic sociology, even though they
differ ideologically. Most of economic theory is premised on the
assumption that social identities of agents do not influence market
outcomes, though there are 'powerful exceptions' that show how
'social identities of economic agents can be central to the determination of their economic outcomes'.[35]

Scholars who adhere to the neo-classical approach resolutely pro-
claim that identities restrict competition in the markets, which in turn
means inefficient markets, and therefore, they conclude that the role
of identities in any economic transaction will eventually wane with
the development of competitive markets. The works of Akerlof,[36]
Lal[37] and Scoville[38] highlight that discrimination in the markets on
the basis of caste is sustained by collective pressure and anticipated
penalty feared by the individual belonging to the upper-caste. These
penalties could be either imaginary or real. The business histories of
Dalit entrepreneurs inform us that the 'threat' of penalties are often
used as an excuse by upper-caste entrepreneurs to force an unequal
exchange relationship with Dalit entrepreneurs. The use of caste identity by upper-caste entrepreneurs, in fact, achieves the institutional
requirement of meeting the demands of the competition from new
player(s) instead of restricting it. The latter has to accept the terms
and conditions set by the former for fear of complete banishment
from the market. The emphasis on the individual as the source of
discrimination is at odds with the experience of Dalit entrepreneurs
in the markets. Instead, they claim that the focus has to be on informal institutions and their influence on formal institutions — both in
the realm of markets and the state — which sustain discrimination.

New Institutional Economics (NIE) addresses this gap and
indicates the role of institutions in influencing market outcomes. It
acknowledges the importance of competition in shaping the markets.
It also recognises the role of informal institutions — religion, customs,
tradition, norms, conventions, etc.[39] — and considers their existence
as a given.[40] However, North,[41] Stiglitz[42] and other scholars suggest
that informal institutions raise transaction costs, thereby restricting
competition, and are hence bound to wane off in the long run. NIE
is also sensitive to the important role of the state in establishing the

Table 6.1 Dominant Theories of State, Markets and Civil Society

Theoretical Lens	Analytical Thrust	Primary Argument	Implications
		Theories of State	
		Society-centred approach	
Marxism	Relative autonomy	a. State power is deployed in the long term interest of the dominant classes; b. The state can pursue policies which can conflict with the interests of the dominant classes in the short run; c. The state intervenes *against capital as well as the working class* — especially when fractions of capital threaten the interests of capital in general.	a. The interest of the dominant class is reflected in the policies of the state; b. The state supports the accumulative endeavours of social groups identified through their class identity; c. Class domination blurs the boundaries between state, market and civil society.
Pluralist-Structural Functional	Plurality of interest groups	a. Government is seen as an arena where interest groups ally with each other to shape public policy.	a. The interests of the plurality of interest groups can influence policies of the state; b. No group can continuously influence the state in the interest of their project of accumulation through markets; c. The reflection of priorities of interest groups within the state is legitimate. Formal boundaries between state, markets and civil society are retained.

(*Table 6.1 continued*)

(*Table 6.1 continued*)

Theoretical Lens	Analytical Thrust	Primary Argument	Implications
		State-centred approach	
Statist	Embedded autonomy	a. Argues against the theoretical primacy of class or capital. b. The state retains the ability to formulate and act on its preferences autonomously (it is embedded as well as autonomous).	a. The state has an ideological purpose and hence strives for universal goals. b. Accumulation is directed by state policies in the interest of the nation, even though individual capitalists have a role. c. Formal boundaries between state, markets and civil society are retained.
		Theories of Markets	
Neo-Classical Approach	Competition	a. The use of identities restricts competition and institutional change in the markets. b. Individuals and not institutions discriminate against other individuals. Individuals tend to conform to social norms, for fear of being penalised by business peers.	a. Identities blur the boundaries between market and civil society, but this is a temporary phenomenon. b. Identity has a role in the market-based accumulation process but the competitive logic of the market will ensure that that this role wanes off in the long run.
New Institutional Economics	Role of institutions	a. Institutions are crucial to determining market outcomes. b. They retain the role of competition.	a. Identities blur the boundaries between market and civil society, but this is a temporary phenomenon. b. Transaction costs will be lowered with the introduction of formal institutions, and accordingly, informal institutions will cease to exist in the long run.

Theories of Civil Society

a. Liberal Democratic/ Free Market/ Freedom	Facilitates accumulation	a. Civil society is a site of accumulation.
		b. Three different views on state:
		  i) life, liberty and property, can only be acquired and legally guaranteed in civil society (Locke), and logically state should uphold the rule of law;
		  ii) State should intervene and temper inequality nurtured in civil society (Hegel);
		  iii) Civil society unleashes the productive potential of individuals; state should not intervene (Smith).
			a) The boundaries between state and civil society on one hand, and state and market on the other, are retained.

Marxist	Facilitates accumulation/ Establishes hegemony	a. Civil society is seen as the site of crass materialism where the right to private property is cemented and private accumulation is carried on. b. Civil society comprises not only all economic relationships but also political and cultural relationships and is the site where consent of the subaltern towards their domination is obtained (Gramsci).	Power derived from class position blurs the boundaries between market and civil society in the interest of the dominant class.
Neo-Marxist	Political society	Political society is different from civil society. The latter is a site for the participation of elite and uses the language of rights and entitlement, whereas the former is the site where subalterns enter in a strategic negotiation with ruling classes for their well-being.	The interests of the subaltern are articulated within the state but through negotiations and bargaining, and this leads to a context specific blurring of boundaries between state and civil society.

Source: Compiled by the author.

institutional framework for reducing transaction costs and promoting competition in the markets. For instance, Stiglitz argues that markets can only function effectively with the parallel development of the modern capitalist state and associated legal institutions.[43]

Therefore, the dominant theories of markets bank on market competition for the demise of the role of identities in influencing market outcomes (as in the case of the neo-classical school) and of formal institutions (as in new institutional economics). Both schools of thought converge on the point that identities/informal institutions are detrimental to growth and market competition. However, what the narratives of Dalit entrepreneurs seem to suggest is that contrary to the generalisations made by the neo-classical school and new institutional economics, modern capitalist markets do not necessarily function through impersonal and secular business norms (see Chapters Three and Four). The strengths of NIE (its recognition of informal institutions) are, in fact, also the source of its weakness because it pins its hopes on competition (similar to the neo-classical school) in the markets as an imperative to economic growth, which is expected to lead to the demise of informal institutions, especially those inspired by social identities (for instance, caste).

How do the dominant theories of civil society differ from the approach of intersectionality?

We have explained in the previous chapter how a. civil society should also be considered as a site of accumulation, and b. caste should be seen as a specifically Indian form of civil society. However, dominant theories of civil society do not seem to agree that civil society is also constituted through social identities like caste. While traditional theorists as diverse as Locke, Hegel, Adam Smith, Marx, and Gramsci recognise civil society as indeed a site of accumulation, they do not think that social identity can be a factor in creating and sustaining inequality or facilitating accumulation in the markets. Additionally, theorists like Gramsci believe that civil society is also a site where a consensus around dominant ideas is manufactured through socio-cultural and political institutions. Likewise, Indian literature on civil society tends to see it as either fighting for the deepening of democratic institutions (a theoretical formulation of Marxists scholars) or as a normative ideal of liberal ideology which is not situated in the concrete social context. In the latter version, civil society is seen as working along with the state to promote universal law and social equality. Others in the same theoretical tradition argue that civil society is represented by secular and open mediating institutions (for instance, universities, banks, newspapers, etc.). Further, civil society, when discussed as political society, allows for an exploration of how subalterns are able to strategically negotiate with the ruling class to claim their entitlements from the state.[44]

Documented business histories of Dalits highlight a different understanding of civil society. Civil society, inspired by the ideology of caste, creates conditions for accumulation in the market for upper-castes but, as a result, also acquires coercive and exclusionary characteristics. Accordingly, civil society articulates the ideology of caste and thereby creates institutionalised norms for regulating the interaction of upper-castes with Dalits. This interaction, so shaped, is always unequal and biased in favour of upper-castes. It also helps develop informal institutionalised norms for regulating market outcomes as well as interactions with the institutions of the state.

Claim II: Social Identity as a Source of Blurring the Boundaries between State, Market and Civil Society

The second claim of the intersectionality approach is that a social identity like caste is able to blur the boundaries between state, markets and civil society. Dominant theories will not entirely agree with this claim.

The theories of state and civil society are characterised by diverse understandings with regard to the ability of any organised interest group to make the lines between state, market and civil society porous. Marxist theorists argue that state policies are not shaped keeping in mind the universal interest but are in fact an institutionalised expression of the particular interests of dominant social classes. Indeed, these formulations acknowledge that the boundaries between state, market and civil society are made porous by the influence of dominant class. This is also true of the concepts of hegemony (consent of subalterns secured through the diffusion and popularisation of the ruling class worldview) and 'political society', which points to the articulation of subaltern interests in the state. The analytical thrust on 'class' prevents these theories of state and civil society from acknowledging the fact that civil/political society is constituted by pronounced vertical and horizontal inequalities which can be better understood through caste, gender and religion inspired inequalities. The case of Dalit entrepreneurs forces us to recognise that the boundaries between state, market and civil society are, more often than not, made porous by the institution of caste. Contrary to this experience, the statist theory of state and corresponding liberal democratic theory of civil society do not entertain the possibility of this porousness. They envision a state which necessarily works for the universal interest, upholds the universality of law, and is independent of forces in the market and civil society. However, another version of the liberal theory of the state — the structural functional approach — upholds the capacity of the organised interest group to create porosity between state and civil society. It also underscores the impossibility of any particular group consistently influencing state action. This is negated by the scores of narratives of our Dalit entrepreneurs, who seem to believe that upper-castes are invariably in a position to articulate their economic interests through the institutions of the state.

Finally, the theories of the markets, accept the possibility that caste/social identity can create porosity between market and civil society. However, they are quick to add that social identity has a temporary influence on economic outcomes in the market. In the long run, its role is bound to weaken and will eventually be wiped off since it restricts competition. This is expected to be accompanied by the resurrection of an autonomous state represented by impersonal formal institutions guiding the economy and society. These formulations will again not pass the test of our empirical evidence that forcefully emphasises that social identities like caste can indeed be used by dominant players to meet the demands of market competition, and it can do so for decades if not centuries, which can hardly be termed as a temporary phenomenon. We have noted that such competition can result in efficient market outcomes for an upper-caste trader or employer, but not for Dalits. However, this does not imply that social identities restrict competition in the markets.

Claim III: Particularity versus Totality

Intersectionality as an approach does not claim to explain the totality of state, market and civil society. It is merely a lens to understand the discrimination against unfavourable inclusion of Dalits in the market. The state, market and civil society are interpreted and analysed through their experiences of adverse inclusion. On the other hand, the dominant theories of state, market and civil society claim to capture the totality of these institutions. It has to be said, though, that if the existing macro theories on state, markets and civil society are not able to make sense of the lived realities and experience of Dalits, then the claim of totality does not hold ground since Dalits numerically represent a substantial proportion of the population.

To conclude this section, we argue that caste identity in a market situation reveals an institutional framework that facilitates the following:

a. A hierarchical concept of social relations with an ideological basis that determines the contours of inter-social group (economic) relationships;

b. Caste helps accumulation by regulating worker participation in the economy, controlling credit, reinforcing caste-inspired norms in the market economy, and providing an effective platform to articulate the interests of its members before the state, and thereby influencing bureaucratic outcomes; hence it should be considered as a social structure of accumulation.

The primary factor driving both a. and b. is the ability of caste identity to create overlaps between state and market, market and civil society, and civil society and state.

Methodological and Conceptual Location of Intersectionality

While proposing intersecting spaces between the state, markets and civil society, to understand discrimination and unfavourable inclusion of Dalit entrepreneurs in the markets, we need to clarify a few conceptual issues.

We need to explain whether we retain or discard the analytical categories of state, market and civil society. Drawing again from feminist literature, we highlight three approaches and subsequently put forth our understanding of the intersecting space between state, market and civil society.

McCall outlines three approaches to studying intersectionality. The first approach rejects any existing dominant categories ('anti-categorical') while the second retains them for strategic purposes ('intercategorical'), and the third starts with the analytical assumption that the complexity of the lived experience of the marginalised can be understood by retaining the categories ('intracategorical') to study intersectionality.[45]

The anticategorical approach implies adopting a theoretical methodology that 'deconstructs analytical category. Social life is considered too irreducibly complex — overfowing with multiple and fluid determinations of both subjects and structures — to make fixed categories'.[46] It questions the very edifice of modern society — its founding philosophies, disciplines, categories and concepts.[47] The theoretical foundations of such a critique are largely drawn from post-modernist and post-structuralist critiques of western philosophy, history and language.[48] In the context of our study, the premise of this approach is that discrimination, cultural misrecognition and socio-economic maldistribution are rooted in institutions nurtured and sustained by the state, markets and civil society, and therefore, the intellectual project of deconstructing these normative categories can contribute to favourable social change. We differ with this approach because this can merely aim to alter the conceptual language embedded in the dominant theoretical discourses of state, markets and civil society and make it more inclusive. However, it does not help to usher in social change. Social change can only be brought about by ensuring that social practices closely correspond to the normative claims of these categories. Therefore, Dalits are decidedly for the existence of these normative categories. In other words, they are against the discriminatory social practices embedded in state, markets and civil society and not against these categories per se.

The second approach referred to by McCall as the 'intercategorical' approach, 'begins with the observation that there are relationships of inequality among already constituted social groups, as imperfect and ever changing they are, and takes those relationships as the centre of analysis. The main task of this approach is to explicate those relationships, and doing so requires the provisional use of categories'.[49] In our context, this can be useful to understand the discrimination experienced by Dalits in the light of the complex dynamics of domination and subordination embedded in the institutional practices of state, market and civil society. However, using these categories provisionally and discarding them once the cause of discrimination and consequent marginalisation has been exposed, leaves little scope for Dalits to imagine the nature of social transformation which they aspire to and the normative institutions which can help them achieve this goal. In the absence of any normative institutional means to claim equality and rectificatory justice, the approach offsets the goals which it supposedly seeks to realise — equality and rectificatory justice.

The third, which is the 'intracategorical approach', takes marginalised intersectional identity as the analytical starting point 'in order to reveal the complexity of lived experience within such groups'.[50] It does not reject the categories but critiques the manner in which they are deployed. The strength of this approach is that, similar to our documentation of the business histories of Dalit entrepreneurs, it takes into account the narratives of their experiences of discrimination, and looks at socio-economic maldistribution and cultural misrecognition due to caste location. These narratives enable us to analyse individual experiences and situate them in a wider socio-economic milieu.

The testimonies of Dalit entrepreneurs inform us how the subordination and discrimination they are subjected to in the market cannot be understood by studying any single category (for instance, state or markets). A rigid or mutually exclusive analysis of state, markets or civil society will invariably fail to take into account the structures and associated processes that sustain discrimination. Here, the primary theoretical question is: why should we retain the analytical categories of state, markets and civil society when our primary concern is to analyse the intersecting spaces between them, which nurture and sustain discrimination? Should we not discard these categories since they are the source of discrimination and marginalisation? Our answer is in the negative due to the reasons enumerated below.

First, the vehement political position of Dalits is that equality and justice have to be seen with reference to a certain normative benchmark. As already discussed, the state is seen as the only political entity which can guarantee them what Guru terms comparative social justice — justice which undermines hierarchical social order and gives primacy to distributive justice — while also being an important source of the imagining and administration of social justice.[51] Likewise, the normative idea of civil society harks to a space where socio-political struggles against historical injustices and the claim for redressal are articulated.[52] The normative idea of the market, meanwhile, is expected to reject ascriptive identities in favour of market forces.[53] In light of this, these categories are not to be rejected but in fact employed in order to claim equality and justice. However, our analysis shows that in practice, the state, markets and civil society are also the sources of discrimination. A normative state is an 'ideal-typical' situation and ideals cannot be realised when social relationships are based on caste. It is a vicious circle, therefore, where the normative is cherished but institutions responsible for ushering in normativity are coloured by the ideology of discrimination and help sustain it. This leads us to our second argument in support of retaining the analytical categories of state, market and civil society.

As we have seen, market outcomes are governed not only by formal/informal institutions present in the markets and state, but also by social institutions, collective behaviour and social values shaped by the ideology of caste. In other words, discrimination and marginalisation are caused at the intersection of state, markets and civil society. The very term intersectionality also denotes that there are spaces outside and beyond the intersection which may be free of discriminatory social practices. This implies that there are elements present in each of these realms which can be, and are, non-discriminatory in nature. And it is this that provides political faith for Dalits to aspire, struggle for and to eventually expect absence of discrimination in the intersecting spaces. Normativity is not a utopian ideal but is born out of their experiences of the political possibility of non-discrimination.

Therefore, from the Dalit standpoint, the recognition of the discrimination spearheaded in intersecting spaces is an important step towards studying the micro-politics[54] of context, relations of structural domination, subordination, discrimination and marginalisation, whereas the retention of the analytical categories of state, market and civil society is indicative of the macro-politics of the struggle and the possibility of equality and rectificatory justice.

Coda: Limits of Intersectionality and the Value of Normativity

We have tried to show that the unfavourable inclusion of Dalits in the market takes place at the intersection of state, market and civil society. This also implies that there are arenas beyond the intersection which may not necessarily be discriminatory. Even among the intersecting spaces, the intensity of discrimination varies. As already noted, we have classified the business endeavours of our Dalit entrepreneurs into five sectors: economic endeavours emerging from their earlier caste professions; those related to professions which were earlier restricted from entering and their pursuit entailed severe sanctions; general economic activities; professions which have emerged due to liberalised markets; and businesses that have arisen by virtue of command of highly specialised skills. As per our interpretation of the narratives of Dalit entrepreneurs, it is safe to conclude that the intensity of discrimination is highest when it comes to individuals pursuing economic endeavours which have emerged from their earlier caste professions and professions earlier socially unavailable to them, followed by general economic ventures. Discrimination also exists in the other two sectors, but at relatively lower intensity. The nature and intensity of discrimination varies across the sectors of the economy, which translates into the varying ability of upper-caste business competitors to invoke caste stereotypes in order to attract clients and discourage them from doing business with Dalits.[55] Dalit entrepreneurs would like to move from the situation of intense discrimination to one of less discrimination, leading to equality with upper-caste business peers in the markets. This is precisely why they believe in the normative idea of democracy as well as the normativity in the praxis of the state.

Democracy as a value promises moral equality. This is a very complex social concept which entails not only the empowered inclusion of each in processes leading to collective decisions and actions,[56] but also a framework of civic society which is able to situate the current socio-economic condition of its constituents in a historical context. In other words, moral equality is not merely about current equality; a genuine democratic morality demands that historical wrongs are acknowledged and remedial actions mandated through the appropriate actions of a democratic state.

Thus, a democratic state is one which is able to protect and promote social relations such that social groups take pride in their distinctive identity. It is in this sense, that Dalits feel threatened by the homogenising tendency of the modern state, where 'particular' and 'minority' social identities are subsumed under the universal, which usually implies the identity represented by the dominant upper-caste Hindus. If the state is able to effectively promote and guard particular identities, it would imply that it can intervene effectively in the domain of civil society through the rule of law and restrict exclusionary tendencies.[57] It is through these measures that the state can check unbridled accumulation that often takes place through illegal means, in the sphere of the markets. This nature of normativity would amount to a state capable of fair, non-partisan and non-arbitrary enforcement of its own legal, political and social code of conduct.

Further, for Dalits, only a democratic state can appreciate their articulation of protest against an oppressive social order, for the protection of their rights, respect for their claim to affirmative action (re-distribution) but, more importantly, recognition of and respect for their agency. Therefore, Dalits would argue against any violent suppression of their demands on the basis of caste.

To sum up, these normative principles of heterogeneity, and administrative and judicial capacity to uphold the rule of law in a non-partisan manner, respect for the right to democratic protest for legitimate demands, along with affirmative action to rectify historical wrongs, together are the only institutional means to draw a dividing line among the state, markets and civil society.

—

Notes

1. Margaret L. Anderson and Patricia Hill Collins (eds), *Race, Class and Gender: An Anthology*, Belmot: Wadsworth Publishing, 2006; Lynn Weber, 'A Conceptual Framework for Understanding Race, Class, Gender and Sexuality', in Sharelene Nagy Hesse Bibber and Michelle Yaisiere (eds), *Feminist Perspective on Social Research*, New York: Oxford University Press, 2004, pp. 121–39; Tracy E. Ore (ed.), *The Social Construction of Difference and Inequality: Race, Class, Gender and Sexuality*, New York: McGraw Hill, 2000.
2. Kimberle Crenshaw, 'De-marginalising the Intersection of Race and Sex: A Black Feminist Critique of Antidiscrimination Doctrine, Feminist Theory and Antiracist Politics', *The University of Chicago Legal Forum*, 1989, 140, pp. 139–67; Kimberle Crenshaw, 'Mapping the Margins: Intersectionality, Identity Politics and Violence Against Women of Colour', *Stanford Law Review*, 1991, 43 (6): 1241–99.
3. Irene Browne and Joya Misra, 'The Intersection of Gender and Race in the Labour Market', *Annual Review of Sociology*, 2003, 29: 487–513.
4. Elizabeth McGibbon and Charmaine McPherson, 'Applying Intersectionality & Complexity Theory to Address the Social Determinants of Women's Health', *Women's Health and Urban Life*, 2011, 10 (1): 59–86.

5. Patricia H. Collins, *Black Feminist Thought: Knowledge, Consciousness, and the Politics of Empowerment*, Boston, MA: Unwin Hyman, 2000.
6. Leslie McCall, 'The Complexity of Intersectionality', *Signs*, 2005, 30 (3): 1771–1800.
7. Crenshaw, 'Mapping the Margins'.
8. Evelyn Glenn, 'The Social Construction and Institutionalization of Gender and Race: An Integrative Framework', in Myra M. Ferree, Judith Lorber, and Beth B. Hess (eds), *Revisioning Gender*, New York: Sage, 1999, pp. 3–43.
9. Celine-Marie Pascale, *Making Sense of Race, Class and Gender: Commonsense, Power and Privilege in the United States*, New York: Routledge, 2007.
10. Crenshaw, 'Mapping the Margins', p. 1246.
11. John Rawls, *A Theory of Justice*, Cambridge: Harvard University Press, 1971.
12. Ronald Dworkin, 'What is Equality? Part 2: Equality of Resources', *Philosophy and Public Affairs*, 1981, 10 (4): 283–345.
13. Amartya Sen, *The Idea of Justice*, Cambridge: Harvard University Press, 2009, p. 19, and detailed arguments on pp. 225–90.
14. Sandra Harding and Kathryn Norberg, 'New Feminist Approaches to Social Science Methodologies: An Introduction', *Signs*, 30 (4): 2009–15.
15. Ibid.
16. Structure here is understood as an enduring set of relationships which are reproduced, but they are also situated in the forces driving historical change and hence are open to change over the long term. Accordingly, structures are constituted by power dynamics between different social groups since the latter are defined in relation to the kind of power one group possesses over other. Derek Layder, 'Power, Structure and Agency', *Journal for the Theory of Social Behaviour*, 1985, 15 (2): 132–33. Caste as per this understanding is a structure constituted by social groups where relationships are reproduced and mediated by power.
17. The capacity of an individual(s) to make autonomous choices.
18. S. Lukes, *Power a Radical View*, London: Macmillan, 1974.
19. Also refer to the concept of structuration; Anthony Giddens, *The Constitution of Society: Outline of the Theory of Structuration*, Cambridge: Polity Press, 1984, pp. 5–25.
20. Irene Rafanell and Hugo Gorringe, 'Consenting to Domination? Theorising Power, Agency and Embodiment with Reference to Caste', *The Sociological Review*, 2010, 58 (4): 604–22.
21. Ibid., p. 612.
22. Jennifer C. Nash, 'Re-thinking Intersectionality', *Feminist Review*, 2008, 89 (1): 3.

23. Bob Jessop, 'Recent Theories of the Capitalist State', *Cambridge Journal of Economics*, 1977, 1 (4): 356.

24. In the Indian context, this view has been empirically examined and put forth most famously by Bardhan. Bardhan lists the three dominant classes in India — the capitalists, the rich farmers, and the bureaucracy — who compete with each other and, as a result, none of them is all-powerful. This in turn makes the state relatively autonomous. See Pranab Bardhan, *The Political Economy of Development in India*, New Delhi: Oxford University Press, 1984. Kaviraj, while using the Gramscian concept of passive revolution, talks about the dynamics of class domination in cases where the dominant classes share power with each other. This again gave the state relative autonomy while heralding the passive revolution. See Sudipta Kaviraj, 'A Critique of the Passive Revolution', *Economic and Political Weekly*, 1989, XXIII (45–47): 2429–44.

25. Also refer to Chapter Five, footnote 42.

26. Jessop, 'Recent Theories of the Capitalist State', p. 363.

27. For details of this approach, see Gabriel Almond, 'A Developmental Approach to Political Systems', *World Politics*, 1965, 2: 183–214; Gabriel A. Almond and James S. Coleman (eds), *The Politics of the Developing Areas*, Princeton, NJ: Princeton University Press, 1960; Gabriel A. Almond and G. Bingham Powell Jr., *Comparative Politics: A Developmental Approach*, Boston, Little Brown: 1966; David Easton, 'An Approach to the Analysis of Political Systems', *World Politics*, 1957, 9 (3): 383–400.

28. Nelson W. Polsby, 'How to Study Community Power: The Pluralist Alternative', August 1960, 22 (3): 474–84.

29. One of the well-known studies on the Indian state shows traces of both the trends — society-centric as well as statist. Rudolph and Rudolph understood the Indian state through the study of organised interest groups. They point out that the Indian state is a reflection of the tussle between demand polity (societal groups dominate over the state) and command polity (the state's hegemony prevails over society). See Lloyd I. Rudolph and Susanne Rudolph, *In Pursuit of Lakshmi: The Political Economy of Indian State*, Chicago: University of Chicago Press, 1987.

30. Peter B. Evans, Dietrich Rueschemeyer and Theda Skocpol (eds), *Bringing the State Back In*, Cambridge: Cambridge University Press, 1985.

31. Theda Skocpol, 'Bringing the State Back in: Strategies of Analysis in Current Research', in Peter B. Evans, Dietrich Rueschemeyer and Theda Skocpol (eds), *Bringing the State Back in*, Cambridge: Cambridge University Press, 1985, p. 10.

32. Embedded autonomy depends on 'an apparently contradictory combination of Weberian bureaucratic insulation with intense immersion in the surrounding social structure'. Both the apparently contradictory elements are required because 'the state that was only autonomous would lack both sources of intelligence and the ability to rely on decentralised private implementation. A state that is only embedded is ripe for capture and dismembering. Only when embeddedness and autonomy are joined together can a state be called developmental'. See Peter B. Evans, *Embedded Autonomy: States and Industrial Transformation*, Princeton, New Jersey: Princeton University Press, 1995, p. 12.

33. Evans, *Embedded Autonomy: States and Industrial Transformation*.

34. Precisely for this reason, Bob Jessop argues that the statist theory 'involves a fundamental theoretical fallacy. It posits clear and unambiguous boundaries between the state apparatus and society, state managers and social forces, and state power and societal power, the state can be studied in isolation from the society . . . (It) excludes . . . logics such as corporatism or policy networks; divisions among state managers due to their ties between state organs and other social spheres; and many forms of overlap between state and society. Bob Jessop, 'The State and State Building', in R.A.W. Rhodes, Sarah A. Binder, and Bert A. Rockman (eds), *The Oxford Handbook of Political Institutions*, New York: Oxford University Press, 2006, p. 119.

35. Ashwini Deshpande, *The Grammar of Caste: Economic Discrimination in Contemporary India*, New Delhi: Oxford University Press, 2011, p. 38.

36. George A. Akerlof, '*The Economics of Caste and of the Rat Race and Other Woeful* Tales', in George A. Akerlof (ed.), *Explorations in Pragmatic Economic*, Oxford: Oxford University Press, 2005, pp. 39–55.

37. Deepak Lal, *Hindu Equilibrium, Volume 1: Cultural Stability and Economic Stagnation, India, c. 1500 BC–AD 1980*, Oxford: Clarendon, 1988.

38. James G. Scoville, 'Labor Market Underpinnings of a Caste Economy: Foiling the Coase Theorem', *American Journal of Economics and Sociology*, October 1996, 55 (4): 385–94.

39. Douglas North defines institutions as 'humanely devised constraints that structure political, economic and social interaction. They consist of both informal constraints (sanctions, taboos, customs, traditions, and codes of conduct), and formal rules (constitutions, laws, property rights)'. Please refer to Douglas C. North, 'Institutions', *The Journal of Economic Perspectives*, 1991, 5 (1): 97–102.

40. Oliver E. Williamson, 'The New Institutional Economics: Taking Stock, Looking Ahead', *Journal of Economic Literature*, September 2000, 38 (3): 596.

41. Douglas North, *Structure and Change in Economic History*, New York: W. W. Norton, 1981; Joseph Stiglitz, 'Formal and Informal Institutions', in Partha Das Gupta and Ismail Serageldin (eds), *Social Capital: A Multifaceted Perspective*, Washington: World Bank, 1999, pp. 59–68.

42. Joseph Stiglitz, 'Formal and Informal Institutions', in Partha Dasgupta and Ismail Serageldin (eds), *Social Capital: A Multifaceted Perspective*, Washington: World Bank, 1999, pp. 59–68; also see, Douglas C. North, *Structure and Change in Economic History*, p. 20.

43. For a detailed discussion on Neo-Classical Economics and New Institutional Economics, please refer to Chapter Three.

44. For a detailed discussion on these theoretical aspects of civil society, refer to Chapter Five.

45. Leslie McCall, 'The Complexity of Intersectionality', *Signs*, 2005, 30 (3): 1771–1800.

46. Ibid., p. 1773.

47. Ibid., p. 1776.

48. See eg., Michael Foucault, *The Archaeology of Knowledge and the Discourse on Language*, New York: Random House, 1972; Jacques Derrida, *of Grammatology*, Gayatri Chakravorty Spivak transl., Baltimore: Johns Hopkins University Press, 1974.

49. McCall, 'The Complexity of Intersectionality', p. 1785.

50. Ibid., p. 1774.

51. Gopal Guru, 'Social Justice', in Gopal Jayal and Pratap Bhanu Mehta (eds), *The Oxford Companion to Politics in India*, New Delhi: Oxford University Press, 2010, pp. 361–81.

52. Ibid., pp. 363–65.

53. Chandra Bhan Prasad, 'Markets and Manu: Economic Reforms and it Impact on Caste in India', *CASI Working Paper Series*, No. 08-01, Center for the Advanced Study of India, University of Pennsylvania, January 2008; A. Ramaiah, 'Dalits to Accept Globalisation: Lessons from the Past and Present', mimeo., Tata Institute of Social Sciences, Mumbai, 2004, http://ssrn.com/abstract=568582 (accessed on 21 May 2009).

54. Micropolitics essentially denotes the use of formal and informal power by individuals and groups to pursue their goals.

55. It is much easier for upper-caste business competitors to dissuade clients from going to Dalit entrepreneurs by invoking entrenched notions of purity and pollution, in sectors like retail and wholesale food, sanitary ware, education, small general shops/workshops. The attacks are invariably open and direct. However, in sectors like information technology, medical health (nursing homes), etc., the language and practice of discrimination is found to be more indirect and subtle.

56. David Held, *Models of Democracy*, Stanford: Stanford University Press, 1996.

57. The writings of Hegel may be relevant in this context. Hegel says that the basis of universal law is the modern state. The essence of the modern state is that the universal is bound up with the complete freedom of its particular members. In his words, 'the universal does not prevail or achieve completion except along with particular interest and through the co-operation of particular knowing and willing'. See G.W.F. Hegel, *Hegel's Philosophy of Right*, Oxford: Clarendon Press, 1967.

SEVEN

Conclusion
Caste and Markets

■

The dominant stream of social science theories tends to suggest that the processes of modernisation and capitalist development will automatically undermine the significance of social identities and their role in affecting economic outcomes. The neo-classical school of economics, for example, points out that social identities restrict market competition, impede institutional change, raise transaction costs, and make markets non-competitive. Market driven economies, thus, would undermine ascription-based social identities. New institutional economics does recognise the role of informal institutions — religion, norms, customs, traditions, etc., but historical evidence seems to suggest the imperative of impersonal/formal institutions to lower transaction costs and hence promote competition, which in turn can lead to growth.

Thus, capitalism as an economic system is expected to usher in a particular kind of market rationality where the role of social identities gradually becomes insignificant. In other words, market outcomes will primarily be shaped at the intersection of demand and supply while secular and formal institutions will regulate the markets in order to avoid any market exigencies.

In the Indian context, several scholars writing on the relationship between caste and market economy agree with the overall underpinnings of neo-classical and new institutional economics, that is, markets have the capacity to diminish the influence of social identities in shaping market outcomes. Markets have also acquired prominence because political democracy (equality through a constitutional guarantee based on the liberal principle of citizenship — one-person-one-vote irrespective of social location) has not met the hopes for economic prosperity.

It is against this backdrop that we have analysed the outcome of the political and economic ambitions of Dalits to enter the market as owners of capital and to trade in various goods and services. Towards this end, we have reconstructed the business histories of 90 Dalit entrepreneurs through detailed interviews of each. The entrepreneurs come from 13 districts located in six states of India. Though these business people are perceived by their immediate community to be successful, many see themselves marginalised in relation to their peers among whom they work, earn their living and survive. The business history of Dalit entrepreneurs has been reconstructed to understand how their involvement in the market has been affected by history, social institutions, collective behaviour or any other factors lying outside the realm of a narrow market exchange.

Table 7.1   Type of Economic Ventures
(Percentages in Parentheses)

Caste related	26 (29)
Earlier restricted and considered taboo	12 (13)
General	36 (40)
Liberalised market	11 (12)
Specialised	5 (6)
Total	90 (100)

Source: Author.

The accompanying table shows the number of businesses in the sample by general economic type. The study classified businesses into five types. The first includes economic ventures inspired by caste location (trade in sanitary ware, bulk washing of clothes for the garment industry, sanitary labour and housekeeping contractors, leather work, hair-cutting saloons, etc). Nearly 30 per cent of our respondents entered the market for goods and services associated with their specific sub-castes. The second type relates to trade in goods and services earlier disallowed to Dalits by the Hindu social order. Only 13 per cent of business persons entered the market for such goods and services (educational coaching, trade in food and food products, priesthood, etc). Around 40 per cent of business people come in the third category, which we have termed general economic ventures (trade in wood and fuel wood, handloom material, grocery shops, etc., as well as big businesses like mining, construction and real estate, production and sale of ceramic ware, etc.). The fourth category, constituting 12 per cent, include newer avenues for business which have been created by the opening up of markets and the ongoing integration of the Indian economy with the global economy (trade in communication, electronics and computers, and real estate). Finally, our fifth category covers economic avenues where participation is contingent on higher education, specialised training and professional degrees. These include economic activities related to medicine and hospital services. We find that such highly skilled and technically qualified business persons constitute a little less than 6 per cent of the total Dalit business persons interviewed.

Discrimination in the study is understood as differential treatment of individuals in similar situations. With the rapid transformation of socio-political structures, the sociological norms of purity and pollution defining the relationships between different castes have changed substantially. Yet, although the norms have acquired new form, the content remains the same — the retention of unequal and hierarchical power relationships between the upper-castes and Dalits. In the context of market relationships, the social relation-ships between Dalits and upper-castes continue to be characterised by social prejudice against Dalits, which is strategically invoked and executed to meet the demands of market competition. The business histories of Dalit business persons indicate that the actual nature of discrimination faced varies in different sectors of the market and often assumes different forms.

As noted earlier, nearly one-fifth of Dalit business persons in our survey trade in goods and services, that is, activities inspired by their caste location. They have earlier worked in a different capac-ity, offering their labour services to the upper-caste owners. Their entry into the markets as owners of capital was treated with con-tempt by their former employers. A common entry barrier involved erecting roadblocks in hiring labour to carry out economic activity. Labourers too, as a group, seem to have gone along with the designs of upper-caste business persons, possibly because their own chances of finding work are mostly controlled by the former. Second, most Dalit business persons faced immense difficulty in securing initial orders for their business. This is generally true for both sanitary and leather business where the market is controlled by the upper-castes. In the case of leather goods, most Dalit entrepreneurs seem to have lost out to big capital and are mostly producing goods on a piece-rate arrangement.

Dalits trading as wholesalers and retailers in the food and beverage business are compelled to supply goods at lower prices. If they refuse, the upper-caste retailers invoke their caste identity and reject their produce. As retailers, they get credit for a shorter period while procuring food items from the wholesalers. Similarly, Dalits often face negative publicity by their business competitors with regard to their 'impure' caste status when trying to attract customers to their own joints. In a few cases, the Dalit owner even had to shift the food establishment to a Dalit locality because of an inability to attract clients from a predominantly upper-caste area. In the category of 'general business' and the new sectors which have come up due to the opening up of the markets, the efforts of the Dalits were hampered by the lack of access to the state's resources. The biggest handicap was their lack of access to social networks that are controlled by the upper-castes which regulate the informal credit market.[1] Short-term informal credit can critically influence the success/failure of any business. Dalit business persons are denied access to these informal networks. Even when they succeed in accessing informal credit, the rate of interest is often much higher than the prevailing market rate. The lack of informal credit or being forced to arrange informal credit at high interest rates, disempowered them to meet the deadlines of lucrative contracts (it may have also helped to scale up their business). Last but not the least, Dalits are unable to rent or buy a strategically important physical space for their businesses due to opposition from upper-caste business competitors.

The final category of businesses, which we have termed as 'specialised', involve Dalits whose previous generation had managed to improve its economic status as a result of the affirmative action policies of the state. Thus they had both the required skills and initial capital to enter into a business as well as sustain themselves. However, all the respondents noted the subtle experience of caste prejudice, claiming that they were not given as much importance as their upper-caste peers commanded. In other words, high class status does not necessarily translate into high social status; caste does come in the way.

Any kind of economic activity is critically influenced by the policies of the state. The role of the modern state is crucial because it establishes and legitimises property rights and governance structures (including labour laws and taxation), regulates credit availability, and also creates and maintains infrastructure (electricity, water, roads, etc.). Dalit entrepreneurs have invariably experienced adverse reactions by state officials whenever they have tried to access the state's resources. In their view, state resources can only be accessed through social networks. They understand social networks as a critical social resource which could enable them to cultivate a relationship with state officials in order to get favourable treatment to enhance their business ventures.

For instance, many of the Dalit entrepreneurs we interviewed were denied credit because they were not considered capable enough to run modern businesses. They were told by officials that they should not waste the state's precious resources because their business was 'destined' to fail, and that instead they should stick to their traditional professions. Dalit entrepreneurs elaborated at length on how kith and kin networks of upper-castes, formed through family contacts and marriage relationships, regularly enable them to access the resources of the state more easily than they can ever manage. These resources range from getting government contracts to ensuring payment of lower sales tax/cess, to flouting municipal laws with ease and without any fear of penalty.

One way to access states resources and tackle officials is through the payment of bribes. In the Dalit entrepreneurs' view, rent-seeking by state officials is rampant and affects every business person, irrespective of caste location. However, what troubles Dalit business persons most is that their upper-caste peers, by virtue of their social network, have to pay lower bribes than they have to. This both reduces their transaction costs and helps them generate a higher surplus. Moreover, it is felt that the upper-castes can access state resources repeatedly, which seems a remote possibility for Dalit business persons.

A telling example of the role of social networks in accessing state resources can be drawn from Madhya Pradesh. The state government had explicitly notified that a specified percentage of total government procurement was to be sourced from Dalit enterprises. Despite being given this exclusive space to do business and earn profit, Dalit entrepreneurs found it difficult to get their payment released. Therefore, many of them had to informally involve upper-caste persons as business partners, whose role was to ensure timely release of payments. In other words, the use of social networks to access the state resources enables the upper-castes to earn money without investing capital in the business, while their absence substantially increases the transaction costs for Dalits.

In several instances, we were told that deliberate inaction by state officials under the influence of upper-caste business competitors increased the transaction cost for Dalits. For instance, licences were not granted to a Dalit brick kiln owner and leather goods trader in Pune and Agra respectively, due to the influence of upper-caste business competitors in both cases. Many Dalit entrepreneurs also informed us that Dalits are often forced to withdraw from the market because of real or potential threats of violence by upper-caste business competitors. State inaction, in such instances, is more palpable because the police routinely refuse to register a first information report.

As is evident from the preceding discussion, Dalit owners of capital experience what Sen[2] describes as 'unfavourable inclusion' in market processes, though the degree of adversity varies with location and sector of the markets. In other words, access to market spaces for Dalits as owners of capital is neither entirely blocked (markets having absolutely rigid entry barriers for Dalits), nor are avenues provided for complete integration as equal players (markets being completely accommodative to the entry of Dalit entrepreneurs). Further, the tendency of market processes towards absolute rigidity or complete accommodation is not only decided by market processes, but equally by the balance of institutional forces in the wider socio-economic and political realms. In other words, if Dalit business persons experience unfavourable inclusion in the market processes, duly aided by the state's inaction, the roots lie in civil society.

It is in the realm of civil society that the ideological architecture of caste relationships is invoked and sustained. It is here that the resources of social networks are drawn to help business endeavours of upper-castes. Again, it is in civil society that potential and actual violence against Dalits is carried out. Therefore, it is important that we understand civil society not only as a site of democratisation but also, following the traditional theorists of civil society — Locke, Adam Smith, Hegel, Marx, and Gramsci — as a site of accumulation. It is in this context that caste must be seen as a specific form of the Indian civil society because on the one hand, caste influences the state (social networks) and on the other, it plays an important role in influencing market outcomes through controlling credit, organising labour and regulating supply and procurement.

In the course of our empirical investigation to reconstruct the business histories of 90 Dalit entrepreneurs, we have tried to explore whether, and to what degree, market outcomes are affected by ascriptive group identity. Overall we found that while Dalits are able to enter the markets as owners of capital, they experience numerous forms of discrimination leading to their unfavourable inclusion in market processes. We argue that multiple forms of discrimination practised against Dalits are developed and sustained at the intersection of state, market and civil society.

The thesis of intersectionality challenges the existing dominant conceptualisation of somewhat rigid analytical boundaries between these institutions — state, market and civil society. It argues in favour of blurred boundaries and the consequent overlapping space which is instrumental in (re)reproducing discrimination/unfavourable inclusion. The intersectional spaces and experiences, though originating in the realm of state, markets and society, on intersecting and interacting, transcend their original character and assume a unique characteristic with its own set of norms, rules and behavioural patterns, different and contradictory to the assumed rationalities of state planning and markets.

Thus, outcomes in the markets are not only governed by formal economic institutions within the markets and state, but are also influenced by social institutions, collective behaviour and social values shaped by the ideology of caste. However, the term intersectionality itself also denotes that there are spaces outside and beyond the intersection that can possibly be free of discriminatory social practices against one or more social groups.

Future Research Agendas

This book marks a certain break from existing literature and provides new empirical information and possibly a new conceptual apparatus to interpret available empirical data and analyse and interpret caste-based discrimination in the context of economic transactions in the markets. However, there are a few crucial gaps that future research must take up. These are as follows:

Pointers for Further Empirical Research

- Does the nature and intensity of discrimination vary between different geographical spaces with varying political formations?

- What are the typical kinds of barriers faced by Dalits entering different sectors of the economy?
- Why is the presence of Dalit women owners of capital negligible?
- What are the other factors like class, gender, religion, and region, which operate along with caste?

Pointers for Further Conceptual Research

Intersecting Spaces

- What are the specific socio-political and economic reasons facilitating the reproduction of social power in the intersecting spaces that results in the adverse inclusion of Dalit owners of capital in the market?

Beyond Intersecting Spaces

This would demand an analytical exploration of the following:

- Role of affirmative action in state provided jobs
- Role of lobbies such as the Dalit Chambers of Commerce

These interrelated sections should form the base on which to build an understanding of the dual nature (oppressive and liberating) of the interaction between market, politics and society. This theorisation should help us develop a framework for understanding the conditions whereby discrimination and adverse inclusion can be further challenged.

Notes

1. In all the sectors covered under this study, access to credit through informal social networks was either not available or available at relatively high interest rates for Dalits.
2. Amartya Sen, 'Social Exclusion: Concept, Application, and Scrutiny', 2000, pp. 14–18, http://www.flacso.org/biblioteca/sen_social_exclusion. pdf (accessed on 2 June 2008).

Bibliography

Abrams, Philip, 'Notes on the Difficulty of Studying the State', *Journal of Historical Sociology*, 1988, 1(1): 58–89.

Ahmad, Imtiaz, and Shashi Bhushan Upadhyay, eds, *Dalit Assertion in Society, Literature and History*, Delhi: New Orient Blackswan, 2010.

Ajay, Gudavarthy, 'Dalit and Naxalite Movements in AP: Solidarity or Hegemony?' *Economic and Political Weekly*, 2005, XL (51): 5410–18.

Akerlof, George, 'The Economics of Caste and of the Rat Race and Other Woeful Tales', in George Akerlof, ed., *Explorations in Pragmatic Economics*, Oxford: Oxford University Press, 2005, pp. 39–55.

———, 'Labour Contracts and Partial Gift Exchange', *The Quarterly Journal of Economics*, 1982, 97(4): 543–69.

———, 'The Market for Lemons: Quality, Uncertainty and the Market Mechanism', *The Quarterly Journal of Economics*, 1970, 84(3): 488–500.

Almond, Gabriel A. and G. Bingham Powell Jr., *Comparative Politics: A Developmental Approach*, Boston: Little Brown, 1966.

Almond, Gabriel A. and James S. Coleman, eds, *The Politics of the Developing Areas*, Princeton, NJ: Princeton University Press, 1960.

Almond, Gabriel A., 'A Developmental Approach to Political Systems', *World Politics*, 1965,(2):183–214.

Aloysius, G., *Nationalism without a Nation in India*, New Delhi: Oxford University Press, 1997.

Ambedkar, B. R., 'Caste in India: The Mechanism, Genesis and Development' in B. R. Ambedkar, *Annihilation of Caste*, Jullander: Bheema Patrika Publication, 1916 [reprinted 1936], http://www.stopfundinghate.org/resources/AmbedkarAnnihilationofCastes.pdf (accessed on 28 February 2011).

———, *Dr. Babasaheb Ambedkar Writing and Speeches*, Section IV, Kalaram Temple Entry Satyagraha, Nasik and Temple Entry Movement, Volume XVII, Government of Maharashtra.

Ananth, Bindu and Nachiket Mor, 'Financial Services Case Study: India', Paper Presented at Organisation of Economic Co-operation and Development (OECD) — World Bank Fifth Services Experts Meeting, 3–4 February, OECD, Paris, p. 5, http://webdomino1.oecd.org/COMNET/ECH/6SEM.nsf/viewHtml/index/$FILE/india_mor.pdf. (accessed on 21 November 2011).

Anderson, Margaret, L. and Patricia Hill Collins, eds, *Race, Class and Gender: An Anthology*, Belmot: Wadsworth Publishing, 2006.

Arora, Saurabh and Bulat Sanditov, 'Caste as Community? Networks of Social Affinity in a South Indian Village', UNU Wider Working Paper, http://www.merit.unu.edu/publications/wppdf/2009/wp2009-037.pdf (accessed on 21 November 2011).

Bandyopadhyay, Sekhar, *Caste, Protest and Identity, in Colonial India: The Namasudras of Bengal*, London: Routledge, 1997.

Banerjee, Abhijit and Esther Duflo, 'The Nature of Credit Constraints. Evidence from an Indian Bank', mimeo., MIT, 2001, http://www.chicagogsb.edu/research/workshops/AppliedEcon/archive/WebArchive 20012002/duflo.pdf (accessed on 9 October 2011).

Banerjee, Abhijit, Shawn Cole and Esther Duflo, 'Banking Reform in India', mimeo., MIT, 2004, http://econ-www.mit.edu/files/508 (accessed on 23 June 2009).

Banerjee, Biswajit and J. B. Knight, 'Caste Discrimination in the Indian Urban Labour Market', *Journal of Development Economics*, 1985, 17(3): 277–307.

Bardhan, Pranab, 'Law and Development' in A. K. Dutt and J. Ros, eds, *International Handbook of Development Economics*, Cheltenham: Elgar, 2008, pp. 381–393.

———, *The Political Economy of Development in India*, New Delhi: Oxford University Press, 1984.

Barney, J., 'Firm Resources and Sustained Competitive Advantage', *Journal of Management*, 1991, 17(1): 99–120.

Basile, Elisabetta and Barbara Harriss-White, 'Corporative Capitalism: Civil Society and the Politics of Accumulation in Small Town India', QEH Working Paper Series — QEHWP S38, Oxford: Queen Elizabeth House, 2000.

Bates, Thomas, 'Gramsci and the Theory of Hegemony', *Journal of the History of Ideas*, 1975, 36 (2): 351–66.

Bauman, Chad M., 'Identity, Conversion, and Violence: Dalits, Adivasis, and the 2007–08 Riots in Orissa', in Joseph Marianus Kujur and Rowena Robinson, eds, *Margins of Faith: Dalit and Tribal Christianity in India*, Thousand Oaks, CA: Sage, 2010, pp. 263–90.

Bayly, Susan, *Caste, Society and Politics in India from the Eighteenth Century to the Modern Age*, Cambridge: Cambridge University Press, 2008.

Becker, G. S., *The Economics of Discrimination*, Chicago: The University of Chicago Press, 1971.

Béteille, André, 'Universities as Public Institutions' *Economic and Political Weekly*, 2005, XL (31): 3377–81.

———, 'Empowerment', *Economic and Political Weekly*, 1999, XXXIV (10 and 11): 589–97.

———, 'Civil Society and Its Institutions', in *Civil Society and Democracy*, ed., C. M. Elliot, Delhi: Oxford University Press, 1995, pp. 191–210.

Bhagwan, Manu and Anne Feldhaus, *Speaking the Truth: Religion, Caste and Subaltern Question in India*, New Delhi: Oxford University Press, 2007.

Bhaumik, Sumon Kumar and Jenifer Piesse, 'A Closer Look at Banks Behaviour in Emerging Credit Markets? Evidence from the Indian banking industry', mimeo., London: Aditya V. Birla India Centre, London Business School, 2004, http://papers.ssrn.com/sol3/papers.cfm?abstract_id=606761#PaperDownload (accessed on 23 March 2010).

Bobbio, Norberto, *Which Socialism? Marxism, Socialism and Democracy*, Cambridge: Polity, 1987.

Borooah, Vani K., Amaresh Dubey and Sriya Iyer, 'The Effectiveness of Jobs Reservation: Caste, Religion and Economic Status in India,' *Development and Change*, 2007, 38(3): 423–45.

Bougle, C., 'The Essence and Reality of Caste System', *Contributions to Indian Sociology*, 1968, 2(1): 17–30.

Bourdieu, Pierre and Jean Claude Passeron, *Reproduction in Education, Society and Culture*, California: Sage, 1977.

Boyer, R., *The Regulation School: A Critical Introduction*, New York: Columbia University Press, 1990.

Bridges, Amy Beth, 'Nicos Poulantsaz and the Marxist Theory of the State', *Politics & Society*, 1974, 4(2): 161–90.

Brown, Radcliffe, 'On Social Structure', *The Journal of the Royal Anthropological Institute of Great Britain and Ireland*, 1940, 70(1): 1–12.

Browne, Irene and Joya Misra, 'The Intersection of Gender and Race in the Labour Market', *Annual Review of Sociology*, 2003, 29: 487–513.

Burt, Ronald S., 'Structural Hole versus Network Closure', in Nancy Lin, Karen Cook, and Ronald S. Burt, eds, *Social Capital: Theory and Research*, New Brunswick: Aldine Transaction, 2001, pp. 31–56.

———, *Structural Holes: The Social Structure of Competition*, Cambridge, MA: Harvard University Press, 1992.

———, *Corporate Profits and Cooptation*, New York: Academic Press, 1983.

Chaco, Pariyaram, *Caste, Business and Entrepreneurship in South India*, Delhi: Kanishka Publishing House, 1991.

Chakraborty, Debashis, D. Shyam Babu and Manashi Chakravorty, 'Atrocities on Dalits: What the District Level Data Say on Society-State Complicity', *Economic and Political Weekly*, 2006, XLI(24): 2478–81.

Chandhoke, Neera, *The Conceits of Civil Society*, New Delhi: Oxford University Press, 2003.

———, 'The Assertion of Civil Society Against the State' in Manoranjan Mohanty, P. N. Mukherjee and Olle Tornquist, eds, *People's Rights: Social Movement and State in the Third World*, New Delhi: Sage, 1998, pp. 23–41.

———, *State and Civil Society: Explorations in Political Theory*, New Delhi: Sage, 1995.

Chatterjee, Partha, 'Community in the East', *Economic and Political Weekly*, 1998, XXXIII(6): 280–87.

———, 'Development Planning in India', in Partha Chatterjee, ed., *State and Politics in India*, New Delhi: Oxford University Press, 1997, pp. 271–97.

Chavan, Pallavi, 'Access to Bank Credit: Implications for Dalit Rural Households', *Economic and Political Weekly*, 2007, XLII(31): 3219–24.

Claessens, Stijn, and Luc Laeven, 'Financial Development, Property Rights, and Growth', *The Journal of Finance*, 2003, 56(6): 2401–36.

Claude, Levi Strauss, 'Social Structure', in Henrietta L. Moore and Todd Sanders, eds, *Anthropology in Theory, Issues in Epistemology*, Oxford: Blackwell Publishing, 2006, pp. 137–52.

Collins, Hill Patricia, *Black Feminist Thought: Knowledge Consciousness, and the Politics of Empowerment*, New York: Routledge, 2000.

Corbridge, Stuart, Glyn Williams, Manoj Srivastava and Rene Veron, *Seeing the State: Governance and Governmentality in India*, Cambridge: Cambridge University Press, 2005.

Crenshaw, Kimberle, 'Mapping the Margins: Intersectionality, Identity Politics and Violence Against Women of Colour', *Stanford Law Review*, 1991, 43(6): 1241–99.

———, 'De-marginalising the Intersection of Race and Sex: A Black Feminist Critique of Antidiscrimination Doctrine, Feminist Theory and Antiracist Politics', *University of Chicago Legal Forum*, 1989, 140: 139–67.

Credit Rating and Information Services of India Limited (CRISIL), http://www.crisil.com/credit-ratings-risk-assessment/crisil-ratings.htm. (accessed on 20 March 2010).

———, 'Insight: CRISL Default Study', 2004–2005, http://www.crisil.com/credit-ratings-risk-assessment/2005-crisil-rating-default-study.pdf (accessed on 20 March 2010).

Derrida, Jacques, *Of Grammatology*, transl. Gayatri Chakravorty Spivak, Baltimore: Johns Hopkins University Press, 1974.

Desai, Sonali and Amresh Dubey, 'Caste in 21st Century India: Competing Narratives', *Economic and Political Weekly*, 2011, XLVI(11): 40–49.

Deshpande, Ashwini and Katherine Newman, 'Where the Path Leads: The Role of Caste in Post-University Employment Expectations', *Economic and Political Weekly*, 2007, XLII: 4133–40.

Deshpande, Ashwini, The *Grammar of Caste: Economic Discrimination in Contemporary India*, New Delhi: Oxford University Press, 2011.

———, *State and Civil Society: Explorations in Political Theory*, New Delhi: Sage, 1995., 'Recasting Economic Inequality', *Review of Social Economy*, 2000, 58(3): 386.

Dirks, Nicholas, 'Castes of Mind', *Representations*, 1992, 37: 56–78.

Doucet, A. and J. Siltanen, *Gender Relations in Canada: Intersectionality and Beyond*, Toronto: Oxford University Press, 2000.

Dubois J. A. Abbe, *Description of the Character, Manners, and Customs of the People of India; and of Their Institutions, Religious and Civil*, 1817, transl. Henry K. Beauchamp, London, p. 29, quoted in Nicholas B. Dirks, 'Caste of Minds', *Representations*, 1992, 37: 56.

Dumont, Louis, *Homo Hierarchicus: An Essay on the Caste System*, Chicago: University of Chicago Press, 1970.

Duncan, Ian, 'Dalits and Politics in Rural North India: The Bahujan Samaj Party in Uttar Pradesh', *Journal of Peasant Studies*, 1999, 27(1): 35–60.

Dworkin, Ronald, 'What is Equality? Part 2: Equality of Resources', *Philosophy and Public Affairs*, 1981, 10(4): 283–345.

Easton, David, 'An Approach to the Analysis of Political Systems', *World Politics*, 1957, 9(3): 383–400.

Evans, Peter B., *Embedded Autonomy: States and Industrial Transformation*, Princeton, New Jersey: Princeton University Press, 1995.

———, Dietrich Rueschemeyer and Theda Skocpol, eds, *Bringing the State Back In*, Cambridge: Cambridge University Press, 1985.

Femia, Joseph, 'Hegemony and Consciousness in the Thought of Antonio Gramsci', *Political Studies*, 1975, 23(1): 29–48.

Foucault, Michel, *The Archaeology of Knowledge and the Discourse on Language*, New York: Random House, 1972.

Frankel, R. Francine, *India's Political Economy, 1947–1977: The Gradual Revolution*, Princeton: Princeton University Press, 1978.

Fraser, Nancy, 'Rethinking Redistribution', *New Left Review*, 2000, 3 May–June, pp. 107–20.

———, 'From Redistribution to Recognition? Dilemmas of Justice in a "Post-Socialist Age"', *New Left Review*, 1995, 212: 68–93.

Fuller, C. J., ed., *Caste Today*, New Delhi: Oxford University Press, 1996.

Gajanan, Mukta, Joshi, 'Access to Credit By Hawkers: What Is Missing? Theory And Evidence From India', D.Phil diss., The Ohio State University, 2005.

Gandhi, M. K., *Varna Vyavastha* (Gujarati), transl. B. R. Ambedkar, quoted in B. R. Ambedkar, *What Congress and Gandhi Have Done to Untouchables*, New Delhi: Gautam Book Centre, 2009 [1945].

Gavaskar, Mahesh, 'Phule's Critique of Brahmin Power' in *Untouchables: Dalits in Modern India*, ed., S. M. Michael, Boulder CO: Lynne Rienner Publishers, 1999, pp. 108–31.

Geetha, V., 'Bereft of Being: The Humiliations of Untouchability', in *Humiliation: Claims and Context*, ed., Gopal Guru, New Delhi: Oxford University Press, 2009, pp. 95–107.

Geetha, V., and S. V. Rajdurai, *Towards a Non Brahmin Millennium: From Iyothee Thass to Periyar*, Calcutta: Samya, 1998.

Ghurye, G. S., *Caste and Race in India*, Mumbai: Popular Prakashan, 1969.

Giddens, Anthony, *The Constitution of Society: Outline of the Theory of Structuration*, Cambridge: Polity Press, 1984.

———, *Central Problems in Social Theory*, Berkeley, CA: University of California Press, 1979.

———, *New Rules of Sociological Methods*, London: Hutchinson, 1976.

Glenn, Evelyn, 'The Social Construction and Institutionalization of Gender and Race: An Integrative Framework', in Myra M. Ferree, Judith Lorber and Beth B. Hess, eds, *Revisioning Gender*, New York: Sage, 1999, pp. 3–43.

Golwalkar, M.S., *We are Nationhood Defined*, Nagpur: Bharat Prakashan, 1934.

Gorringe, Hugo, *Untouchable Citizens: Dalit Movement and Democratisation in Tamil Nadu*, New Delhi: Sage, 2005.

Gouldner, Alvin, *The Two Marxisms: Contradictions and Anomalies in the Development of Theory*, London: Macmillan Press, 1980.

Government of India, Ministry of Finance, http://www.smallindustryindia. com/publications/reserveditems/dereserve.htm (accessed on 23 June 2011).

———, 2009–10, *Economic Survey*, New Delhi: Ministry of Finance, 2010.

———, *The Challenge of Employment: An Informal Sector Perspective*, Vol. I, National Commission for Enterprises in Unorganised Sector, New Delhi, 2009.

———, 2006, *Social, Economic and Educational Status of Indian Muslims*, New Delhi: Ministry of Minority Affairs, 2006.

Government of Madhya Pradesh, *The Bhopal Declaration*, http://www. ambedkar.org/ (accessed on 30 June 2010).

———, *The Bhopal Conference: Charting A New Course For Dalits For The 21st Century*, Bhopal, 2002.

Gramsci, Antonio, *Selections from the Prison Notebooks*, transl., Quentin Hoare and Geoffrey Nowell Smith, London: Lawrence and Wishart, 1971.

Granovetter, Mark, 'The Impact of Social Structure on Economic Outcomes', *Journal of Economic Perspectives*, 2005, 19(1): 33–50.

———, 'Economic Institutions as Social Construction: A Framework of Analysis', *Acta Sociologica*, 1992, 35(1): 3–11.

———, 'Economic Action and Social Structure: The Problem of Embeddedness', *American Journal of Sociology*, 1985, 91(3): 481–510.

———, 'The Strength of Weak Ties: A Network Theory Revisited', *Sociological Theory*, 1983, 1: 201–33.

———, 'The Strength of Weak Ties,' *American Journal of Sociology*, 1973, 78(6): 1360–80.

Gupta, Akhil, 'Blurred Boundaries: The Discourse of Corruption, the Culture of Politics, and the Imagined State', *American Ethnologist*, 1995, 22(2): 375–402.

Gupta, Dipankar, *Interrogating Caste: Understanding Hierarchy and Difference in Indian Society*, New Delhi: Penguin, 2000.

———, 'Civil Society in the Indian Context: Letting the State off the Hook', *Contemporary Sociology*, 1999, 26(3): 305–07.

Gupta, Smita, 'State Finances and Dalits', mimeo., New Delhi: Institute for Human Development, 2007.

Guru, Gopal and Anuradha Chakravarty, 'Who are the Country's Poor: Social Movement Politics and Dalit Poverty', in Raka Ray and Fainsod Katzenstein, eds, *Social Movements in India: Poverty, Power and Politics*, Oxford: Rowman and Littelfield Publishers, 2005, pp. 135–60.

Guru, Gopal, 'Social Justice', in Niraja Jayal and Pratap Bhanu Mehta, eds, *The Oxford Companion to Politics in India'*, New Delhi: Oxford University Press, 2010.

———, 'The Language of Dalit-Bahujan Political Discourse', in Manoranjan Mohanty, ed., *Class, Caste, Gender*, New Delhi: Sage, 2004a.

———, 'Dalit Vision of India: From Bahishkrut to Inclusive Bharat', *Futures*, 2004b, vol. 36.

———, 'Understanding Violence against Dalits in Marathwada', *Economic and Political Weekly*, 1994, XXIX(9): 469–72.

Harding, Sandra and Kathryn Norberg, 'New Feminist Approaches to Social Science Methodologies: An Introduction', *Signs*, 2005, 30(4): 2009–15.

Harriss-White, Barbara and Aseem Prakash, 'Social Discrimination in India: A Case for Economic Citizenship', IHD-Oxfam Working Paper Series, New Delhi: Institute for Human Development, 2010.

Harriss-White, Barbara, *India Working: Essays on Society and Economy*, Cambridge: Cambridge University Press, 2003.

Hegel, F. G. W., *Hegel's Philosophy of Right*, transl. T. M. Knox, Oxford: Clarendon Press, 1967.

Held, David, *Models of Democracy*, Stanford: Stanford University Press, 1996.

Himanshu, 'Employment and Wages of Dalits', mimeo., Centre De Science Humaines, http://www.csh-delhi.com/team/downloads/publiperso/Emp_wages_Dalits_himanshu.pdf (accessed on 27 September 2011).

Iheduru, C. O., 'Social Concentration, Labour Unions and the Creation of a Black Bourgeoisie in South Africa', *Commonwealth & Comparative Politics*, 2002, 40(2): 47–85.

Inden, Robert, *Imagining India*, Oxford: Oxford University Press, 1990.

Institute for Human Development, *India Labour and Employment Report 2014: Workers in the Era of Globalisation*, New Delhi: Academic Foundation, 2014.

Iyer, Lakshmi, Tarun Khanna, and Ashutosh Varshney, 'Caste and Entrepreneurship in India', Harvard Business School Working Paper, http://www.hbs.edu/research/pdf/12-028.pdf (accessed on 11 January 2012).

Jaffrelot, Christophe, *India's Silent Revolution: The Rise of Low Caste in North India*, London: Hurst and Company, 2003.

———, *The Hindu Nationalist Movement and Indian Politics: 1925–1990s*, New Delhi: Penguin Books, 1996.

———, 'Hindu Nationalism: Strategic Syncretism in Ideology Building', *Economic and Political Weekly*, 1993, XXVIII(12–13): 517–24.

Jayal, Niraja Gopal, 'Five Caveats to Citizenship', mimeo., New Delhi: Jawaharlal Nehru University, 1999.

Jeffrey, Craig and Jens Lerche, 'Stating the Difference: State, Discourse and Class Reproduction in Uttar Pradesh, India', *Development and Change*, 2000, 4: 857–78.

Jeffrey, Craig, Roger Jeffery and Patricia Jeffery, 'Degrees without Freedom: The Impact of Formal Education on Dalit Young Men in North India', *Development and Change*, 2004, 35(5): 963–86.

Jessop, Bob, 'The Social Embeddedness of the Economy and its Implications for Economic Governance', http://eprints.cddc.vt.edu/digitalfordism/fordism_materials/jessop2.htm (accessed on 21 August 2011).

———, 'The State and State Building' in R. A. W. Rhodes, Sarah A. Binder, and Bert A. Rockman, eds, *The Oxford Handbook of Political Institutions*, New York: Oxford University Press, 2006, pp. 111–30.

———, 'Recent Theories of the Capitalist State', *Cambridge Journal of Economics*, 1977, 1(4): 353–73.

Jetley, S., 'Education and Occupational Mobility: A UP Village', *Economic and Political Weekly*, 1969, IV(17): 725–27.

Jodhka, Surinder S., 'Caste in the Periphery', *Seminar*, 2001, http://www.india-seminar.com/2001/508/508%20surinder%20s.%20jodhka.htm (accessed on 16 July 2011).

———, 'Dalits in Business: Self-Employed Scheduled Castes in North-West India', *Economic and Political Weekly*, 2010, XLV(11): 488–500.

———, 'Prejudice Without Pollution? Scheduled Castes in Contemporary Punjab', *Journal of Indian School of Political Economy*, 2000, 12(3–4): 381–404.

Jodhka, Surinder S., and Murli Dhar, 'Cow, Caste and Communal Politics: Dalit Killings in Jhajjar', *Economic and Political Weekly*, 2003, XXXVIII(3): 174–76.

Joshi, Barbara R., ed., *Untouchables: Voice of Dalit Liberation Movement*, London: Zed Books, 1986.

Joshi, Sanjay, 'Republicizing Religiosity: Modernity, Religion and the Middle Class', in *The Invention of Religion: Rethinking Belief in Politics and History*, eds, Derek R. Peterson and Daren R. Walhof, New Jersey: Rutgers University Press, 2002, pp. 79–99.

Kannan, K. P., 'Dualism, Informality and Social Inequality: An Informal Economy Perspective of the Challenge of Inclusive Development in India', *Indian Journal of Labour Economics*, 2009, 52(1): 1–32.

Kannan, K. P., and G. Raveendran, 'India's Common People: The Regional Profile', *Economic and Political Weekly*, 2011, XXXVIII(6): 60–73.

Kapoor, Dip, 'Gendered-Caste Violations and the Cultural Politics of Voice in Rural Orissa, India', *Gender, Place & Culture*, 2007, 14(5): 609–16.

Kaviraj, Sudipta, 'On State, Society and Discourse in India', in *Development: Critical Concepts in Social Science*, ed., Stuart Corbridge, London and New York: Routledge, 2000, pp. 426–43.

Kaviraj, Sudipta, 'A Critique of the Passive Revolution', *Economic and Political Weekly*, 1989, XXIII(45–7): 2429–44.

Khapre, Shubhangi, 'Young Dalits are More Pragmatic' DNA, 16 April, 2006, http://www.dnaindia.com/mumbai/special_young-dalits-are-more-pragmatic_1024353 (accessed on 26 September 2011).

Khare, R. S., *Normative Culture and Kinship. Essays on Hindu Categories, Processes and Perspectives*, New Delhi: Vikas Publishing House, 1983.

Khilnani, Sunil, 'The Development of Civil Society', in Sudipta Kaviraj and Sunil Khilnani, eds, Cambridge: Cambridge University Press, 2001, pp. 11–32.

Kothari, Rajni, *State Against Democracy: In Search of Humane Governance*, Delhi: Ajanta, 1988.

Kotlowski, Dean, 'Black Power-Nixon Style: The Nixon Administration and Minority Business Enterprise', *Business History Review*, 1998, 72(3): 409–45.

Kotz, David M., 'Interpreting Social Structure of Accumulation Theory', in David M. Kotz,Terrence McDonough and Michael Reich, eds, *Interpreting the Social Structure of Accumulation Theory*, Cambridge: Cambridge University Press, 1994a, pp. 50–71.

———,'The Regulation Theory and Social Structure of Accumulation Approach' in David M. Kotz, Terrence McDonough and Michael Reich, eds, *The Social Structures of Accumulation: The Political Economy of Growth and Crisis*, Cambridge: Cambridge University Press, 1994b, pp. 85–98.

Krekel, R., 'Unequal Opportunity Structure and Labour Market Segmentation', *Sociology*, 1980, 4 : 525–49.

Kuan-Hsing, Chen, 'Civil Society and Min-Jian: On Political Society and Popular Democracy', *Cultural Studies*, 2003, 17(6): 877–96.

Kumar, Sanjay, 'Civil Society in Society', *Economic and Political Weekly*, 2005, XXXV(31): 2276–79.

Lal, Deepak, *Hindu Equilibrium, Volume 1: Cultural Stability and Economic Stagnation: India, c. 1500 BC–AD 1980*, Oxford: Clarendon Press; New York: Oxford University Press, 1988.

Layder, Derek, 'Power, Structure and Agency', *Journal for the Theory of Social Behaviour*, 1985, 15(2): 132–33.

Leblang, David A., 'Property Rights, Democracy and Economic Growth', *Political Research Quarterly*, 1996, 49(1): 5–26.

Lee, Joel and S. K. Thorat, 'Dalits and the Right to Food: Discrimination and Exclusion in Food Related Government Programs', mimeo., New Delhi: Indian Institute of Dalit Studies, 2007.

Lin, Nan, 'Social Resources and Occupational Status Attainment', in R. L. Breiger, ed., *Social Mobility and Social Structure*, New York: Cambridge University Press, 1990, pp. 247–71.

———, 'Social Resource and Instrumental Action', in Peter Marsden and Lin, eds, *Social Structure and Network Analysis*, Beverly Hills: Sage, 1982, pp. 131–45.

Locke, John, 'An Essay Concerning the True Original, Extent and End of Civil Government', in Earnest Barker, ed., *Social Contract: Locke Hume Rousseau; With an Introduction by Earnest Barker*, London: Oxford University Press, 1960, pp. 3–166.

Lukes, S., *Power: A Radical View*, London: Macmillan, 1974.

Madan, T. N., 'Whither Indian Secularism?' *Modern Asian Studies*, 1993, 27(3): 667–97.

Mahajan, Gurpreet, 'Civil Society and its Avatars: What about Freedom and Democracy', *Economic and Political Weekly*, 1997, XXXIV(20): 1188–96.

Mahalingam, Ramaswami, 'Essentialism, Culture, and Power: Representations of Social Class', *Journal of Social Issues*, 2003, 59(4): 733–49.

Mann, A. S., and L. R. Kelley, 'Standing at the Crossroads of Modernist Thought: Collins, Smith, and the New Feminist Epistemologies', 1997, *Gender and Society*, 11(4): 391–408.

Marx, Karl, *A Critique of the German Ideology*, Moscow: Progress Publishers, 1968, http://www.marxists.org/archive/marx/works/download/Marx_The_German_Ideology.pdf (accessed on 28 July 2010).

———, *On The Jewish Question*, Paris: *Deutsch-Französische Jahrbücher*, 1844, http://www.marxists.org/archive/marx/works/1844/jewish-question/ (accessed on 28 July 2010).

McCall, Leslie, 'The Complexity of Intersectionality', *Signs: Journal of Women in Culture and Society*, 2005, 30(3): 1771–800.

McGibbon, Elizabeth and Charmaine McPherson, 'Applying Intersectionality & Complexity Theory to Address the Social Determinants of Women's Health', *Women's Health and Urban Life*, 2011, 10(1): 59–86.

Mehrotra, Santosh, 'Well-being and Caste in Uttar Pradesh: Why UP Is Not Like Tamil Nadu', *Economic and Political Weekly*, 2006, XL(40): 4261–71.

Mencher, Joan P., 'The Caste System Upside Down, or The Not-So-Mysterious East', *Current Anthropology*, 1974, 15(4): 469–93.

Michelutti, Lucia, 'We (Yadavs) are a Caste of Politicians: Caste and Modern Politics in a North Indian Town', *Contributions to Indian Sociology*, 2004, 38: 43–71.

Migdal, Joel S., 'The State in Society: An Approach to Struggles for Domination', in Joel S. Migdal, Atul Kohli and Vivienne Shue, eds, *State Power and Social Forces: Domination and Transformation in the Third World*, Cambridge: Cambridge University Press, 1994, pp. 7–33.

Miliband, Ralph, *The State in a Capitalist Society*, London: Weidenfeld and Nicoloson, 1969.

Mills, Charles W., 'Re-Theorizing Justice: Some Comments on Amartya Sen's 'The Idea of Justice', *Indian Journal of Human Development*, 2011, 5(1): 148–49.

Mohanty, Manoranjan, 'Social Movement in Creative Society: Of Autonomy and Interconnections', in Manoranjan Mohanty, P. N. Mukherjee and Olle Tornquist, eds, *People's Rights: Social Movement and State in the Third World*, New Delhi: Sage, 1998, pp. 63–78.

Mor, Nachiket, 'Expanding Access to Financial Services — Where do we go from here?', Centre for Micro Finance Research Working Paper Series, Chennai: IFMR Trust, http://www.ifmr.ac.in/pdf/workingpapers/expandingAccess.pdf (accessed on 23 March 2008).

Morris Jones, H.W., *The Government and Politics of India*, London: Hutchinson University Library, 1964.

Nafziger, Wayne E. and Terrell Dek, 'Entrepreneurial Human Capital and the Long-Run Survival of Firms in India', *World Development*, 1996, 24(4): 689–96.

Namboodiripad, E. M. S., 'Caste Conflicts and Growing Unity of Popular Democratic Process', *Economic and Political Weekly*, 1979, VII/VIII, Annual Number: 329–36.

Narayan, Badri, *Women Heroes and Dalit Assertion in North India: Culture, Identity and Politics*, New Delhi: Sage, 2006.

Narula, Smita, *Broken People: Caste Violence Against India's 'Untouchables'*, New Delhi: Human Rights Watch, 1999.

Nash, Jennifer, C., 'Re-thinking Intersectionality', *Feminist Review*, 2008, 89(1): 1–15.

Nathan, Dev, Sandip Sarkar, Hareshwar Dayal and Sunil Mishra, 'Development and Deprivation of Scheduled Tribes', *Economic and Political Weekly*, 2006, XLVI: 4824–27.

National Commission for Enterprises in the Unorganized Sector, Government of India, *The Challenge of Employment*, New Delhi: Government of India, 2006.

Nigam, Aditya, 'In Search of a Bourgeoisie: Dalit Politics Enters a New Phase', *Economic and Political Weekly*, 2002, XXXVIII(13): 1190–93.

———, 'Secularism, Modernity, Nation', *Economic and Political Weekly*, 2000, XXXV(48): 4256–68.

Nixon, Richard letter to Anthony Maxwell, 31 October 1972, folder: Ex Fg 21–17, Office of Minority Business Enterprises [2 of 2], box 7, FG 21- Department of Commerce, Central Files, Nixon Presidential Materials, quoted in Dean Kotlowski, 'Black Power-Nixon Style: The Nixon Administration and Minority Business Enterprise', *The Business History Review*, 1998, 72(3): 409–45.

North, Douglas, C., 'The New Institutional Economics and Third World Development', in *The New Institutional Economics and Third World Development,* eds, John Harriss, Jane Hunter and Colin M. Lewis, London: Routledge, 1995, pp. 17–26.

———, 'Institutions and Economic Theory', *The American Economist*, 1992, 1: 36–52.

———, 'Institutions', *The Journal of Economic Perspectives*, 1991, 5(1): 97–102.

———, *Institutions, Institutional Change and Economic Performance*, Cambridge: Cambridge University Press, 1990.

———, *Structure and Change in Economic History*, New York: W. W. Norton, 1981.

O'Hanlon, Rosalind, *Caste, Conflict and Ideology: Mahatma Jotirao Phule and Low Caste Protest in Nineteenth-Century Western India*, Cambridge: Cambridge University Press, 1985.

O'Neill, Onora, and Edward Nell, 'Justice under Socialism', in James Sterba, ed., *Justice: Alternative Political Perspective*, Belmont: Wadsworth, 1980, pp. 196–217.

Omvedt, Gail, 'Globalisation & Indian Tradition', http://www.ambedkar. org/News/Globalisation.htm (accessed on 28 February 2011).

———, *Seeking Begumpura: The Social Vision of Anti Caste Intellectuals*, New Delhi: Navayana Publishing, 2008.

———, *Dalit Visions: The Anti-Caste Movement and the Construction of an Indian Identity*, New Delhi: Orient Longman, 1995.

———, 'Peasants, Dalits and Women: Democracy and India's new Social Movements', *Journal of Contemporary Asia*, 1994a, 24(1): 34–48.

———, *Dalits and the Democratic Revolution: Dr Ambedkar and the Dalit Movement in Colonial India*, New Delhi: Sage, 1994b.

———, 'Dalit Literature in Maharashtra: Literature of Social Protest and Revolt in Western India', *Comparative Studies of South Asia, Africa and the Middle East*, Fall, 1987, 1&2: 78–85.

Oommen, T. K., 'Civil Society: Religion, Caste and Language in India', *Sociological Bulletin*, September 2001, 50(2): 219–35.

Ore, Tracy E., ed., *The Social Construction of Difference and Inequality: Race, Class, Gender and Sexuality*, New York: McGraw Hill, 2000.

Pai, Sudha, *Developmental State and the Dalit Question in Madhya Pradesh: Congress Response*, New Delhi: Routledge, 2012.

Pai, Sudha, *Dalit Assertion and the Unfinished Democratic Revolution: The Bahujan Samaj Party in Uttar Pradesh*, New Delhi: Sage, 2002.

Palshikar, Suhas, 'Caste Politics through the Prism of Region', in Rajendra Vora and Anne Feldhaus, eds, *Region, Culture and Politics in India*, New Delhi: Manohar, 2006, pp. 271–90.

Pandian, M. S., 'One Step Outside Modernity: Caste, Identity Politics and Public Sphere', mimeo., Amsterdam/Dakar: South-South Exchange Programme for Research on the History of Development (SEPHIS) and the Council for the Development of Social Science Research in Africa (CODESRIA), 2001.

———, 'Dalit Assertion in Tamil Nadu', *Journal of Indian School of Political Economy*, 2000, 3 & 4: 501–17.

Panini, M. K., 'The Political Economy of Caste', in M. N. Srinivas, *Caste: Its Twentieth Century Avtar*, New Delhi: Viking, 1996.

Parekh, Bhiku, *Colonialism, Tradition and Reform: An Analysis of Gandhi's Political Discourse*, New Delhi: Sage, 1989.

Parry, Jonathan, 'Lords of Labour: Working and Shirking in Bhilai', *Contributions to Indian Sociology*, 1999, 33(1–2): 108–40.

Pascale, Celine-Marie, *Making Sense of Race, Class and Gender: Common-sense, Power and Privilege in the United States*, New York: Routledge, 2007.

Patil, Sharad, 'Dialectics of Caste and Class Conflicts', *Economic and Political Weekly*, 1979, Annual Number, XIV(7/8): 287–96.

Phule, Jyotirao, *Shetkaryaca Asud (The Whipcord of the Cultivators)*, transl. Gail Omvedt and Bharat Patankar, http://ambedkar.org/ (accessed on 21 May 2009).

Podolny, J., 'A Status Based Model of Market Competition', *The American Journal of Sociology*, 1993, 98(4): 829–72.

Podolny, Joel M. and Karen L. Page, 'Network from Organisation', *Annual Review of Sociology*, 1998, 24: 57–76.

Polanki, Pallavi, 'Untouchability Declassified', *Open Magazine*, 2010, 11: 43–51.

Polanyi, Karl, *The Great Transformation: The Political and Economic Origins of Our Times*, Boston: Beacon Press, 1957.

Polsby, Nelson, W., 'How to Study Community Power: The Pluralist Alternative', *Journal of Politics*, 1960, 22(3): 474–84.

Porter, M. E., *Competitive Strategy*, New York: Free Press, 1980.

Poulantsaz, N., *Political Power and Social Classes*, London: New Left Books, 1973.

Poulantsaz, N., *State, Power, Socialism*, London: Verso, 1978.

Prakash, Aseem, 'Re-imagination of the State and Gujarat Electoral Verdict', *Economic and Political Weekly*, 2003, XXXVIII: 1601–10.

Prasad, Amar Nath and M. B. Gaijan, eds, *Dalit Literature: A Critical Exploration*, New Delhi: Sarup and Sons, 2007.

Prasad, Chandra Bhan, 'Markets and Manu: Economic Reforms and its Impact on Caste in India', *CASI Working Paper Series*, No. 08-01, Center for the Advanced Study of India, University of Pennsylvania, January, 2008.

Rafanell, Iren and Hugo Gorringe, 'Consenting to Domination? Theorising Power, Agency and Embodiment with Reference to Caste', *The Sociological Review*, 2010, 58(4): 604–22.

Rajadurai, S. V. and V. Geetha, *Towards a Non-Brahmin Millennium: From Iyothee Thass to Periyar*, Calcutta: Samya, 1998.

Ram, Ronki, 'Untouchability, Dalit Consciousness, and the Ad Dharm Movement in Punjab', *Contributions to Indian Sociology*, 2004, 38(3): 323–49.

Ramaiah, A., 'Dalits to Accept Globalisation: Lessons from the Past and Present', mimeo., Mumbai: Tata Institute of Social Sciences, 2004, http://ssrn.com/abstract=568582 (accessed on 28 February 2011).

Rao, Anupama, *The Caste Question: Dalits and Politics of Modern India*, Ranikhet: Permanent Black, 2011.

Rauch, James E. and Gary G. Hamilton, 'Networks and Markets: Concepts for Bridging Disciplines', in James E. Rauch and Alessandra Casella, eds, *Networks and Markets: Concepts for Bridging Disciplines*, New York: Russell Sage Foundation, 2001, pp. 1–29.

Rawls, John, *A Theory of Justice*, Cambridge: Harvard University Press, 1971.

Reserve Bank of India, Guidelines of, http://rbi.org.in/rbi-sourcefiles/lending rate/home.html (accessed on 30 June 2012).

Robeyns, Ingrid, 'Is Nancy Fraser's Critique of Theories of Distributive Justice Justified?' *Constellations*, 2003, 4: 538–54.

Rodrigues, Valerian, 'Justice as the Lens: Interrogating Rawls through Sen and Ambedkar', *Indian Journal of Human Development*, 2011, 5(1): 155–57.

Roy, Ajit, 'Caste and Class: An Interlinked View', *Economic and Political Weekly*, 1979, Annual Number, VII/VIII: 297–312.

Rudolph, Lloyd, I. and Susanne Hoeber Rudolph, *In Pursuit of Lakshmi: The Political Economy of Indian State*, Chicago: University of Chicago Press, 1987.

———, *The Modernity of Indian Tradition*, Chicago: University of Chicago Press, 1967.

Runciman, W. G., 'Processes, End States and Social Justice', *Philosophical Quarterly*, 1978, 28: 37–45.

Saberwal, Satish, 'Democracy and Civil Society in India: Integral or Accidental', *Sociological Bulletin*, September 2001, 50: 193–205.

Sahu, Geetanjoy, 'Mining in the Niyamgiri Hills and Tribal Rights', *Economic and Political Weekly*, 2008, XLIII(15): 19–21.

Said, Edward W., *Orientalism*, New Delhi: Penguin Books, 1995.

———, *Culture and Imperialism*, London: Chatto and Windus, 1993.

Sangvai, Sanjay, 'No Full Stops for the Narmada: Life After the Verdict', *Economic and Political Weekly*, 2001, XLIX: 4524–26.

Sarkar, Sumit, *Writing Social History*, New Delhi: Oxford University Press, 1998.

Savarkar, V. D., *Who is a Hindu?* Bombay: S. S. Savarkar, 1969.

Scott, James C., *Seeing Like a State: How Certain Schemes to Improve the Human Conditions Have Failed*, New Haven: Yale University Press, 1998.

———, *Domination and the Arts of Resistance: Hidden Transcripts*, New Haven: Yale University Press, 1990.

———, *Weapons of the Weak: Everyday Forms of Peasant Resistance*, New Haven: Yale University Press, 1985.

———, *The Moral Economy of Peasant: Rebellion and Subsistence in South East Asia*, New Haven: Yale University Press, 1976.

Scoville, James, G., 'Labor Market Underpinnings of a Caste Economy: Foiling the Coase Theorem', *American Journal of Economics and Sociology*, 1996, 55(4): 385–94.

Sen, Amartya and Bernard Williams, eds, *Utilitarianism and Beyond*, Cambridge: Cambridge University Press, 1982.

Sen, Amartya, *The Idea of Justice*, Cambridge: Harvard University Press, 2009.

———, 'Social Exclusion: Concept, Application, and Scrutiny', Social Development, 2000, , http://www.flacso.org/biblioteca/sen_social_exclusion. pdf (accessed on 2 June 2008).

Shah, Ghanshyam, Harsh Mander, S. K. Thorat, Satish Deshpande, and Amita Baviskar, eds, *Untouchability in Rural India*, New Delhi: Sage, 2006.

Shah, Mayank and Ram Monder, 'Supplier Diversity and Minority Business Enterprise Development: A Case Study of Three US Multinationals', *Supply Chain Management: An International Journal*, 2006, 1: 75–81.

Sivanandan, P., 'Caste, Class and Economic Opportunity in Kerala: An Empirical Analysis,' *Economic and Political Weekly*, 1979, XIV(7/8): 475–80.

Skocpol, Theda, 'Bringing the State Back In: Strategies of Analysis in Current Research', in Peter B. Evans, Dietrich Rueschemeyer, and Theda Skocpol, eds, *Bringing the State Back In*, Cambridge: Cambridge University Press, 1985, pp. 3–43.

Smith, Adam, *Wealth of Nations*, North Carolina: Hayes Barton Press, 2005.

Somers, Margaret R. and Gloria D. Gibson, 'Reclaiming The Epistemological 'Other': Narrative and Social Construction of Identity', CSST Working Papers No. 94, Ann Arbor: The University of Michigan, 1993, http:// deepblue.lib.umich.edu/bitstream/2027.42/51265/1/499.pdf (accessed on 26 September 2011).

Southall, Roger, 'The ANC & Black Capitalism in South Africa', *Review of African Political Economy*, 2004, 31(100): 313–28.

Srinivas, M. N., *Caste: Its Twentieth Century Avatar*, New Delhi: Viking, 1996.

———, *Social Change in Modern India*, New Delhi: Orient Longman, 1972.

———, 'Varna and Caste', in *Caste in Modern India and Other Essays*, M. N. Srinivas, Bombay: Asia Publishing House, 1962, pp. 63–69.

Srinivas, M. N., and André Béteille, 'Networks in Indian Social Structure', *Man*, 1964, 64: 165–68.

Stiglitz, Joseph, 'Formal and Informal Institutions', in Partha Das Gupta and Ismail Serageldin, eds, *Social Capital: A Multifaceted Perspective*, Washington: World Bank, 1999, pp. 59–68.

Taylor, Charles, 'The Politics of Recognition', in Ajay Heble, Dona Palmateer Pennee, and J. R. Tim Struthers, eds, *New Contexts of Canadian Criticism'*, Ontario: Broadview Press, 1997, pp. 98–131.

Teltumbde, Anand, 'Pursuing Equality in the Land of Hierarchy: Positive Discrimination Policies in India', mimeo., New Delhi: Institute for Human Development, 2007.

———, *Ambedkar in and for the Post-Ambedkar Dalit Movement*, Pune: Sugawa Prakashan, 1997.

Thorat, Amit, 'Ethnicity, 'Caste and Religion: Implications for Poverty Outcomes', *Economic and Political Weekly*, 2010, XLV(51): 47–53.

Thorat, S. K., 'Caste, Social Exclusion and Poverty Linkages — Concept, Measurement and Empirical Evidence', mimeo., New Delhi: Indian Institute of Dalit Studies, 2008.

———, 'Caste System and Economic Discrimination: Lessons from Theories', in Sukhadeo Thorat, Aryama and Prashant Negi, eds, *Reservation and Private Sector: Quest for Equal Opportunity and Growth*, New Delhi: Indian Institute of Dalit Studies and Rawat Publications, 2005, pp. 73–80.

Thorat, S. K. and Chittaranjan Senapati, 'Reservation Policy in India- Dimensions and Issues', Working Paper Series, Vol. I, No. 02, New Delhi: Indian Institute of Dalit Studies, 2006.

Trivedi, Kumar Prashant, 'Violence and Atrocities Against Dalit Women in Rural Uttar Pradesh', *Journal of Indian School of Political Economy*, 2007, 1&2: 65–92.

Vanaik, Achin, *The Painful Transition: Bourgeois Democracy in India*, London: Verso, 1990.

Varshney, Ashutosh, 'Is India Becoming More Democratic? *The Journal of Asian Studies*, 2000, 59(1): 3–25.

Vijay, G., and G. Ajay, 'Civil Society, State and Social Movements', *Economic and Political Weekly*, 2000, XXXV(12): 1035–36.

Vincentnathan, S. George, 'Caste Politics, Violence, and the Panchayat in a South Indian Community', *Comparative Studies in Society and History*, 1996, 383: 484–509.

Wakankar, Milind, *Subalternity and Religion: The Pre-History of Dalit Empowerment in South Asia*, New York: Routledge, 2010.

Weber, Lynn, 'A Conceptual Framework for Understanding Race, Class, Gender and Sexuality', in Sharelene Nagy, Hesse Bibber and Michelle Yaisiere, eds, *Feminist Perspective on Social Research*, New York: Oxford University Press, 2004, pp. 121–39.

Weber, Max, 'Politics as Vocation', in H. H. Gerth and C. Wright Mills, eds, *From Max Weber: Essays in Sociology*, New York: Oxford University Press, 1946, pp. 77–128.

Webster, C. B., 'Who is a Dalit', in S. M. Michael, ed., *Dalits in Modern India: Vision and Values*, New Delhi: Sage, 1999, pp. 76–90.

Weems Jr., E. Robert and Lewis Randolph, 'The Ideological Origins of Richard M. Nixon's 'Black Capitalism' Initiative', http://web.ebscohost. com/ehost/pdf?vid=2&hid=107&sid=073e804f-932e-4523-80fc-1292ad813570%40sessionmgr102 (accessed on 2 June 2008).

Weiner, Myron, *Political Change in South Asia*, Calcutta: Firma K. L. Mukhopadhyay, 1963.

White, Harrison, C., 'Where Do Markets Come From?' *The American Journal of Sociology*, 1981, 87(3): 517–47.

Williamson, Oliver E. and Marika Vicziany, *The Untouchables: Subordination, Poverty and the State in Modern India*, Cambridge: Cambridge University Press, 2005.

Williamson, Oliver, E., 'The New Institutional Economics: Taking Stock, Looking Ahead', *Journal of Economic Literature*, 2000, 38(3): 595–613.

———, *The Economic Institutions of Capitalism*, New York: Free Press, 1985.

Wood, Allen, 'The Marxian Critique of Justice', *Philosophy and Public Affairs*, Spring, 1972, 1(3): 244–82.

World Bank, *India's Employment Challenge: Creating Jobs, Helping Workers*, New Delhi: Oxford University Press, 2010.

World Development Report, *Building Institutions for Markets*, New York: Oxford University Press for World Bank, 2002.

Yadav, Yogendra, 'Understanding the Second Democratic Upsurge: Trends of Bahujan Participation in Electoral Politics in the 1990s', in Francine R. Frankel, Zoya Hasan, Rajeev Bhargava and Balveer Arora, eds, *Transforming India: Social and Political Dynamics of Democracy*, Delhi: Oxford University Press, 2000, pp. 120–45.

Yagnik, Achyut and Anil Bhatt, 'The Anti-Dalit Agitation in Gujarat', *Comparative Studies of South Asia, Africa and the Middle*, 1984, 4(1): 45–60.

Young, Marion Iris, *Intersecting Voices: Dilemmas of Gender Political Philosophy*, Princeton: Princeton University Press, 1997.

Young, Marion Iris, Justice *and the Politics of Difference*, New Jersey: Princeton University Press, 1990.

Zelliot, Eleanor 'Dalit Literature, Language and Identity', in Braj Kachru, Yamuna Kachru and S. N. Sridhar, eds, *Language in South Asia*, Cambridge: Cambridge University Press, 2008.

———, *From Untouchable to Dalit: Essays on the Ambedkar Movement*, New Delhi: Manohar, 1992.

———, 'Perspectives on the Dalit Cultural Movement: Editor's Introduction', *Comparative Studies of South Asia, Africa and the Middle East Fall*, 1987, 7(1 &2): 2–64.

About the Author

Aseem Prakash is Associate Professor and Chairperson, School of Public Policy and Governance, Tata Institute of Social Sciences, Hyderabad. His doctorate is from the Centre for Political Studies, Jawaharlal Nehru University, New Delhi. He has been working on the informality and formality of markets for more than a decade and is currently focused on studying the regulation of small town capitalism.

Index

Abrams, Philip, 121, 150
agency and social power argument
    of intersectionality, 204–05
Akerlof, George, 58–59
Ambedkar, B. R., 64
ati-shudras, 1
autonomy, 207

Bardhan, Pranab, 127, 139,
    158*n*33, 224*n*24
Basile, Elisabetta, 148, 185
Becker, Gary, 57
Béteille, André, 145, 147, 180
Bhat-brahmins, 1
Bhopal Declaration, 120
Black Capitalism, 155*n*11–155*n*12
bourgeoisie liberal principle of citi-
    zenship, 2
Brahminical colonialism, 2
bribes, 232
British colonialism, 2
Browne, Irene, 200
bureaucracy, 123, 131–32, 135,
    137, 140, 142, 157*n*30, 224*n*24
Burt, Ronald, 168–69
business alliances with upper castes,
    100–02
business histories
    of Dalit entrepreneurs, 4–5,
        229–32
    documentation of, 7–12
    narrative analyses of Dalit
        entrepreneurs, 8–12

capital accumulation, 87
capitalism as an economic system,
    228

capitalist economies, 63
caste, construction of
    caste as civil society, 179–87
    caste-inspired social networks,
        174, 176–79
    coercive and manipulative form
        of caste, 178
    collectivisation spirit of caste,
        178
    Dalit perspective, 30–36
    defence of *varna*, 27–28
    distinction between *varna* and
        jati, 25
    exclusionary role of caste, 177
    hierarchy among caste groups,
        25–26
    ideological force of *dharma* or
        religion, 26
    as ideology, 64–65
    impermeability, 58
    inevitability, 58–59
    organic social blocks, 28–29
    Orientalist perspective, 24–25
    permanence, 59
    sanskritisation, 25–26
    as a social system, 26
    structure–agency debate, 38–40
    structure of social power,
        37–38
    as a superstructure, 26–27
    upper caste identity, 178
caste-inspired social networks, 174,
    176–79
    blurring between state, market
        and civil society, 177
    caste as an institutional avenue
        to networks, 177

convergence between hierarchical notion of social structure and economic interests, 177
socio-economic norms, 177–78
caste-related economic activities, 100–01
caste system, principle of, 3
Chatterjee, Partha, 2, 126–27, 157n30, 158n31, 192n35
civil society
  assurance of non-discrimination, 179–80
  capital accumulation in, 185
  caste as a form of, 185–87
  dominant form of, 181, 185
  dominant theories of, 211–14
  hierarchy of social relationships in, 185–86
  institutions, 167
  under *laissez faire* conditions, 182–83
  liberal democratic perspective, 179–80
  Locke, Adam Smith and Hegel, perspectives of, 182–83
  Marxist understanding of, 180, 183
  normative ideals, 180
  Partha Chatterjee's arguments, 194n47
  political and cultural relationships in, 184
  political negotiations and transactions, 181, 192n35
  regulation of credit and labour supply, 186
  in shaping accumulative instincts, 181
  as site of crass materialism, 183–84
class-based inequality, 183
closed social networks, 179
comparative justice, 42

competitive multi-party system, 159n38
corruption in socio-political processes, 138–42, 232
Credit Rating Information Services of India Limited (CRISIL), 78
credit regime to Dalit business-persons, 75–87, 232
  bank's governance regime, 79
  community exclusion from credit, 84–85
  credit denial, perception of Dalit entrepreneurs, 82–87, 99–100
  credit index-based lending, 82
  credit rating exercise, 77–79
  criterion for extending credit, 77–78
  de-capping of interest rates, 78
  'faulty' regulatory regime, 80–82
  financial transactions in terms of 'trust' or 'culture of fear,' 81–82
  interest rate ceilings and, 78
  lack of institutional and informal credit for Dalit-operated petty business, 99–100
  neo-classical school on credit markets, 80–82
  'rational' and 'scientific' credit index-based decisions, 81
Crenshaw, Kimberle, 200
cultural capital, 146, 178–179

Dalit bourgeoisie, 3
Dalit business-persons. *see also* Dalit entrepreneurs
  automobile workshop owner, 144–45
  availability of credit, 75–87
  caste-related trade and commerce, 69

categories of businesses, 69
ceramic manufacturing unit, 73, 86, 135–36
educational coaching institute, 72–73
food entrepreneurs, 71–72
fruit wholesaler, 196–198
laundry owner, 84–85, 123–24, 138, 149
leather goods manufacturer, 70–71, 76, 96, 112n54, 135, 144
marginalisation experience, 70
market entry and market operations, 84–87
'mid'-sized wholesale food and beverages businesses, 71
nursing home, 73–74, 85
perception of markets, 87–105
sample interviewed, 67. *see also* credit regime to Dalit business-persons
sanitaryware trade, 69, 83, 96, 100–02
type and size of economic ventures, 68
Dalit discourse, 2
Dalit entrepreneurs, 4, 184. *see also* Dalit business-persons
business histories of, 4–5
class-based inequality against, 183
livelihood earned in the market, 4
in a market networks, 172
state and, 209
weak position of, 176
Dalit identity, 36–37, 41
Dalit Indian Chamber of Commerce and Industry (DICCI), 55
'Dalit Panthers' manifesto of 1973, 23
Dalits

as an analytical category, 22–23
as a homogenous group, 23
meaning of term, 23
perspectives on caste construction, 30–36
political agency of, 36–46
as a single social category, 23
as a social group, 22–23
Dalit youth venture, 56
Deshpande, Ashwini, 57, 59
dialectic of control, 39
discrimination against Dalits
approach of intersectionality, 199–222
Munna's testimony, 196–98
distributional notion of justice, 42, 53n72
distribution *per se*, 42
domestic de-regulation, 80
dominant classes in India, 224n24
dynamic component of social networks, 174–76

economic relationships, caste identity and, 88
economic ventures, types of, 229–32
elite political culture, 157n23
endogamy, institution of, 148–49
epistemic superiority argument of intersectionality, 206
Evans, Peter, 209
exclusionary role of caste, 177
exclusion of Dalits from policy processes, 134–37
ex-untouchables, 23

free market policies, 3, 147

graded inequality, 38
Gramsci, Antonio, 184, 214, 233
Granovetter, Mark, 62, 168
Gujarat Industrial Development Corporation (GIDC), 125–26

Harriss-White, Barbara, 64, 137, 143, 147–48, 162, 185
Hegel, G. W. F., 182–83, 214, 233
hierarchy of state departments, 132–33
Homo Hierarchicus, 26
Huntington, Samuel, 139

institutional economics, 60–61
interconnectedness argument of intersectionality, 202
intersectionality, thesis of, 199–222, 234
    agency and social power argument, 204–05
    central tenets, 202
    challenges at state, market and civil society, 201, 203, 206–17
    denial of credit, 199–222
    epistemic superiority argument, 206
    from feminist studies, 200–02
    implications on practical politics, 201
    interconnectedness argument, 202
    limits of, 220–22
    McCall's approaches, 217–19
    methodological and conceptual location of, 217–20
    particularity *vs* totality, 216–17
    social determinants of women's health, analysis of, 201
    social exclusion *vs* discrimination argument, 203–04
    social identity, stress on, 207–15
    subordination and marginalisation, 218–19
Investment Information and Credit Rating Agency (ICRA), 78

Kamble, Milind, 55

Kannan, K. P., 56
Khan, Mushtaq, 141

Lin, Nan, 168
Locke, John, 182–83, 214, 233

market-based accumulation processes, 167
    accommodative model of, 90
    social networks, role of, 167–79
market discrimination, 56–66
    basis of caste as an ideology, 64–65
    caste-based, 57
    economic discriminatory practices, 57
    experience of Dalit businesspersons, 66–74
    labour, 57
    neo-classical school of thought, 59–60, 65
    in new institutional economics, 60–61, 65–66
    'social embeddedness' school of thought, 62–63, 66
    statistical discrimination, 58
market operations, aspects of, 89
market outcomes, 57–61, 65, 87–88, 103, 149, 152, 167–68, 175
markets, defined, 5–6
markets and market-based transactions, experiences of Dalit entrepreneurs
    access to market spaces, 90
    alliance with upper castes, 100–02
    brick kiln owner, 96–98
    building contractor, 88–89
    courier company owner, 96–97
    degree of hostility toward Dalits, 89
    handloom business and boutique owner, 98

impediments created by former employers, 90–92

labour contractor, 89

lack of institutional and informal credit for Dalit-operated petty business, 99–100

leather goods manufacturer, 96

prejudices, 91

'pure' goods and 'impure' caste, 93–95

real estate contractor, 119

relations with non-Dalits, 88–90

role of social network in restricting business resources, 95–99

social networks, 102–05

Marx, Karl, 180, 183, 208, 214, 233

mass political culture, 157n23

McCall, Leslie, 217–19

Miliband, Ralph, 193n42

Misra, Joya, 200

Myrdal, Gunnar, 139

Namasudras, 1

narrative analysis, 9–12

neo-classical economics, 87, 110n33, 210, 228

on credit markets, 80–82

market discrimination, 59–60, 65

new institutional economics, 60–61, 65–66, 82, 87, 110n33, 210–14, 228

Nigam, Aditya, 136

non-competition, 147

normative component of social networks, 170–71

maintenance of hierarchy in relationships, 170–71

privileges and rights, 171

normative principles of caste, 170

North, Douglas, 60–61, 210

Omvedt, Gail, 3

oppression, 45

Page, K. L., 95

Pandian, M. S. S., 136

Panini, 3

passive exclusion, 136

patron-client politics, 141

Phule, Jotirao, 1

Podolny, J., 62, 95

Polanyi, Karl, 62

political agency of Dalits

important and interrelated properties, 37

question of social justice, 41–46

structural power of caste and, 37–40

political democracy, 2–3

Poulantsaz, N., 193n42

poverty in India, 154n6

profitability of Dalit-owned economic enterprises, 172–73

'pure' goods and 'impure' caste, 93–95

rectificatory justice, 43

relative autonomy, 207

relative worth, 41

rent-giving, 141–42

rent-seeking, 139–42

resource component of social networks, 172–74

'risk based pricing' (RBP), principles of, 78

sanskritisation, 25–26

Santhanam Committee Report, 139

Sardar Sarovar Project, 156n21

Sarkar, Sumit, 136

Sen, Amartya, 136, 233

shudras, 1

Smith, Adam, 182–83, 214, 233

social acceptance of caste system, 59
social alliances, 174
social assertion of Dalits, 85
social capital, 146, 148
social embeddedness, 63, 87, 167–68
   of market relationships, 173
social equality, 1
social exclusion *vs* discrimination argument of intersectionality, 203–04
social identity (ies)
   defined, 6–7
   role in market, 207–15
social justice, notion of, 41–46
   characteristic features, 43–44
   compensation, 44–45
   context of socio-cultural and economic subordination of Dalit labour, 43–44
   distributional theories of, 42
   norms and practice, 45
   recognition and redistribution of resources, 42, 44–46
   in terms of relative worth, 41
   utilitarian view, 42
social networks, role in business outcomes, 96, 102–05, 232–33
   accumulation strategies and labour regulation practices, 98–99
   based on ascriptive ties, 103
   based on business alliances with upper castes, 103–05
   on the basis of caste location and regional identity, 97, 99
   dynamic component, 174–76
   economic relationships embedded in social networks, 168
   flow of information, 169
   fostering of close relationships, 174
   in Indian context, 169
   in market-based accumulation processes, 167–79
   normative component, 170–71
   as a relation-centred approach, 169–170
   resource component, 172–74
   resource raising networks, 96–98
   reward and punishment through, 169
   role in facilitating economic endeavours, 169
   strength of weak ties, 168
   structural component, 171–72
   as vehicles for political mobilisation, 176
   weak networks, 102–05
social resources, 168
social structure of accumulation, 14, 64, 66, 87, 88, 102, 105, 112n49, 153, 185, 217
social ties in markets, 171
South Africa, black capitalist class of, 155n11
state simplification, theses of
   'anti' and 'compensatory' discrimination policies, 137
   blurred boundaries between the state and civil Society, 137–45
   caste, role in socio-political processes, 137–45
   caste and articulation of dominant economic interests, 140–42, 145–46
   class interest, upholding of, 183, 193n42
   de-linking of state department from statecraft and state officials, 131–34
   exclusion from policy processes, 134–37
   forms of regulatory control and corruption, 138–41

Marxist theories, 208
regime of 'discretionary control' and regulation, 139
role of ascriptive identities in shaping ideology, 208
role of family and its relationship with caste, 145–49
of state's hierarchy, 132–33
unfavourable inclusion, reasons for, 131, 134–37
upper castes social affinity, significance of, 145–49
verbal negotiations, 134
state-system and Dalit business, 121–27, 158n34–158n35
caste character of the state, 137–45, 152–53
inability to comprehend state action, 125–27
insensitive policies, 123–25
normative construct of the state, 151–52
political inclusion and economic exclusion, 127–49
state as an abstract institution, 122–27, 150
verbal negotiations, 134
Stiglitz, Joseph, 210
Strauss, Levi, 88
strength of weak ties, concept of, 168
Structural Adjustment Programmes, 140

structural component of social networks, 171–72
norms and shared rules, 171
structural determinism, 39
structuration, theory of, 39, 171–72
super-subordination, hierarchical system of, 131
Swadeshi movement, 1
symbolic violence, 38

Thass, Iyothee, 1
'traditional marginality' of the Dalits, 1
trust, 170

uncertainty, 170
unfavourable inclusion in market processes, 199, 201–02, 207, 216–17, 220, 233
untouchability, 38
upper caste-controlled social networks, 176
upper caste employers, impediments to hinder Dalit entrepreneurs, 90–92
upper caste entrepreneurs, 171, 173

varna scheme, 2

Weber, Max, 131–32
White, Harrison C., 62

Related Titles

Caste in Contemporary India (2015)
Surinder S. Jodhka
978-1-138-82243-6

Seva, *Saviour and State: Caste Politics, Tribal Welfare and Capitalist Development* (2015)
R. Srivatsan
978-1-138-79609-6

Dalits in Neoliberal India: Mobility or Marginalisation? (2014)
Editor: Clarinda Still
978-1-138-02024-5

Hindi Dalit Literature and the Politics of Representation (2014)
Sarah Beth Hunt
978-0-415-73629-9

Constructing Indian Christianities: Culture, Conversion and Caste (2014)
Editors: Chad M. Bauman and Richard Fox Young
978-1-138-02018-4

Retro-modern India: Forging the Low-caste Self (2010)
Manuela Cotti
978-0-415-56311-6

The Structure of Indian Society: Then and Now (2010)
A. M. Shah
978-0-415-58622-1

The Vernacularisation of Democracy: Politics, Caste and Religion in India (2008)
Lucia Michelutti
978-0-415-46732-2

For Product Safety Concerns and Information please contact our EU
representative GPSR@taylorandfrancis.com Taylor & Francis Verlag GmbH,
Kaufingerstraße 24, 80331 München, Germany

Printed and bound by CPI Group (UK) Ltd, Croydon, CR0 4YY
08/05/2025
01864357-0001